Luminos is the open access monograph publishing program
from UC Press. Luminos provides a framework for preserving
and reinvigorating monograph publishing for the future
and increases the reach and visibility of important scholarly
work. Titles published in the UC Press Luminos model are
published with the same high standards for selection, peer
review, production, and marketing as those in our traditional
program. www.luminosoa.org

The Place of Devotion

SOUTH ASIA ACROSS THE DISCIPLINES

South Asia Across the Disciplines is a series devoted to publishing first books across a wide range of South Asian studies, including art, history, philology or textual studies, philosophy, religion, and the interpretive social sciences. Series authors all share the goal of opening up new archives and suggesting new methods and approaches, while demonstrating that South Asian scholarship can be at once deep in expertise and broad in appeal.

Series Editor: Muzaffar Alam, Robert Goldman, and Gauri Viswanathan

Founding Editors: Dipesh Chakrabarty, Sheldon Pollock, and Sanjay Subrahmanyam

Funded by a grant from the Andrew W. Mellon Foundation and jointly published by the University of California Press, the University of Chicago Press, and Columbia University Press.

The Place of Devotion

Siting and Experiencing Divinity in Bengal-Vaishnavism

Sukanya Sarbadhikary

UNIVERSITY OF CALIFORNIA PRESS

University of California Press, one of the most
distinguished university presses in the United States,
enriches lives around the world by advancing scholarship
in the humanities, social sciences, and natural sciences.
Its activities are supported by the UC Press Foundation
and by philanthropic contributions from individuals and
institutions. For more information, visit www.ucpress.edu.

University of California Press
Oakland, California

Suggested citation: Sarbadhikary, Sukanya. *The Place of
Devotion: Siting and Experiencing Divinity in Bengal-
Vaishnavism.* Oakland: University of California Press,
2015. doi: http://dx.doi.org/10.1525/luminos.2

Library of Congress Cataloging-in-Publication Data

Sarbadhikary, Sukanya, 1983- author.
    The place of devotion : siting and experiencing
divinity in Bengal-Vaishnavism / Sukanya
Sarbadhikary.—First edition.
        pages cm. — (South Asia across the disciplines)
Includes bibliographical references and index.
      ISBN 978-0-520-28771-6 (pbk. : alk. paper) —
ISBN 0-520-28771-1 (pbk. : alk. paper) —
ISBN 978-0-520-96266-8 (ebook) —
ISBN 0-520-96266-4 (ebook)
        1. Vaishnavism—India—Bengal. 2. Sacred space—
India—Bengal. 3. Anthropology of religion—India—
Bengal. I. Title. II. Series: South Asia across the
disciplines.
    BL1284.532.B46S37 2015
    294.5'35095414—dc23
2015007907

24 23 22 21 20 19 18 17 16 15
10 9 8 7 6 5 4 3 2 1

To the sounds and silences of faith

Contents

Acknowledgments

One can see and smell the flower, but it becomes the most difficult task to discern whether the sunlight, soil, seed, environment, or gardener played the most significant role in giving it its life and breath. Similarly, I believe, writing the acknowledgements for a book is a most challenging exercise since identifying the encouragement, labor, and love of the many people who have inspired it is next to impossible. So whether or not I name them, my most sincere gratitude extends to all those who have loved and taught me, who have unknowingly shaped my thoughts, emotions, and being, all of which have gone entirely into conceiving this book.

However, I take this opportunity to thank those who have directly helped me in conceptualizing and writing the book. I must begin with the soul of the book: the people of Navadvip and Mayapur, who allowed me into their rich and sophisticated devotional lives, who taught me that people, their beliefs, and above all their unstinting faith, are greater teachers than books. Their words, worship, songs, and rhythms have transformed me in ways that are irreversible.

I have been fortunate to have Susan Bayly as my supervisor in Cambridge. Her utmost sincerity and involvement with this work have sometimes even surpassed my own. I am most grateful to her for our fruitful discussions whenever I needed them, and for reading and commenting on various drafts of my PhD dissertation, which forms the spine of this book. She continuously helped me better my articulations of the complex devotional worldviews of my Vaishnava interlocutors. James Laidlaw and Joanna Cook, examiners of my PhD dissertation, have also been inspirational figures, whose most careful reading of the work and critical appreciation and input helped enormously in reworking the dissertation for the book. My supervisor and examiners were essentially instrumental in nurturing my confidence in the future potential of my research.

I thank Trinity College, Gates Cambridge Trust, and Overseas Research Studentship for their generous support during my PhD years in Cambridge. I also thank the Richards Fund, Smuts Memorial Fund, and William Wyse Fund for their additional support during the primary fifteen months of my fieldwork, between July 2009 and September 2010.

I thank Ashok Ray and Kalpana Ray for their warmest hospitality during this period of my fieldwork, and during all subsequent visits.

Words and gratitude can never be enough to acknowledge the inspiration I have been blessed with by Arindam Chakrabarti. He taught me the simplest of truths: that just as smell cannot be understood without smelling, faith cannot be understood without believing. My fifteen months in the field, and my work with Vaishnavas generally, consumed my senses, faith, and knowledge. I would not have understood devotion without my ardent teacher.

Sibaji Bandopadhyay was the first person to hear about, empathize with, criticize, and refine my initial analyses of the fieldwork material and my conceptualizations of *gupta* (veiled) Vrindavan. Without those key guidelines, this book would not have the shape it currently does.

Many undergraduate and postgraduate teachers have shaped and influenced my intellectual orientations. I especially thank Arindam Chakrabarti, Avijit Pathak, Dalia Chakrabarty, Dipankar Gupta, Partha Chatterjee, Pradip Datta, Prasanta Ray, Sibaji Bandopadhyay, Soumyabrata Choudhury, Susan Visvanathan, Tapati Guha-Thakurta, Udaya Kumar, and V. Sujatha.

A number of people read and commented on chapters of the book, and others gave their feedback on critical ethnographic and theoretical dimensions of the work during conversations or presentations in seminars and conferences between 2010 and 2014. I thank Anirban Das, Arindam Chakrabarti, Bhaskar Mukhopadhyay, Bodhisattva Kar, Chris Pinney, David Sneath, Deepak Mehta, Dipesh Chakrabarty, Edward Rodrigues, Ferdia Stone-Davis, James Laidlaw, Leo Howe, Maitrayee Chaudhuri, Manish Thakur, Partha Chatterjee, Prathama Banerjee, Rajesh Kasturirangan, Rich Freeman, Sanjay Srivastava, Sibaji Bandopadhyay, Sudipta Kaviraj, Sumathy Ramaswamy, S. S. Jodhka,

Tapati Guha-Thakurta, Urmila Mohan, and two anonymous referees of *Contributions to Indian Sociology*. I also thank my colleagues who participated in the writing-up seminars in the Department of Social Anthropology, Cambridge, and my friends Rohan Deb Roy, Sayam Ghosh, and Upal Chakrabarti for commenting on chapters.

I am especially grateful to Partha Chatterjee. He read and critically commented on chapters whenever I asked. He also had the inspiring patience to go through the entire manuscript and provide his invaluable suggestions at every step. I will always remain thankful for his continuous support. I hope I can be as sincere as he is, some day.

I intended my work to be just a little beginning in explorations of South Asian devotion, and I am immensely indebted to the editors of South Asia Across the Disciplines for considering my work fit for this vibrant series. I also extend utmost gratitude to Tony K. Stewart and the anonymous referee of the book manuscript for their most nuanced and critical insights on my work. It is in trying to do full justice to their comments that the book has taken its existing character. While I thank both reviewers for their extensive and intensive comments, I remain thoroughly obliged to Tony K. Stewart for being in touch with and encouraging me throughout the revision process, for furnishing me with invaluable scholarly advice and help whenever I needed it, and especially for his extremely insightful appreciation of my work. It would not be an exaggeration to say that I have had reviewers who were able to generate in me a renewed respect for my research.

I thank Presidency University for granting me leave to finish working on the book manuscript.

I thank Reed Malcolm and the entire editorial team of the University of California Press for their relentless help.

I thank my students, Devi, Radhika, Sandipan, and Sayan for helping me in the final stages of the editorial work for the manuscript.

My emotional strength would not be possible without the continuous lessons I have learned from friends. They have helped me in ways that neither they nor I will ever be able to comprehend fully. But friends have been many; friendships, few. These rare friendships have helped me think, emote, write, and survive.

My family and in-laws have been extremely supportive all throughout my writing process, especially when I have been down and stressed.

Finally, it seems both essential and impossible to thank my parents and my husband for just being the way they are, for being with me. My book is not merely a piece of writing for me: it has been a part of my soul for all this time. And my soul would not function without these three people.

The only impossible task I do not wish to face in life is to know how to thank my parents. An acknowledgement is not the space for them, yet I could not do without this sentence.

I have read out loud to Upal even the commas and full-stops of the book, shouted at him whenever my brain stopped working, made him stay up at night whenever I was tense, and treated him to much love whenever a new idea flashed. He always made me laugh when I took myself too seriously, and reminded me to be intensely serious about my self and passions, whenever I drifted. I would not be able to write without Upal's steady love and sharp intellectual insights into my work. His honest simplicity is a constant reminder of faith and faithfulness.

Passion, pedagogy, and devotion are never separate. So, writing this book is in itself a mode of gratitude to my teachers, family, friends, Upal, and the world of devotion at large.

Postscript. I conceived my son while working on the final stages of the book, and he was born just months before I completed it. My "conceptions" developed together; my son grew with my thoughts. We've named him Darshan, insight. I hope he will carry with him the life of my thoughts.

Note on Transliteration

I have not used diacritics in the text, to avoid cluttering it. So I have generally spelled Bengali and Sanskrit words as they would be pronounced in English, except words which are now relatively common in the English-speaking world. I have glossed the meanings of vernacular terms in their first usage. However, for the reader's convenience, I have also provided a separate glossary of vernacular terms which appear more than once in the text. All translations of informants' quotes and poems are my own, and the interviews were transcribed by me.

CHAPTER I

Introduction: Siting and Experiencing Divinity in Bengal-Vaishnavism

BACKGROUND

The anthropology of Hinduism has amply established that Hindus have a strong involvement with sacred geography. The Hindu sacred topography is dotted with innumerable pilgrimage places, and popular Hinduism is abundant with spatial imaginings. Thus, Shiva and his partner, the mother goddess, live in the Himalayas; goddesses descend to earth as beautiful rivers; the goddess Kali's body parts are imagined to have fallen in various sites of Hindu geography, sanctifying them as sacred centers; and yogis meditate in forests. Bengal similarly has a thriving culture of exalting sacred centers and pilgrimage places, one of the most important being the Navadvip-Mayapur sacred complex, Bengal's greatest site of guru-centered Vaishnavite pilgrimage and devotional life. While one would ordinarily associate Hindu pilgrimage centers with a single place, for instance, Ayodhya, Vrindavan, or Banaras, and while the anthropology of South Asian pilgrimage has largely been single-place-centered, Navadvip and Mayapur, situated on opposite banks of the river Ganga in the Nadia District of West Bengal, are both famous as the birthplace(s) of the medieval saint, Chaitanya (1486–1533), who popularized Vaishnavism on the greatest scale in eastern India, and are thus of massive simultaneous importance to pilgrims in contemporary Bengal. For devotees, the medieval town of Navadvip represents a Vaishnava place of antique pilgrimage crammed with centuries-old temples and ashrams, and Mayapur, a small village rapidly developed since the nineteenth century, contrarily represents the glossy headquarters site of ISKCON (the International Society for Krishna Consciousness), India's most famous globalized, high-profile, modernized guru movement.

My fieldwork in Navadvip and Mayapur, however, predominantly involved carrying out an intensive study of different kinds of very rich everyday spiritual lives engaged in by the large number of ascetic-renouncers and householder devotees who reside in these places. Within a few months in the field I grasped that there are four very different kinds of Vaishnavas who live in Navadvip-Mayapur, each with its own highly distinctive focus in worship. They include the glossy globalized ISKCON devotees; the much-stigmatized quasi-tantric, poor, illiterate Vaishnavas who practice sexual-yogic religious rituals; the knowledgeable ascetic renouncers living in secluded ashrams; and finally the householder Brahmin priests who are the owners of Navadvip's large and famous temples. I wanted to explore what it was that made Vaishnavism so many things yet still somehow one. What made my fieldwork particularly exciting was that I was able to relate this classic question in the anthropology of Hinduism, that is, whether Hinduism (in this case Vaishnavism specifically) is one thing or many, in a new way, to broader concerns in the anthropology of space and place on one hand, and the anthropology of emotions and affect on the other. This was possible because I realized that the radically contrasting ways in which devotees embody Vaishnavism in Navadvip-Mayapur are interestingly related, since all Vaishnavas pursue versions of a mode of spiritual engagement that they experience as a form of intensely emotional place-making, a process of attaining an ecstatic devotional goal they all think of as Vrindavan. For Vaishnavas, therefore, Vrindavan is not only a place-name but even almost a shorthand term for intense states of devotional exaltation.

While Vaishnavism, a critical strand of devotional Hinduism, refers to the worship of the deity Vishnu and his incarnations, in Bengal, Krishna, his lover Radha, and Chaitanya are revered as the supreme divinities. Radha and Krishna are never worshipped as independent deities in Bengal, but always together, as the divine couple embroiled in the most passionate erotic relationship in their cosmic abode, Vrindavan. Thus, Bengali temples worship *vigrahas* (idols) of the two deities together, and devotees always refer to them in the same breath, as Radha-Krishna: the couple united in love.[1] Furthermore, the Radha-Krishna sacred aesthetic is not only incomplete but also impossible without the imagining of Vrindavan. Bengal-Vaishnavas also consider Chaitanya to be the dual manifestation of Radha-Krishna, the deities enjoying their intense union in and through his body.[2]

These distinct beliefs and practices are bound within the sophisticated philosophy of Bengal-Vaishnavism: *achintya-bhed-abhed* (simultaneous difference/dualism/separation and non-difference/monism/union, a simultaneity that is inconceivable by profane sensibilities). This unique relationship of difference/non-difference exists between the supreme deity, Krishna, and his world, including Vrindavan, where he is manifest, and his lovers or devotees, including Radha. The theology asserts that of Krishna's intrinsic energies, one amounts to the cosmic pleasure principle (*hladini sakti*), which underlies any manifestation of bliss, including the pleasurable relations Krishna enjoys with his entourage. Since these relations are essentially part of Krishna's own nature, they are non-different from him, while because they are also different from him, he can engage in intense sensuous relationships with them. This explains why Radha-Krishna and Vrindavan are represented as always-enmeshed entities. The theology further explains that the utmost divine irony was that Krishna, the repertoire of greatest possible bliss, was unable to taste his own sweetness (*madhurya*), though Radha, by virtue of being his supreme lover, could. With a fine stroke of imagination, the two thus decided to incarnate in the same body, to taste each other's love (*prem*) in the same site. So Chaitanya was literally born as the perfect embodiment of *achinty-abhedabhed* between Radha-Krishna.[3] Since Krishna's devotees, a part of his own divine nature, bound with him in the same relation of difference/non-difference, are also potentially able to realize the intense pleasure principle, so the ultimate purpose of Bengal-Vaishnavas is to drown themselves in the refined erotic ocean which blissfully merges Krishna and his world. Partaking in Vrindavan's pleasures becomes their goal.

Thus, while South Asian *bhakti* (devotional) traditions in general are widely characterized as personalized devotion with the aim of arousing intense emotional relations with deities, Chaitanyaite devotion holds a special place in this regard. It puts the utmost premium on devotees' being able to experience these divine erotic moods at their own most embodied, visceral levels.

Engagement with the Philosophy of Place

My two, initially distinct, aims of fieldwork were to study on the one hand the different pilgrimage processes of Navadvip and Mayapur and senses of place engendered therein, and on the other hand the devotional lives of Navadvip-Mayapur's resident devotees. The most revealing aspect of my fifteen months of fieldwork in the two places during 2009–10, however, was that the connection between my two ethnographic aims was much closer than I had thought. For Bengal-Vaishnavas, senses of place are not limited to physical pilgrimage geographies but interestingly intertwined with their religious practices. My two fieldwork aims thus ultimately merged because distinctive dimensions of place-experience and sensuous apprehensions of divinity through varied spiritual practices overlap, such that devotees experience sacred geography not only in external physical sites but also in interiorized affective spaces of their bodies, minds, imagination, and senses. So my concern is with the exact nature of the rigorous affective and bodily disciplines enacted by different Vaishnavas through regimes of personal and collective practice, and the significant relationships of these practices with the cultivation of senses of place. These practices range from, for instance, spiritual arts of musical exaltation, to the cultivation of impassioned erotic identification with Radha-Krishna and their enactment of cosmic arousal in Vrindavan. So I locate my book within a diverse set of concerns in the anthropology of religion (especially Hinduism), the anthropology and philosophy of place, and the anthropology and philosophy of emotions, affect, and the senses.

The various spiritual practices I document in this book have the aim of transporting or translocating devotees to Radha-Krishna's cosmic abode, celestial Vrindavan, which is characterized by devotees as a site at once of sensuous delight, divine sexuality, and spiritual bliss. Transportation to celestial Vrindavan, as discussed through the different chapters, implies different things: traversing Navadvip-Mayapur during pilgrimage; serving the deities emplaced there; visualizing Vrindavan in imagination; hearing Vrindavan's acoustics; and being able to apprehend within one's own bodily interiors the erotic heightening that Radha-Krishna experiences in Vrindavan. Thus, my book analyzes complex intertwinings of affect, cultivated emotion, and physical stimulation of sensory capacities, including hearing, visualization, and sexual arousal, all known to be central to Radha-Krishna-centered devotion, but which I explore in connection with different senses of place. I seek to establish that for Bengal-Vaishnavas the process of being a spiritually active devotee is crucially rooted in different ways of realizing specific sensory awareness of Vrindavan; and the various kinds of intense physicality associated with the experience of Vrindavan are what this book documents and analyzes.

FIGURE 1. Idols of Radha-Krishna and their girlfriends with Vrindavan's scenery in the background.

For Bengal-Vaishnavas, Vrindavan is not only the famous and active North Indian Vaishnavite pilgrimage town with its hundreds of temples and practitioner Vaishnavas, but more centrally the deities' cosmic abode, celestial Vrindavan, alternatively referred to as Vraja or Goloka, meaning "the place of senses." The physical town of Vrindavan is considered by devotees the earthly manifestation of celestial Vrindavan. This celestial site of divine activities is imagined by them to be a rustic paradise, a beautiful forested area cut across by the rippling river Yamuna, where spring is the eternal season, where the deity-consort enact their daily and eternal passionate love-plays (*lilas*), and where their attractive handmaidens serve them and sing melodies in their praise. Many Indian households display the famous oleograph with the best-known Vrindavan image: Krishna dancing with his lovers in the dark forest and love-bower on a full-moon night with beautiful peacocks in the background. For all Bengal-Vaishnavas, Radha-Krishna devotionalism is indeed impossible without the imagining of this sensuous place.

Stewart (2005, 267) argues similarly that imagining celestial Vrindavan's spatial environment is a prelude to establishing relations with deities, since the deities' romance is necessarily conceptualized as being emplaced in Vrindavan; and Entwistle (1991, 88) says that this idea of Vrindavan is a mode of "pastoralization" in which the aesthetics

FIGURE 2. Evening temple-sermon in Navadvip.

of imagining the land is a kind of participation with the intention of traveling to the same place after death.

A sense of place is indeed crucial for many Hindu after-life beliefs, for instance the wish to be transported to Vishnu's heaven on death. The sacred place as soteriological destination provides a sense of religious belonging and security, and theistic Hindu traditions benefit from tangible references to where and how deities reside. Contrary to monistic Vedantist traditions where the soul is considered to eventually merge with the disembodied almighty, dualist traditions assert the reality of embodied deities and the places they reside in, and the distinct relations devotees embody with them before and after death.

In Navadvip and Mayapur temples, for an hour every morning or evening, scores of devotees gather to hear gurus read Sanskrit verses from a ninth-century Vaishnava text, the *Bhagavata Purana*, and explain their meanings in Bengali.

While the *Bhagavad Gita*, which exalts Krishna as the *Mahabharata*'s warrior-god, is popular among many North Indian devotional groups and appropriated by Hindu nationalist-militant organizations like the Rashtriya Swayamsevak Sangh or RSS (Horstmann 1995; Malinar 1995), Bengal-Vaishnavas, while respecting the *Gita*, more centrally celebrate the *Bhagavatam*. Hardy's (1983) classic work shows how the *Bhagavatam*, which narrates stories of "sweet devotion," of Krishna's childhood and adolescence spent in Vrindavan, became the historical harbinger of "emotional Krishna *bhakti*." So Bengali devotees hear about Radha-Krishna's daily routine in celestial Vrindavan—when they wake up together in the forest bowers after their nocturnal passionate love-acts, what they do in their respective homes through the day, how and where they meet for their secret trysts (since Radha is married to another man), and details of their emotions during periods of intense union and separation. Devotees know these stories by heart but still regularly flock to temples to relish them together. The daily routine of serving deities in all Nadia temples also mirrors the deities' routine in Vrindavan as described in the *Bhagavatam*. Bengal's Vaishnava calendar also celebrates monthly festivals commemorating Radha-Krishna's special activities in celestial Vrindavan, for instance Holi, the colorful spring festival in February/March, or Ras, Krishna's circle-dance with his lovers on the autumnal full-moon night in November. Vrindavan is thus a one-word representation for the entire emotional apparatus which makes divine activities possible and worthy of spiritual apprehension by Bengal-Vaishnava devotees.

While Bengal-Vaishnavas conceptualize celestial Vrindavan, the quintessential place of love, as the destination they want to reach after lives of spiritual perfection, they also claim to experience glimpses of the deity-consort and their own devotional selves emplaced in and serving them in celestial Vrindavan, during their present lives' devotional practices. Their spiritual telos is therefore capable of manifesting itself in their practices of the present, and Bengal-Vaishnavas have three distinct senses of place: the celestial after-life destination; the Navadvip-Mayapur sacred topography where they reside; and devotional practices which help them apprehend sensuous pleasures of the divine place within their own minds, bodies, and senses. It is the second and third of these senses of place which this book analyzes in detail. Thus, unlike Ayodhya, Banaras, and other South Asian pilgrimage places which become important for pilgrims as sites where for instance some key manifestation of divinity occurred, say where Ram was born, or where death-rituals may be performed, in Navadvip-Mayapur we encounter forms of place-awareness which are cultivated in sites far exceeding and more complicated than physical, geographical ones. So, while Hindu pilgrimage centers often derive their importance from being associated with providing devotees the potential of "crossing over" from the present life to the next,[4] in light of the distinctiveness of Bengal-Vaishnava practices, to which Entwistle's (1991) account of Vrindavan as a goal for devotees' *after-life* attainment does not do full justice, what has not been fully documented by other scholars is the complexity of Vrindavan's significance in the *ongoing* spiritual lives of devotees.

Thus, the main question my book seeks to answer is what sites and senses of place beyond physical geographical ones can do to our notions of space/place, affect, and sanctity. While I build on the anthropology of religion/Hinduism and pilgrimage which foregrounds senses of place in relation to the sanctity of physically located spaces, I argue that this is not all, and attention to complexities of place and affect as interacting dimensions of religious experience, by conceptualizing senses of sacred place interiorized in devotees' minds and bodies, can contribute to diverse anthropological interests in devotional Hinduism, sacred geography, senses of place, and cultivation of affective interiors of the body and mind. The analyses of the book congeal with increasing nuances as the narrative progresses. Traveling through both exterior and interior landscapes, I show that the practitioner inhabits Krishna's world through every daily religious practice. The synesthesia that results from the overlap of these different planes of experience confirms the intensely transformative power of Vaishnava ritual processes.

The ways in which Vrindavan is experienced are not homogeneous, however, and there are contestations among devotees about the ideal mode of apprehending celestial Vrindavan. These different place-experiences demonstrate the political complexity and plurality of Vaishnava subjectivities in contemporary Bengal. I demonstrate that different Vaishnava groups, while borrowing from the same discursive tenets of Bengal-Vaishnavism, emphasize opposing interpretations of devotional emotions, how these emotions are cultivated and affectively experienced, and their significant ways of embodying Vrindavan.

For all Bengal-Vaishnavas, reverence for sacred geography begins with physical landscapes. Thus, since Chaitanya is worshipped as the dual incarnation of Radha-Krishna, devotees refer to and sanctify the Nadia region, Chaitanya's birthplace, as *gupta*-Vrindavan, where *gupta* means "veiled." That is, since Chaitanya is the embodiment of Radha-Krishna's love, so devotees venerate his birthplace as undifferentiated from Radha-Krishna's passion-abode, Vrindavan. The notion of *gupta*-Vrindavan is crucial for this book as both a descriptive and an analytical category and refers not only to Nadia's landscape but even to interiorized spaces of the body or mind, cultivated and experienced by devotees as Radha-Krishna's *lila-sthal* (playground). Referring to these sites as veiled-Vrindavan signifies that they conceal the spiritual/erotic essence of celestial Vrindavan, which is potentially accessible to those who cultivate appropriate spiritual techniques. Thus, the notion of the veil as covering or obscuring is a metaphor for the perceptions of the devotee before his or her connection with the place or meaning of Vrindavan is brought to light. My central concern in this book is with the techniques and experiences of unveiling and emplacement in these diverse affective spaces, a key dimension of Vaishnava spirituality not generally recognized in the literature on devotional Hinduism.

Different practices help different groups of devotees experience Vrindavan in distinct ritual sites including but far surpassing physical geographies: in different ways of relating to Nadia's consecrated landscape; through services rendered toward the physical place, Mayapur; in the interiors of the body-mind through sensuous imagination; in corporeal interiors through intense sexual arousal; and through intensely experienced aural sensations of spiritual music. All my informants, though representing different kinds of Vaishnavisms, affirmed that through their different devotional practices, Radha-Krishna's cosmic presence in Vrindavan becomes *prakat* (unveiled/apparent) in these very sites. So, while Sax (1990) and Mason (2009, 16–17) have demonstrated, regarding Ramlila in Ayodhya and Raslila in Vrindavan, respectively, that these Vaishnavite theatrical performances carry an emotional import which transports audiences to the corresponding celestial places, for Bengal-Vaishnavas the difference between spiritual reality and theatricality is blurred. Their differential practices claim to manifest Vrindavan in their everyday lives, in their very sites of ritual performances.[5]

Crucial implications follow from this. While all devotees living in Navadvip-Mayapur consider their physical locales of residence, and the North Indian town of Vrindavan, sacrosanct, some also emphasize potent ways of experiencing celestial Vrindavan's sacrality in interiorized sites. Thus, one may well be walking on noisy roads and still consider oneself, in one's imagination, to be in Vrindavan, and one's imagination in this case *is* the sacred place, spiritually as important as the physical town or the Vrindavan heavens. Thus, the sense of place for Bengal-Vaishnavas is marked by the potential of constant reproduction or proliferation, and the different levels of this very complex layered geography, from cosmic heavens to physical places to interiorized affective spaces, are all experienced as equally real.

I grew up hearing innumerable Bengali songs which convey the senses of "I carry Krishna in my heart," "I have stopped searching for

Vrindavan for it is here inside me," and so on, but I understood only after intensive fieldwork that rather than being merely poetic and metaphoric references these literally derive from Vaishnava experiences of place as interiorized in devotees' bodies/minds, that is, the sacred place as both sedentary and itinerant, and of Vaishnavas' devotional selves as both dwellers and travellers. I demonstrate through the different chapters, therefore, that senses of place are not necessarily only embedded in physical locales, and that even when disembedded they are experienced as thoroughly embodied.

In addition to devotees' experiences of physical geographies, therefore, through the different chapters I also discuss Vaishnava understandings of the place-*in*-the-body/mind and so on, that is, the body-as-place, the mind-as-place, and the auditory sense as apprehending senses of place. So, while the contemporary anthropology of place and embodiment, following Edward Casey's (1993) philosophy, is dominated by the idea of body-in-place, my book seeks to extend his formulations by also analyzing cultural constructions and experiences of place *in* the body, mind, and so on. My analyses have resonance with Gaston Bachelard's notions of space. In *The Poetics of Space* (1994, xxxvi) he talks about the "topography of our intimate being," locating the fullest possible experiences of place and space, from the most intimate to the most immense, within the interiority of the self. Thus, he too articulates the notion of a "layered geography" (viii) and demonstrates, especially with respect to imagination, that senses of place can equally be non-physical.

Bachelard's philosophy, although much lauded, has recently been criticized as subjectivist and mentalistic. Casey (1998, 295) for instance says that Bachelard's philosophy, or "psychography," with its emphasis on the "psychical topography and the inner structure of inhabitation," relies much on ideas of the psyche and does not account for embodied experiences of the body-in-place (1993, 306). In fact, both the anthropology of place and the anthropology of emotions, affect, and senses have recently criticized studies of interiority, primarily on two related grounds: first, that they highlight dimensions of the mind and consciousness rather than embodied experience, and second, that they assume the idea of the autonomous, bounded, sovereign, thinking subject (Ahmed 2004; Hirschkind 2006, 28–29).

However, Bachelard's ideas hold much relevance for my work in thinking about people's notions of space and place as both exterior and interior to the self. But in contrast to Bachelard and in agreement with the recent anthropology of place and affect, I show that Vaishnava place-experiences in every instance are thoroughly embodied rather than relying only on abstract mental dimensions. Also, in many cases these interiorized embodied experiences are intensely affective, that is, they arise from pre-conscious or supra-conscious and pre- or supra-subjective levels of bodily and mental dispositions. As gushes of sensation, these affective excesses overwhelm consciousness and therefore also the sense of subjective autonomy. Thus, I argue that the anthropology of place and affect have much to gain from conceptualizing people's relations with both external geographies and interiorized spaces of the mind, body, and senses, and I seek to demonstrate throughout the book that interiorized place-experiences, rather than being biased toward the Cartesian dualist category of the mind, are also experienced as thoroughly embodied and affective.

Engagement with the Anthropology of Hinduism

I grew up observing that many fellow Calcuttans from educated, professional, upper-middle-class backgrounds criticize Vaishnavas, calling them over-affected and hyper-emotional at best and debased at worst. They make fun of Krishna's popular image as the flirtatious lad of Vrindavan; they laugh at how Vaishnavas roll around and cry out with emotion when listening to devotional music describing Radha-Krishna's spiritual/erotic activities (*kirtan*), and at their admitting the poorest and low-caste people into their religion. Urban Bengali films have ample comic songs parodying *kirtan* tunes, and references to fake gurus as almost always Vaishnava. Also, many urban people who disparage Vaishnavas associate them with dirty sexual practices.

These understandings have insistent pasts. The colonial stereotype, especially among the Western-educated Indian elite, was that the heightened emotionalism associated with the worship of Krishna, the lover-god, was improper for zealous nation-building, while the aggressive masculine vigor associated with Ram-worshipping cults was appropriate.[6] There was also the Vedantic assertion that Hinduism is high and exalted only when disembodied, and Krishna cults, with their emphasis on erotic love between deities and on sensuous devotion, were seen as licentious.

In colonial Bengal, similarly, the urban, educated middle class (*bhadralok*) displayed ambivalent responses toward Vaishnavism. While Chaitanya's charismatic personality was celebrated, the *bhadralok* had internalized notions of puritanical religiosity via their colonial education, and a great part of their anxiety centered on the embodied and therefore emasculating tendencies of Chaitanyaite devotionalism.[7] In this milieu, during the late nineteenth century in Calcutta, a Western-educated colonial bureaucrat, Kedarnath Datta, decided to redefine and consolidate a new Vaishnavism which would no longer be associated with what many of his contemporaries represented as excess emotionalism, and which would have urban, upper-caste, educated devotees, instead of its usual influence among rural people and "prostitutes, beggars and untouchables" (Fuller 2003, 207). Datta's version of Vaishnavism was extremely popular in urban Bengal, and it was the precursor to modern reformist Vaishnava institutions, the Gaudiya Math (established in 1918) and ISKCON (established in 1966). Calcuttans' opinions of Vaishnavism were in fact tempered by Tagore's compositions resembling Vaishnava songs and the increasing influence of Gaudiya Math and ISKCON among them.

My fieldwork, however, exposed me to many faces of Vaishnavism. While Mayapur's religious landscape is permeated with the kind of Vaishnavism represented by ISKCON and Gaudiya Math, the champions of reformist Vaishnavism, this is far from the entire gamut of Nadia's or rural Bengal's devotional variety. The river Ganga is like a divider of devotionalism, and on the opposite side, in Navadvip, I found Vaishnava groups which represent wild diversities in celebrating "alternative Krishnas" (Beck 2005). Navadvip's Vaishnavisms have no shame of their sensuous pasts, and retained their intense religions all through the colonial period. Their relationships with Vrindavan are exalted only when affective, their religion considered high only when embodied. Rather than any aggressive masculinist bias, their practices emphasize the need to cultivate feminine subjectivities and moods as Krishna's lovers or Radha's handmaidens. So my concerns about Bengal-Vaishnava devotionalism differ from the analytical tropes of older studies of Vaishnavism and Hinduism.

Fuller (2003, 187–91) infers that with the ascent of Kedarnath Datta's puritanical Vaishnavism as the unequivocal modern progressive fulfillment of religion, ISKCON and Gaudiya Math became most powerful in Bengal, with the marginalization of other Vaishnavas, including traditional Vaishnavas of Navadvip. I argue that his inference has an urban bias toward what he calls the "bhadralok habitus" (203). It is not entirely correct to assume that the predominant form of religion to study in Bengal is that of the puritanical urban minority, since their pursuits are not representative of the wider Bengali religious world.

However, my focus on the emotive articulations of *bhakti*, while primarily built on ethnographic evidence, is also heavily influenced by the philosophical history of Vaishnavism. Bengal-Vaishnavism ascribes singular importance to the worship of Krishna's "sweeter" moods (*madhurya*), as opposed to his kingly warrior moods (*aishwarya*), and accordingly to cultivating emotional relationships with him. Hardy (1983) argues that "emotional Krishna *bhakti*," a later historical development, evolved with the popularity of the *Bhagavata Purana*, as the psychological merger of aesthetic, erotic, and ecstatic devotional levels. Intellectual, non-emotional *bhakti* which focused on yogic concentration on the divine, as propounded in the *Gita* for instance, received more scholarly attention, however.

But studies of Hinduism which downplayed emotion severely restricted its epistemological possibilities. It is important to recognize the productive analytical capacity of emotion, especially when it is the structuring principle of religion, as in Bengal-Vaishnavism, while also to avoid reified understandings of emotion, by highlighting traditions of debate over it.

The distinctiveness of Bengal-Vaishnavism is that the different groups constitute an intensely competitive topography of contested emotions, each claiming to represent the ideal mode of being Vaishnava. Their debates include contestations over the best way to experience the sacred place, the best way to love Radha-Krishna and place themselves in relation to their sexuality, and the role of the body in devotion. So the situation in Navadvip-Mayapur differs from that of Ayodhya and Vrindavan described by van der Veer (1987, 1989) and Brooks (1989), where inherently very different modes of religiosity—of feminine/ecstatic and militant, and of modern (ISKCON) and traditional varieties, respectively—cohabit peacefully.

My ethnography thus posed the crucial question central to studies of debated traditions of religion, that is, who is a "true" Vaishnava, or which mode of religiosity is "true." This question of authenticity can be viewed through three possible lenses, and each suggests that all forms of Bengal-Vaishnavisms are equally true, and thus that the search for authenticity is a non-question in the first place. First, in terms of religious truth as textual fidelity, all groups of Bengal-Vaishnavas borrow heavily from the same discursive corpus, especially the *Bhagavatam*, the *Gita*, and *Chaitanya Charitamrita*, Chaitanya's chief biography, although they offer different interpretations of the texts. Second, since all groups maintain strict self-definitions as Vaishnavas and in fact as the only true representatives of Vaishnavism, I follow the anthropological impulse of taking people's narratives seriously, and theorizing their claims to ultimate legitimacy. Third, if truth is understood in terms of the immediate effects which religion has, then the practices of all kinds of Vaishnavas impact the real corporeal bases of devotees' bodies and sensibilities. This thread proves to be most critical in the book's analyses.

My specific engagements with the anthropology of Hinduism thus range from issues concerning the relation between devotion and embodiment—including sensory dimensions of *bhakti* explored through religious music, feminine modes of worship, and dimensions of tantric religiosity—to issues of modern globalized religions and long-standing traditions of pilgrimage. Also, while it has widely been asserted that South Asian devotional traditions are associated with intensely corporeal and sensuous apprehensions of the divine, this book deals with the absolute specifics of how *exactly* the devotees' sensuality and sexuality interact with their senses of sacrality. Unlike what has been explored in earlier studies, I deal with nuanced details of how different kinds of Vaishnavas use their bodies, minds, and senses, in both similar and starkly dissimilar ways, to establish relations with Radha-Krishna, and to sense the sacred place, Vrindavan; that is, how they construct and experience multiple (and contested) Vaishnava subjectivities.

My exploration of the intrinsic and intricate relations among senses of place, affect, and devotion also contribute to two related and persistent debates in the history and anthropology of (South Asian) religions: that is, what enables the continuity of some South Asian devotional traditions over centuries (in this case, four centuries), and more generally, how religious discourses sustain and perpetuate themselves in and through bodily practices. These, however, are issues which I raise in the conclusion of the book, issues which help me analyze the respective conditions of experience which constitute the simultaneous importance, popularity, and continuity of the extremely different kinds of Bengal-Vaishnavisms. In concluding my work, I argue that despite radical differences among them, common to all Bengal-Vaishnava groups is a proliferative impulse which is embodied in and strengthened by their different practices of place-experience and affective community formation. The most complex practices of each of the Bengal-Vaishnava groups are worth book-length analyses, and an ethnographic comparison in a single work of all the different religious perspectives they bring forth has hitherto not been attempted.

THE FIELD

Navadvip is one of the oldest Bengali towns, known since the medieval period as a center of Sanskrit learning and the dwelling-place of famous Vaishnava practitioners (Mondol 2002; Radi 2004). All Bengalis immediately associate Navadvip with traditional, knowledgeable Vaishnavas. Today it is a municipal town with primarily a lower-middle-class population, and like other Bengali towns, it is small, and not as developed or well-equipped as the cities. It is better-off than the surrounding villages in Nadia, however. It has very narrow lanes with open drains and old houses, and the town center is bustling with busy marketplaces and loud, honking rickshaws. Small schools, municipality offices, sweet-shops, and shops selling brass and handloomed products, Navadvip's traditional industrial goods, are common all over the town. Dotted over the entire town, almost in every narrow lane, with maximum concentration in the area between the main railway station to the south, another railway station to the west, and the riverbanks or *ghats* to the east, are more than hundred temples and ashrams, and Navadvip has a busy pilgrimage life all year.

Generally close to the town center and amid busy pilgrimage routes are *goswami* temples with centuries-old idols of Radha-Krishna, Chaitanya, and/or his important associates. One of the four major sets of devotee-followers of distinctive Vaishnava traditions I studied were the *goswamis*, who are economically relatively comfortable by semi-urban standards, often college-educated, married, householder Brahmin-priests, who own and live within their large temple compounds, or in well-built houses adjacent to the temples. They claim to be blood descendants of Chaitanya's important associates, and this makes them gurus of utmost importance.[8] They have innumerable disciples in the outskirts of Calcutta, in the towns and villages of many North Indian states, including West Bengal, Orissa, Assam, and even in Bangladesh.

The two *goswami* lineages which dominate Navadvip are descendants of Chaitanya's brother-in-law, and Chaitanya's major associate, Nityananda. Both date back to the sixteenth or seventeenth century, and each claims 300–350 members in Navadvip.[9] Although they do not constitute a very big proportion of the town's population, *goswamis* are most respected among people as very scholarly and representative of traditional Vaishnavism. Most *goswamis* earn their living from temple fees paid by pilgrims, and oratory on sacred Vaishnava texts, and these days many members of *goswami* families are also occupied in nonreligious and medium-paid jobs like clerical services and school teaching, and some in higher-paid jobs in Navadvip, Calcutta, and other towns and cities. Many *goswamis* perform *puja* and are invited to render discourses on spiritual topics from the *Bhagavatam*, *Gita*, and Chaitanya's biographies in different temples and devotees' houses in Vaishnava-predominant places such as Bengal, Vrindavan, and Puri, and devotee-listeners pay voluntary sums during these occasions. *Goswami* women mostly take care of their homes, but like their husbands, can be gurus to initiated disciples.

Mostly away from the town center, in isolated quiet areas, are small ashrams known as Vaishnava *akhras*, meaning places for spiritual discussion, where ascetic renunciate men known as *babajis* live in small groups. It is difficult to exactly quantify how many hundreds of *babajis* live in Navadvip. In addition to the basil-seed necklaces (*tulsi-mala*) and vertical forehead designs made of clay (*tilak*) which are common to all Vaishnavas, *babajis* wear a white loincloth (*dor-koupin*) and carry a white or grey shawl. They are mostly poor, and in some ashrams I have seen wealthy devotees donate blankets to them during winter. *Babajis* are initiated into Chaitanyaite-Vaishnavism through senior renunciate gurus, and like *goswamis*, claim that their spiritual lineages date back to the sixteenth or seventeenth century. They live relatively secluded lives doing ashram work throughout the day and dedicating most of their time to personal spiritual practice. Some *akhras* are also temples and run on pilgrims' donations. Many *babajis* maintain the tradition of Vaishnava *vairagis* (renouncers) and go begging in Navadvip. Those *goswamis* and *babajis* who are more popular as gurus are away from Navadvip for extensive periods, rendering sermons and preaching in different areas of Bengal, Assam, Bangladesh, and so on.

Apart from economic disparities, the main difference between *goswamis* and *babajis* is that *goswamis* are householders and *babajis*, renunciates. Thus one is born into and initiated in a *goswami* family, but one joins a guru to become a *babaji*, and *goswamis* wear the brahmanical sacred thread while renouncer-*babajis* denounce the caste system. Despite this, these two Vaishnava groups generally share peaceful relations. They together claim to represent Chaitanya's authentic teachings, and have similar religious practices, which I document and analyze in this book. *Babajis* invite important *goswamis* to festivals in their *akhras*, and vice versa. However, both groups despise another group claiming to be Vaishnava, the *sahajiyas*, who also feature significantly in my study. They refused to even talk much about *sahajiyas*. During our conversations they repeatedly emphasized that *sahajiyas* "do dirty things" and that due to them Vaishnavism "got a bad name among educated people." They kept saying, "*Sahajiyas* don't live in our Navadvip. They are not Vaishnavas at all." "Their" Navadvip is identified as a sanitized sacred space belonging to *goswamis* and *babajis*, while *sahajiya*-Vaishnavas indeed live in the town's outskirts.

All along Navadvip's railroad tracks, partly within Nadia and partly in the adjacent district, Bardhamman, *sahajiyas* live in thatched huts. They belong to Bengal's lowest castes and classes, and own no major temple. It is difficult to assess their exact numbers, although they say there are roughly around 250 (or more) couples in the area. Thus, although fewer in number than *goswamis* or *babajis*, they have a substantial presence. *Sahajiyas* are repudiated by others because they are the only Vaishnava group in Bengal which allows women to take renunciation and permits cohabitation with partners even after renunciation. Thus, householder and renouncer *sahajiyas* follow similar lifestyles, and very often men and women cohabit without getting married. *Sahajiyas* live very modest lives. Renouncer *sahajiyas* mostly go begging (*madhukori*) in the mornings to nearby villages, and some earn money through ad hoc masonry, farming, and so on. Those *sahajiyas* who are gurus have innumerable disciples in rural Bengal, and earn by lecturing on Bengal-Vaishnava scriptures in the rural interior.

Nadia's look and feel changes completely, however, as one crosses the river to Mayapur. Mayapur is a small, quiet, serene, and clean village with large stretches of green fields. In 1894, Kedarnath Datta identified a particular spot in Mayapur as Chaitanya's birthplace and built a temple there—in opposition to a group of *babajis* who insisted that the birthplace was in Navadvip (see chapter 2). Since then Mayapur has witnessed a rapid increase in pilgrimage and the growth of a series of massive, glossy temples, and in the late 1960s the Vaishnava guru A. C. Bhaktivedanta popularized in America the reformed Vaishnavism initiated by Kedarnath Datta, founded ISKCON, and declared its headquarters in Mayapur. ISKCON's devotionalism also occupies an important position in my book.

ISKCON has thousands of devotees all over the world, and middle-class and rich followers in Indian cities, who donate huge sums of money and contribute to Mayapur's and ISKCON's development of sites and spaces, which need effective management, embellishment, and upkeep. A large number of foreign devotees live in ISKCON's headquarters enclosure. Unprecedented in any other East Indian village, amidst the rural ambience, ISKCON, in addition to its colossal, opulent temples, offers its resident-devotees and pilgrims posh guest-houses, fast-food restaurants, ATM facilities, and international education.

The Navadvip-Mayapur region is thus an interesting complex of varied religious, social, and economic differences.

Nadia's Vaishnava population and pilgrimage have increased significantly since the 1970s. This is both because of ISKCON's establishment and because a number of *sahajiyas* and *babajis* migrated here from Bangladesh after the 1971 war. Nadia shares a border with Bangladesh on its east, and a significant number of refugee Vaishnavas chose Navadvip because of its age-long reputation as an important Vaishnava center. Although Nadia already had a thriving Vaishnava culture, it witnessed a sudden vibrancy in the competitive socio-religious topography, with greater numbers of *goswamis, babajis, sahajiyas,* and ISKCON devotees beginning to inhabit a concentrated geography, embodying different kinds of Vaishnavisms, and claiming to be ideal representatives of the religion. All four of the Vaishnava groups I discuss in the book derive their chief means of economic and religious sustenance from increasing numbers of disciples, and claims to the best form of Vaishnavism serve as important means to attract disciples. Each group articulates similar religious principles while displaying subtle mechanisms of explaining the others' interpretations as at best inadequate and at worst illegitimate.

Despite sharp economic discrepancies, however, no Vaishnava group has been able to displace the religious/social authority of the others. This is because rather than economic wealth, many disciples seek in their gurus scriptural knowledge, emotional intensity, and/or the capacity to teach devotees how to experience Vrindavan. Different Vaishnava groups appeal to different kinds of devotees. While ISKCON is more popular among the urban elite and international patron-devotees, *goswamis* and *babajis* have some devotees in Calcutta and in Bengali towns, mostly among those who are not extremely well-off but are educated and who relate to the traditional, scriptural Vaishnavism these groups represent. They also have substantial numbers of disciples, comparable to the massive extent of *sahajiya* popularity, in rural Bengal. While ISKCON can boast of worldwide popularity and influence as a globalized religious movement, *goswamis* and *babajis* boast of their long genealogy of past gurus and tremendous scriptural knowledge, and *sahajiyas,* of their strong religious convictions and ever-increasing popularity in rural Bengal.

Despite their differences, Vaishnava groups are marked by an ideological equality which this book explores in detail: their competitive relations in asserting ritual superiority as being "true" Vaishnavas. Also, although all my informants recognized that Vaishnavism is a distinct Hindu *sampradaya* (sect/tradition), they consider this more of a factual detail, and are rather more comfortable with the notion of Vaishnavism as an experiential disposition and mode of personhood marked by ego-effacement, humility, and an intense relationship with Radha-Krishna in Vrindavan.

SENSES OF PLACE

Nadia's landscape, known as *gupta*-Vrindavan, is revered by all Vaishnavas as the abode of Chaitanya's and thereby Radha-Krishna's earthly manifestation, and every Vaishnava group experiences emotive attachment toward the sacred lands in ways that are particular to their varied modes of devotional self-definition. Practitioners express their love of the landscape through historical and mythical stories about temples/ashrams they own in the landscape. In chapter 2, I seek to demonstrate that there are inherent relationships between the devotional self-experiences of contesting Vaishnava groups and the narrativized landscape which is inhabited and constituted simultaneously through the telling of these stories. There are conflicts among Vaishnava practitioners over their claims to Nadia's physical topography, which also reflect debates about true modes of embodying devotion. The location of Chaitanya's birthplace, for instance, has been disputed between Mayapur Vaishnavas and a group of Navadvip *babajis* since the late nineteenth century. Also, all Vaishnavas (except *sahajiyas*, who own no temple), emphasize the paramount importance of their own temples/ashrams and their histories, as embodiments of their kinds of devotion, and this serves as a most important method of attracting pilgrims to become their potential disciples in the economic and political competition for sacred space. Pilgrims flock to Nadia from various parts of Bengal, Assam, Manipur, Vrindavan, Orissa, and now, thanks to ISKCON's influence, from other parts of India and the world. Due to their unrelenting affection for the consecrated lands, however, pilgrims, in the last instance, instead of being caught up in these political debates over specific sites, exhibit passionate engagement with the entire landscape.

My most distinctive revelation during fieldwork, however, was that Vaishnavite devotional life in Bengal is characterized by an immense

diversity of ways in which the sacred place, Vrindavan, is conceptualized and experienced, of which historicizing and narrativizing the
physical landscape is only one component. Vaishnavas also choose
to experience the sacrality and passions of Radha-Krishna's love in
Vrindavan in other ritual sites. The mark of spiritual ascendancy,
most Vaishnavas assert, is in witnessing Radha-Krishna and glimpses of
Vrindavan *within* themselves, that is, in sensing the sacred place within
themselves. Which group identifies and cultivates which site as veiled-
Vrindavan, that is, what unveils itself as the ideal location for spiritual
emplacement, is determined according to practitioners' varying social
and political positions.

Goswamis and *babajis* have spiritual practices in common and take
great pride in the fact that they have preserved these practices, con-
solidated by their spiritual ancestors, continuously since the medieval
period. An important aspect of this pride is in their claimed sanitiza-
tion of religion. They reiterate how after Chaitanya's death a number
of religious groups (such as *sahajiyas*) developed which misinterpreted
Vaishnava teachings to foreground "dirty," indulgent practices. They
practiced sex with gurus and identified coital pleasure with experiencing the same erotic pleasures as Radha-Krishna. *Goswamis* and *babajis*
define their spirituality in clear opposition to these groups. However,
they admit that the best way to sense Vrindavan pleasures is to experience divine passions. In chapter 3, I analyze how they resolve this
contradiction by locating Vrindavan in their imagination, imagination deemed to be passionately embodied without being carnal. They
emphasize that devotees must rejoice in divine sensuality by vividly
imagining Radha-Krishna's erotic *lilas* (love-plays), but that direct
sexual experience must be reserved for the deities. Thus, they imagine themselves as Radha's young handmaidens, who arrange Radha-
Krishna's secret erotic trysts in Vrindavan's forests, and even witness
them in detail, but never desire similar relations with Krishna. They
say that this is the best way to experience erotic passions without
allowing them to disrupt a devotee's humility. They regard their *manas*
(the intermediate space between mind and heart) as the ideal spiritual
site, veiled-Vrindavan, which unveils the deities' *lilas* in every passionate detail through disciplined imagination. Thus they say *"ei manas-
e Vrindavan prakat hoy"*: Vrindavan becomes apparent in the mind-
heart; or simply, the mind/heart is Vrindavan.

All Vaishnavas are socialized into a common discursive theme, an
analytical distinction devotees are taught to make, and which I heard

being reiterated an ample number of times by gurus during morning and evening classes on Vaishnava scriptures in Nadia temples. This distinction is between *vaidhi bhakti* (disciplined devotion), the daily ritual discipline devotees must commit to—for instance, listening to *Bhagavatam* explanations from gurus, chanting deities' names, performing *puja*, and so on—and *raganuga bhakti* (passionate devotion), which develops after sustained practice of disciplined devotion and refers to emotional relationships devotees cultivate and experience in relation to Krishna. These may be in the mood of Krishna's mother, cowherd friend, servant, or Radha-Krishna's friend-handmaiden who rejoices in their erotic pleasures. Bengal-Vaishnavas consider the last variety to be spiritually the most rewarding. Like other key discursive concepts, Bengal-Vaishnavas borrow the distinction between *vaidhi bhakti* and *raganuga bhakti* from the theorizations of Rupa Goswami, one of the chief theologians and aestheticians deployed by Chaitanya to consolidate Bengal-Vaishnava philosophy in the sixteenth century. In Rupa Goswami's classificatory framework of *bhakti*, both *vaidhi* and *raganuga* constitute *sadhana bhakti*, devotion which is born from active effort (De 1986, 171–73; Haberman 2003, 19).

Clearly, *goswamis'* and *babajis'* practice of witnessing Radha-Krishna's passionate activities in their imagination is an expression of *raganuga* devotion. However, the group they define their practices against is the *sahajiyas*, who make identical claims of embodying *raganuga* devotion and experiencing intense sensual delight. Yet, although embodying the same Vaishnava discourses, their practices are radically different, and all other Vaishnavas detest them as morally repugnant. *Sahajiyas* live a life confined to themselves. They do not flag their identities as *sahajiyas* when they go begging, and if any other Vaishnava identifies a person as a *sahajiya*, they avoid her at all costs. While Mayapur's ISKCON devotees do not interact with Navadvip's *goswamis* and *babajis*, their social lives have some inevitable crossroads, for instance when ISKCON brings pilgrims to visit some important *goswami* temple, or when, during my fieldwork, *goswamis*, *babajis*, and ISKCON all concurred in their criticism of a Bengali film that had just been released and which made fun of Vaishnavas in a particular song. But *sahajiyas* are a glaring absence on all such occasions.

For their part, however, *sahajiyas* claim to be the true Vaishnavas. They draw a distinction between the practices of *goswamis*, *babajis*, and ISKCON—which they call *shushko bhajan* (dry worship)—and their own practices, *ras-er sadhan* (juicy worship). For instance, *sahajiyas* associate the *goswami-babaji* practice of experiencing Vrindavan in imagination, or imagining deities' erotic encounters, with indirect intuitions of Vrindavan and therefore inferior devotional experiences. *Sahajiyas*, in contrast, cultivate and venerate their physical bodies as *gupta*-Vrindavan and claim to unveil and directly experience Radha-Krishna's passions in Vrindavan within their corporeal interiors, through yogic breathing routines, ingestion rituals, and sexual relationships with partners and gurus. *Rasa* means "viscous juice" and is interpreted by other Vaishnavas aesthetically as concentrated love toward Radha-Krishna. But *sahajiyas* emphasize that the best way to embody divine love is to interpret Vaishnava philosophical concepts as literally as possible. Thus, they understand *rasa* to mean male and female bodily excreta like sperm, menstrual blood, and urine, each of which is an embodiment of deities according to them, and in exchanging these body-fluids among themselves through yogic sex or ingestion, Vrindavan love, as fluid, flows among devotees' bodies. Thus, *sahajiyas* say *"ei dehe-i Vrindavan"*: Vrindavan is in the body-itself; or simply, the body is Vrindavan. I analyze *sahajiyas'* experiences of the body-as-place in chapter 4.

While many studies view *sahajiyas* and other similar Bengali religious groups as "subaltern" and their practices resistant to ideological intervention by mainstream religious groups, my fieldwork rather suggests that Navadvip's *sahajiyas* are religious actors in an equal, competitive political field, where every Vaishnava group claims to be the best representative of Vaishnavism.[10] Sarkar (2011, 347) uses the term "affective subalternity" to describe the devotional experiences of an eighteenth-century low-caste Vaishnava group in Bengal. My *sahajiya* friends, however, associate their affect with devotion but not any subaltern location. Thus, I avoid paradigms of subalternity when discussing the *sahajiyas*.

My strategy had been to work in Navadvip with *goswamis*, *babajis*, and *sahajiyas* first, and then do fieldwork in Mayapur. I worked in a milieu of extreme mutual disparagement, with each group claiming to be the true Vaishnavas and viewing the others with suspicion. All Vaishnavas more or less took for granted that I should study only their practices, the only true Vaishnavism(s). So I had to maintain diplomacy in not letting any group feel that for me they were analytically only as important as the others. I worked with one group at a time, giving them my full attention and the time to become familiar with me and discuss their philosophy and practices, and giving myself the time to understand their most complex devotional experiences.

Working with ISKCON in Mayapur after working in Navadvip was interesting since ISKCON devotees stress the absolute inappropriateness of passionate devotion in contemporary times. They assert that all Navadvip Vaishnavas are on different levels of esoterism which unnecessarily complicate devotion. I show in chapter 5 that contrary to the specialist emphases of the other Vaishnavas and their esoteric practices of the body and mind which require long periods of intense training and practice, ISKCON emphasizes a religion that is clear, pragmatic, and definitely non-esoteric, and which has the utmost capacity to communicate with all sections of society. *Bhakti*, according to them, should be a form of regular ritual discipline (*vaidhi*) rather than passionate embodiment (*raganuga*). They admit the theoretical importance of *raganuga bhakti*, but insist that only very elevated personalities can practice it or even discuss it. Thus, rather than experiencing Vrindavan pleasures within their mental or corporeal interiors, they experience the pleasures of serving Radha-Krishna in Vrindavan by collectively serving the physical veiled-Vrindavan, Mayapur, which is both the earthly manifestation of celestial Vrindavan and the site of the devotees' physical residence. Thus, ISKCON devotees envision perfect devotion as disciplined and lavish services toward the deities' physical abode, for instance building huge temples and beautifying them, developing the roads in Mayapur for pilgrims, providing basic food and education to poor villagers, publishing high-quality devotional books and journals, and encouraging more and more people to become Radha-Krishna's devotees by preaching Krishna Consciousness all over the world from Mayapur, ISKCON's headquarters.

Navadvip's Vaishnavas consider ISKCON spiritually immature, commercialized, even fake. They say that their own religions are capable of moving beyond the veneration of physical lands to more subtle, sophisticated, and elevated senses of the spiritual place, while ISKCON remains confined in superficial indicators and early devotional stages. However, ISKCON devotees, like other Vaishnavas, emphasize the absolute importance of affective identification with Radha-Krishna. While they assert that devotional emotions must not be passionate to the extent that devotees engage with the deities' sexuality, they also emphasize the need to love Radha-Krishna in the most embodied and subservient ways. Thus, for instance, all ISKCON devotees congregate every evening in the main temple in Mayapur's headquarters enclosure to sing and dance together, staring at the life-size idols of Radha-Krishna; and unfailingly, these musical sessions end up being most sensuous and ecstatic, with devotees vigorously jumping together and shouting the deities' names.

Indeed, despite marked differences among Vaishnavas with respect to their place-experiences and understandings of devotion, music is absolutely central to all Vaishnavas' religious lives. Vaishnava sacred music, *kirtan*, refers to two distinct practices in the Bengal-Vaishnava context, which I analyze in chapter 6: repetitive chanting of the deity-consort's names—either mentally to oneself, keeping count on one's *jap-mala* (chanting-bead necklace), or musically in groups—and songs performed by trained musician-devotees for devotee-audiences. These songs' lyrics explicitly describe Radha-Krishna's passionate activities in Vrindavan. All Vaishnava devotees agree that both forms of *kirtan* manifest Vrindavan's sensory bliss in the very site of sonic utterance, transforming it into celestial Vrindavan. They have a common saying that *"nam o nami abhinna"*, the name and the named are the same: uttering the deities' names (or activities) makes them apparent in the site of naming. So they say, "Wherever there is *kirtan*, there is Vrindavan," signifying yet another way in which the sacred place is experienced, that is, heard through music. This reminds one of Feld's (1996, 91) assertion that perceptual experiences are central to conceptualizations of place. When devotees congregate to chant Radha-Krishna's names, ecstatic rhythms are played on drums, the continuously escalating music is swayed to by participants, and the entire sonic atmosphere creates the most sensually pleasurable experience. This explains why every site in which communal singing takes place is revered as Vrindavan, Vrindavan itself imagined to be the site of the utmost spiritual and sensuous ecstasy.

THEORETICAL REFLECTIONS

So, through the next five chapters of the book I document and analyze five different senses of place, five ways in which Vrindavan is experienced by different Bengal-Vaishnavas. My fieldwork sensitized me to a myriad different ways in which a sacred place may be conceptualized and experienced: as an embedded geographical locale where devotees live and pilgrims visit; as complex working of imagination, written in practices of the body, heard through music, and desired as an after-life destination. Thus, mappable external physical geographies may not be exhaustive of senses of place. Bengal-Vaishnavas foreground practices through which the sacred place is literally felt everywhere: in interiorized spaces (of the mind-heart or body), outside the body in the landscape, and on the body-surface as sensations on the skin. This all-pervading dimension of place-experience renders the body's boundaries porous, that is, it engenders the body's capacity to open itself to both the place outside and the place inside.

In analyzing Vaishnavas' place-experiences, I have been influenced by phenomenological approaches to place-studies and the anthropology of emotions, affect, and senses.

People's experiential relations with the places they inhabit have been theorized by philosophers and anthropologists for a long time. Influenced by Heidegger's (1975) emphasis on the absolute centrality of the dwelling experience, Casey (1993, 315; 2001) formulated the idea of "implacement," or inhabitation in the place-world. Casey, however, criticized Heidegger's general formulation of being-in-the-world as vague and disembodied and argued for replacing it with the more concrete and situated notion of being-in-place, thus highlighting the necessary relations between the body and place (1993, xv, 313, 1998, 292, 2001). A plethora of phenomenological approaches to place followed in anthropology—phenomenology defined in this case as ways in which people experience and understand the places they inhabit (Tilley 1994, 11, 2008).[11]

My ethnography shows not only that place-experiences may be embodied and debated but also that places, when felt in imagination, body, or through music, rather than being limited to bounded physical geographies, acquire the unique capacity of mobility. Vrindavan is experienced both in Nadia's physical lands and as travelling with the devotee in her imagination, or body, or musical sensibilities, as the case may be. Thus, my work avoids both homogenized and static approaches to place-experiences. I agree with anthropologists who have cautioned against emphasizing overtly bounded notions of place. Appadurai (1988) and Rodman (2003) suggest for instance that paying attention to people's own contested senses of place or "multilocalities" helps avoid enclosed ideas of place.

However, while the anthropology of place mostly focuses only on senses of external physical spaces, some have hinted at other possibilities. Thus, Bender and Winer (2001, 6) point out that while we live in one place, there are others in hearsay and imagination, and Dawson and Johnson (2001) show that migration is as much a cognitive movement as a physical one, thus arguing that movement need not always mean physical dislocation. Yet anthropology largely remains confined to studies of external spaces, and this also stems from philosophical traditions which are critical of exploration of spaces interior to the individual. For instance, by "topoanalysis" Bachelard (1994) referred to the study of "sites of our intimate lives," by which he meant senses of place interior to the self. Casey's (1993, 103) critique of Bachelard's approach to place-experience is similar to his critique of Heidegger's formulations as being inadequately embodied. He says that Bachelard's focus on interiority is mentalistic, and argues for instance that imagination can provide no genuine sense of inhabitation. Thus, Casey primarily foregrounds the importance of understanding the body-in-place, that is, the body's intimate relations with external places it inhabits.

However, my fieldwork material, as discussed above, suggests that Bachelard's analyses are most relevant. So I argue that an anthropologist must be sensitive to and document people's own senses of place-experience, including when they are conceptualized as interiorized spaces. Thus, in this book I analyze how devotees cultivate and experience their minds-as-places, bodies-as-places, and so on. My work seeks to contribute to the anthropology of place by showing how places can have all-pervasive or enveloping relationships with people, with the capacity to affect both how people negotiate with external physical topographies and how they experience senses of place as interior to them. Extending Bachelard and influenced by Casey, however, I also show how interiorized place-experiences are intensely embodied.

By bringing together dimensions of place and embodiment, my book thus also contributes to classic issues concerning the study of South Asian sacred places. While the academic common sense has mostly concerned itself with the study of either pilgrimage places central to the devotional cartography of South Asia or the theological dimensions of imagined after-life destinations, a careful analysis of the ways in which Vrindavan is embodied and even internalized within devotees' bodily and mental capacities, and sexual and auditory senses, shows that notions of cosmological spaces do not necessarily remain only distant and abstract. The sense of sacred place, or emplacement in Vrindavan, becomes synonymous with cultivating devotional capacities of the body and mind as well. Vrindavan becomes not only a Vaishnava's constant companion but also the central marker of her subjectivity. It is this interface of place and affect, the all-pervading experience of a soteriological destination, which defines faith in the context of Bengal-Vaishnavism.

My analyses of the extremely diverse and intensely sensuous place-experiences (which are sometimes conceptualized as external reality and sometimes introjected into inner sensory capacities of the religious subject) also engage centrally with anthropological debates on emotions and affect. The general understanding is that words can be translated, but emotions cannot (Leavitt 1996, 515). This raises the crucial question for an anthropologist: how to understand another's emotions.

Throughout my fieldwork and after, I kept trying to understand whether Vaishnavas' relations with Vrindavan are emotional, that is discursively constituted, or affective, that is felt as more spontaneous experiences.[12] Analyzing the case of ISKCON was easier since they explicitly stress that love for deities should be manifested as externalized services toward the physical place and not internalized into the recesses of the body-mind. They clearly emphasize that this is what senior gurus teach them and especially what is written in the books of A. C. Bhaktivedanta, their founder guru, which they follow word by word. These books contain details of for instance how devotees should feel for and express their love toward Radha-Krishna. Thus ISKCON devotees make it clear that religious emotions are social prescriptions and therefore rigidly constituted. It was the experiences of the other groups that were difficult to conceptualize.

Imagination, sexual pleasure, and musical ecstasy may be said to have both universal relevance and cultural articulations. Whether emotions are universal in nature or culturally shaped has been a central debate since the 1980s. Foucault (1988) and Asad (1983, 1987, 1993, 83–124, 159–203) represent one end of the debate, arguing that (religious) subjects and emotive and moral dispositions are strictly constructed out of social discourses and disciplinary practices. The constructionists' influence was substantial in anthropology, and a number of studies followed which, although emphasized the importance of dissolving mind–body binaries and foregrounded the role of bodily practices, argued that emotions are primarily socially/discursively constructed—with however a prime ground for such discursive articulations being bodily practices.[13] Others argued against overtly representationalist paradigms in studying emotional and sensory experiences and put forward diverse approaches to bourgeoning studies of embodiment, which try to treat the phenomenological or sensory realities as independent objects of study, relatively distinct from the ideological elements which constitute them.[14] Recently, Wulff (2007) has argued that the above debate has been resolved and that the emerging consensus is that social constructionist and universal (biological) approaches to emotion must cohere.

These debates have also influenced the anthropology of devotional Hinduism. Thus, van der Veer (1989, 464) says that in Hindu culture emotions are learned and cultivated through discourse.[15] McDaniel (1989) and Stewart (2005), on the other hand, have demonstrated more spontaneous sensory dimensions of devotional experiences.

Recently, new debates have arisen with respect to the "affective turn" in theory.[16] This perspective may be productively engaged as the most sophisticated interrogation of and afterword to both phenomenological and discursive paradigms. Following the works of Deleuze and Guattari (2004) and Massumi (2002), affect is understood as pre- or non-linguistic, ineffable, visceral, oceanic sensations which overwhelm the subject and are not immediately grasped intellectually by her consciousness. Affect, in other words, is pre-subjective or supra-subjective. While emotions, which are linguistic formulations of already-felt affective sensations on the skin, get conceptually ingrained in consciousness and memory, affect, although sensorily as powerful as emotions, is "faster than the word," and thus escapes consciousness (Massumi 2002, 4). Affect is pre-conscious because it does not register in the brain (7), and supra-conscious because its intensity is "unassimilable" in any linguistic structure of thinking (5). Thus, the affective domain has "autonomy" from linguistic constructions. However, that is also what makes it a most challenging task to conceptualize and *write* about affective realities in ethnographic contexts.

Thus, affect theorists avoid paradigms of subjectivism and criticize earlier works on emotion which focused on dimensions of interiority, since interiority is associated with the formation and assertion of a conscious, autonomous self/subject (Ahmed 2004). As do philosophers of place, affect theorists associate studies of interiority with a bias toward Cartesian dualism (especially with respect to the mind and consciousness) and additionally with foregrounding notions of a bounded, thinking subject. Yet, all my interlocutors, despite different senses of place, even interior ones, spoke of thoroughly embodied practices. Indeed, my ethnography suggests that not only may interiorized experiences of place be embodied (that is, not mentalistic and abstract), but they may also be experienced at intensely affective, extra-conscious and supra-subjective levels. Thus, I agree with Halliburton (2002, 1126) that anthropologists should be sensitive to "local phenomenology," or what Feld (1996, 91) calls "social phenomenology," that is, context-specific dimensions of knowledge and experience—and with Navaro-Yashin (2009) that affect should be situated and understood within ethnographic contexts, since her interlocutors, like mine, were also vocal about (conceptually contradictory) notions of both embodied emotions and interiority.[17]

However, given these debates variously posed between construction-ism and universalism, discourse and embodiment, and emotion and affect, the question I asked myself is whether the various Vaishnava place-experiences are socially constructed or more primal and affective, and the simple answer is that they are both. My interlocutors in the field taught me to think that these academic distinctions and debates often get reworked in ethnographic settings. This is not because they could not relate to my complex questions, but because they felt that the debates were misplaced.

Emotions, all Vaishnavas I know agree, are learned. Reading Vaishnava texts, listening to gurus explain verses from the *Gita*, the *Bhagavatam*, and Chaitanya's biographies during morning and evening temple-sermons, and discussions among fellow-devotees are important ways of learning how to conceptualize Vrindavan, the analytical differences between disciplined and passionate devotion, the importance of the body's sensory capacities in feeling the pleasures of serving Radha-Krishna with love, and techniques of experiencing the deities' passions within themselves. Bengal-Vaishnavism is indeed a thoroughly scripted religion, with discursive specifications and complex classifications of different kinds of emotional states of deities and devotees (McDaniel 1995, 48), which practitioners must learn to understand and cultivate. My informants were extremely eloquent (even about the most intimate matters) and had clarified answers to my questions. Their confidence, however, stemmed from both their immaculate knowledge of Vaishnava literature and the intensely felt immediacy and clarity of spiritual/bodily experiences. Thus, they invoke the concept of *kay-mana-vakya*, or the simultaneous importance of the body, mind, and discourse, in experiencing devotion.

However, there were emotional aspects that were most difficult for me to understand and for them to talk about. Their difficulty, I understood later, was due not to any lack of understanding but to the immediacy and obviousness they associated with ineffable experiences which cannot easily be brought into language. And that is the domain of affect. For instance, I kept wondering whether there is anything specific to the *manas* (mind-heart) which helps *goswamis* and *babajis* experience it as the sacred place, Vrindavan, through their imagination. This was something intensely visceral, therefore obvious, and thus a non-question to them. Eventually, one day, after thinking as hard as I was about this question, a senior *goswami*, my close friend, said, "We remember people. It means we *keep* them in our minds/hearts. We can do that because these are also places. It remains to us, whether we can experience it as Vrindavan." In fact, in Bengali, "to remember" is literally *mon-e* (in heart/mind) *rakha* (to keep): to keep in the mind/heart. Similarly, *sahajiyas* explained that breath and food can "pass through us" because our bodies have a space-like quality. Once, a *sahajiya* man, amused at my thinking hard about this, said, "But you eat too. Don't you understand this?" Thus, affective experiences were sometimes not spoken about also because practitioners thought I should easily and automatically understand shared experiential realities. They expected me to "feel along with them" (Leavitt 1996, 530). Feeling along with them, therefore, in this book, I analyze in detail how sensory experiences of sound, breath, and imagination, for instance, are felt by the devotees' affective interiors.

Thus, one of my main concerns throughout the book is to show that Bengal-Vaishnavas' varied senses of place are both discursively shaped and affectively experienced. I agree with Cook (2010b) that (ascetic) interiority is engendered through social and disciplinary practices, and with Hirschkind (2006) that discursive practices produce ethical substrates which inform affective behavior. So, in every chapter I analyze varied discursive practices through which senses of place are cultivated. However, I also try to articulate more visceral, ineffable dimensions of those sensory place-experiences. This is also conceptually sustainable since affect is not pre-social. It always carries contextual memories of past socialities in the brain and flesh (Massumi 2002, 8). However, unlike Cook and Hirschkind, I also delve into the "asocial" (8) aspects of devotional affects, and their characteristics which are in excess of social dictates.

So, while both Cook and Hirschkind, in a Foucauldian vein, treat the affective domain as an unambiguous product of discursive techniques, I try to maintain analytical autonomy for both the discursive and affective modalities of religion. I argue not only that the discursive (in)forms and gives articulation to the affective, but also that devotion and senses of place can assert and sustain themselves especially when sedimented in the affective capacities of the body. Although heavily influenced by Hirschkind in this matter, I extend his analysis to argue that the affective may also make the discursive possible and sustainable. My analysis also hopes to especially contribute to South Asian studies, since affect has not yet been adequately theorized in the context of South Asian devotion.

What has however been very well conceptualized in the context of Bengal-Vaishnavism is the link of devotional sentiments with classical

Sanskrit aesthetics. These interpretive frameworks, that is, understanding devotion through the lens of contemporary Western debates concerning emotions/affect on one hand and discussions in Indian philosophy on the other, are very distinct and cannot be compared. I want to make a very rough attempt in this regard, however, for the first time. Common to the religious experiences of all groups of Bengal-Vaishnavas is an intense sensory and aesthetic appreciation of divinity, such that the domains of religion and aesthetics are not really separate. This is what makes Bengal-Vaishnavism interpretable within the discourse on *rasa*, or the theory of "rasaesthetics." Bengal-Vaishnavism is extremely rich in its textual heritage, and textual discourses even constitute a central element of the religious practices. Indeed, the terms and discourses all my interlocutors use borrow heavily from rasaesthetics, which they are encultured into through their very active discursive culture of temple sermons by gurus and other collective discussions. They directly referred to many of these texts in discussing their practices with me. For instance, the *Chaitanya Charitamrita* makes heavy use of the concepts and ideas of Rupa Goswami's rasaesthetics, and my interlocutors regularly discuss this text among themselves and are thus highly aware of these theoretical frameworks. Thus, a brief discussion of the central ideas of rasaesthetics will help contextualize the discussions of later chapters.

The theology, philosophy, poetics, and aesthetics of Bengal-Vaishnavism developed through the influence of Sanskrit love-poetry and especially Bharata's poetics. *Bhakti rasa* developed in this context as the intermediary between the devotional paradigm of the *Bhagavata Purana* (emotional *bhakti* or love) and the aesthetic theory of Bharata's *Natyashastra* (*rasa*). While classical *rasa* theory developed through centuries of debates among scholars like Bharata, Abhinavagupta, Bhatta Nayak, and Bhoja, the most important philosophical sources for Bengal-Vaishnavas are the works of the medieval scholars Rupa and Jiva Goswami. In his magnum opus, *Bhakti Rasamrita Sindhu* (see Haberman 2003), Rupa Goswami tried to formulate and understand devotional sentiments as correlates of forms of pure literary enjoyment described in Sanskrit poetics (*rasa*), wherein the refined devotee becomes the sophisticated literary connoisseur. More specifically, a direct relationship was established between devotion and erotic sensations.

The two critical terms for rasaesthetics are *bhava* and *rasa*. *Bhava* refers to certain latent or dormant emotive predispositions, which in appropriate poetic/discursive contexts transform into the concentrated joy of aesthetic sensations (*rasa*). *Rasa*, which literally means juice or essence, and in this context the taste of divine sensations, is constituted and garnished through different devotional practices and realized as ecstatic sentiments and sensations by the devotee's refined and cultivated body.

This *rasa*, as a physiological and psychological phenomenon, is most complex. It is a subjective experience, which, while affecting the material senses of a person, is simultaneously, and more significantly, of an impersonal order. Its supremacy as a pure sentiment lies in its sparkling, bright, objective universality.[18] When the dormant emotions receive discursive stimuli and transform to the essence of devotional sentiments, *rasa* "cracks the hard shell of 'I'" (Haberman 2003, xl). This sensation of *rasa* also eludes contemplation or consciousness in its power of "abundant amazement" (385).[19]

While affect is being thoroughly discussed in other contexts, it has not yet been sufficiently theorized or compared in studies of South Asian devotion. However, I propose not an equivalence but a correspondence, in three ways, between what has been identified in classical aesthetics as *rasa* and what I theorize as affect. First, like affect, *rasa* needs a social context or occasions of repeated discursive practice for its articulation. It is not pre-social. Second, like affect, *rasa*, since it is in excess of contemplation, has an aspect of ineffability. And third, both are incompatible with the sense of an ego or "I," due to the impersonality of *rasa* and the supra-individuality of affect.

Studying affect ethnographically makes it essential for the anthropologist to place herself in the emotional life-world of her people. My understanding of methodology was significantly reworked during fieldwork. It is possible neither to sit and "observe" nor to "participate" when someone else is imagining, or experiencing the sacred place in her body while having sex. Thus, a great part of my fieldwork benefitted from intimate relationships with people and frequent, long conversations with them. However, my interlocutors expected a different kind of inter-subjective participation from me during our conversations, an intuitive participation that relied on understandings of shared experience. I call this conversing with the body. The word *intuition* is instructive here since it conveys an intermediary sense between conception and sensation. Borrowing rasaesthetic language, I too was a connoisseur who tried to sympathetically partake in devotees' emotions and sensations: in the vibrations of the bliss of their (im)personal joy. *Goswamis* and *babajis* sometimes suggested for instance that I hear songs vividly describing Radha-Krishna's (erotic) encounters before speaking with them the next time. In the subsequent conversation they would want me to first tell them whether I could imagine what was being described in the songs and how I felt about it. Or, *sahajiyas* would literally sit with a straight spine, pull in their breath and show how body-muscles flex and straighten with proper inhalation, and ask me to repeat the process. When they felt I was catching up they would ask whether I felt my breath moving inside me, that is, whether I sensed my own body-as-place.

The distance between my objective anthropological position and Vaishnava experience was narrowed the most during collective musical occasions. I am a singer myself and had immediate interest in *kirtan*. My participations in musical gatherings organized in various temples, devotees' houses, or roadside *pandals* were therefore more conventionally anthropological than participation in another's imagination or body. I personally felt the extreme sensuous delight of collective chanting, and my analyses of *kirtan* follow closely from my autoethnographic affective responses to the music. While my reactions to worded songs describing Radha-Krishna's passions were learned, since throughout fieldwork I had discovered various ways of appreciating the meanings and sentiments of these descriptions, my reactions to chanting sounds were more spontaneous. With the continuously escalating rhythm I found my limbs swaying artlessly, while my eyes remained shut and my lips repeated the deities' names. When I opened my eyes to see everyone else responding in exactly the same manner, I was convinced of Leavitt's (1996, 530) notion of the anthropologist's relations of sympathy, rather than ethnocentric empathy, with her subjects.

Place, discourse, and affect thus form the critical analytical tropes in this book, to revisit persistent questions and concerns centering around Vaishnavism particularly and South Asian devotional traditions more generally.

CHAPTER 2

Discovering *Gupta*-Vrindavan: Finding Selves and Places in the Storied Landscape

INTRODUCTION: TRAVELLING STORIES, TELLING LANDS

It was March, and Nadia's most important Vaishnava festival, Dol, was being celebrated. Thousands of pilgrims had gathered in Navadvip and Mayapur. Dol (or Holi) is the colorful spring festival observed by Bengal-Vaishnavas both as a commemoration of Radha-Krishna's passionate play with colors in Vrindavan and as Chaitanya's birthday.

Although Nadia has a busy pilgrimage life all year, the months of February and March reach pinnacles of devotee participation. The grand circumambulation of Nadia annually organized by ISKCON had ended a couple of days ago. Pilgrims were now visiting the numerous temples in Navadvip and Mayapur, attending elaborate *pujas*, daubing temple grounds with colors, attending sermons and musical gatherings, and buying pictures and idols from pilgrimage-markets. The devotees' pilgrimage enthusiasm during these times, to use Entwistle's (1991, 83) term and a typical Vaishnava metaphor, is like a "swarm of bees" savoring the land's tastes.

The town's narrow lanes were packed with people. There was hardly space for rickshaws or cycle-vans to move. This led to a complete acoustic pandemonium, in which the loud honks of vehicles mixed with

Parts of this chapter were published as an article (Sarbadhikary 2013).

FIGURE 3. Navadvip's narrow lanes crowded by rickshaws.

loudspeakers listing dos and don'ts for pilgrims. From a distance *kirtan* echoes resonated over the Ganga, with hundreds singing on the ferry-boats crossing from Mayapur to Navadvip and vice versa.

It was seven in the evening, but the heat was still unbearable. My limbs were exhausted after the day's walk. I looked for a place to sit. All over Mayapur's rural fields pilgrims had laid their *saris* down to sleep and were cooking dinner on little stoves. I joined a group of ladies who had travelled overnight from Assam. I complained about my aching legs and tired ears, when one of them said, "We come here every year during Dol, leaving our families and fields. We are on our feet for over ten hours a day . . . , but never complain! You will stop feeling any pain once you realize the importance of these lands. These are the roads on which Mahaprabhu [Chaitanya] walked and still walks. . . . This is *gupta*-Vrindavan. . . . The temples here tell us different stories [*ghatanar katha*] of Mahaprabhu's life. In walking through these lands and hearing the stories [*katha*], we are able to understand his ongoing *lilas* [divine play]." At this point another woman joined in with a couplet often quoted by devotees. "'Even today Gour[1] does the same *lilas*, which only lucky ones can witness.' You are seeing only the physical lands. If you listen carefully to the stories [*kahini*] with an honest heart, the lands will reveal themselves to you—you will see the shadows of eternal Vrindavan."

FIGURE 4. Boats ferrying pilgrims between Navadvip and Mayapur.

My exploration of Bengal-Vaishnava devotional life as a complex layering of sacred geography begins with stories of the significance of the visible, mappable physical spaces and structures in Bengal's most distinctive composite sacred space of the two neighboring pilgrimage complexes, Navadvip and Mayapur. So it becomes important to understand the place of devotional stories or narratives in the lives of both resident committed Vaishnava practitioners and ordinary pilgrims. Chaitanyaite devotion in particular and Hindu *bhakti* traditions in general are to a large extent story-centered religiosities, since devotees relish narratives glorifying gods and goddesses, their life-events, and historical and mythical stories about famous temples built in their honor.

The term *story*, as used here, is a translation of various Bengali words devotees use to refer to narratives about Chaitanya's *lilas* (divine activities) and about Nadia's sacred topography embodied in its different temples and ashrams. Thus, *ghatana* refers to events, *katha* to words and stories, and *kahini* to stories, often epical ones. Devotees never use the term *galpo* to refer to divine narratives, because it carries the implication of artificial or "made-up" stories. Thus, the stories devotees hear during pilgrimage about Chaitanya's divine life and Nadia's sacrality are considered by them to be spiritual narratives which transport their selves to the real times and places of the saint's life.

The stories are narrated by different Vaishnavas—the householder *goswamis* and renunciate *babajis* of Navadvip, and modern religious institutions, the Gaudiya Math and ISKCON of Mayapur—about the temples/ashrams they own. All Vaishnava practitioners derive a large part of their livelihoods from revenue generated through devotees' pilgrimage to their temples/ashrams; thus, one of their major devotional activities is to popularize stories associated with their temples. Thus, in contrast to Vaishnava place-experiences which deal with more esoteric dimensions of sensations in interiorized spaces of practitioners' minds or bodies, storying Nadia deals with the public face of Vaishnavism, since practitioners engage in articulate exegesis, claims, and counter-claims regarding the different temples/ashrams that inhabit and constitute the landscape.

Storying begins with efforts by different Vaishnavas to historicize Nadia's landscape, which followed from a kind of modern invention, a literal-minded response to colonial historicizing, a kind of after-life of Bengali intellectuals feeling that they need to adopt a quasi-Western historical narrative for sacred places. These public, accessible ways of narrativizing and historicizing landscapes constitute the truth-claims of different Vaishnavas about Chaitanya's birth-site and other sites. But the scientific, text-centered kind of conventional archival documentation of facts is only one aspect of storying the landscape. It is not as if what is on the map or what is historically identifiable is all that is there when thinking of pilgrimage places. Storying equally involves the circulation of mythical narratives of a kind of personified space, for instance of Nadia's mythogeographic space grieving Chaitanya's absence.

Bengal-Vaishnavas' complex engagement with the storied landscape also entails their belief, as exemplified by my informant, that listening to the landscape stories involves a subtle process of unveiling, of establishing affective relationships with another place, with celestial Vrindavan. As I have mentioned, pilgrims and residents of Navadvip-Mayapur refer to these places as *gupta* (veiled) Vrindavans. Although scholars have discussed the Hindu tradition of linking "lesser" regional pilgrimage places with "greater" national ones,[2] Bengal-Vaishnavas do not draw any hierarchy between Nadia and Vrindavan. They consider Nadia Vrindavan's silhouette or mirror-reflection. For Vaishnavas, Vrindavan is not only a physical town in Uttar Pradesh but also the celestial embodied expression of Radha-Krishna's love, the eternal site of their passionate love-play. Nadia was Chaitanya's birthplace, and he spent 24 years there before becoming a renunciate and leaving for Puri. Devotees worship Chaitanya as Radha-Krishna's manifestation, the deities enjoying their erotic union in his body; thus, Chaitanya's birthplace is revered as offering the same spiritual ecstasies as Vrindavan.[3] While devotees aspire to do pilgrimage in both Nadia and Vrindavan, many poor devotees told me that their experiences in Nadia were sufficient; although they could not afford to visit Vrindavan, Nadia offered them the same spiritual delight. Thus, the historicized space engulfed by Navadvip-Mayapur also offers devotees a subtle spiritual experience such that going to Nadia is conceptualized by them as also travelling to Vrindavan. I have often heard devotees refer to Nadia town-paths as roads of or to Vrindavan, and to the Bhagirathi (Ganga) River, which separates Navadvip and Mayapur, as the Yamuna.

The term *gupta* means both "secret" and "veiled." But Bengal-Vaishnavas use it in the sense of a veil, *gupta*-Vrindavan therefore implying a veiled landscape, which can be unveiled through the appropriate spiritual techniques, in this case through the telling of and listening to stories. Thus, I use the term *storied* also in the sense of a spiritual layering of geography, to analyze the distinctive feature of Navadvip-Mayapur's physical sacred topography as a region revered and spatially conceptualized as a hidden, yet spiritually accessible manifestation of a cosmic site of spiritual truth and experience.

The sacred physical landscape holds immense importance for all Vaishnavas, and they embody intense relations with it. Till a decade ago there used to be a festival called Dhulot in Navadvip, when devotees would lie on and roll around on the ground for hours, allowing their bodies to become smeared with dust (*dhulo*). Navadvip's resident practitioners reminisce that Dhulot was the ideal occasion to establish tactile relations with *gupta*-Vrindavan, where the saint left his traces.

Although Dhulot is no longer celebrated, embodied relations with the lands, in terms of walking and sensing the landscape, is still the most important way devotees experience the material region. It was in my relentless strolls through the towns (sometimes with pilgrims, sometimes alone), in spending hours listening to stories of different temples as recounted by temple-attendants, local people, and tour guides, and in reading *sthan-mahatyas*[4] given out by temple-attendants and town elders that I was able to comprehend what it means to participate in *gupta*-Vrindavan.

Nadia's landscape manifests its essence, devotees say, through the countless stories narrated in temples about Chaitanya's *lilas*—temple-attendants often claiming that their temples were built at the exact sites of those *lilas*—which devotees hear with rapt attention during their pilgrimage. Thus the invisible manifests *in* the visible, and veiled-Vrindavan unveils itself through temples embodying Chaitanya's life, ashrams narrating his grace, and public debates, including disputes about Chaitanya's birthplace, searching and locating the saint's *lilab-humi* (lands of divine play) for the public. Both affective and contested relations with the sacred lands are thus expressed by practitioners through different discourses about their temples and ashrams. The narratives sometimes hunt out lost sacred sites, and sometimes legitimize existing buildings. However, the buildings or sites do not create the sense of belonging in the chronotope of the saint's divine activities as much as they embody it and "gather" a landscape for the community (Heidegger 1975, 152).

Such acts of narration are also ways of discovering and asserting religious selves. Multiple appropriations of the sacred lands by religious practitioners demonstrate contested ways of being Vaishnava. While an intense affective attachment to the physical lands is common to all Vaishnava groups, so are competitions in social, political, and economic claims to the landscape, religion, and pilgrims. Organization and marketing of the pilgrimage industry is certainly the most important way in which pilgrims are attracted and potential disciples secured from among them. The contrasting versions of narratives of the landscape are significant strategies of displaying the authenticity of one's particular Vaishnava group within the contesting field and attracting pilgrims to become disciples of *goswamis, babajis,* or ISKCON. Disciples are absolutely necessary for the economic and religious maintenance of spiritual lineages. Pilgrimage is an ideal time when Vaishnava groups come in contact with hundreds of potential disciples and narrate the stories of their temples/ashrams to them. Especially during important festivals, hundreds of pilgrims at a time may be initiated into their particular form of Vaishnavism by *goswamis, babajis,* or ISKCON. Temple courtyards overflow with people, as the guru sits on a pedestal and initiates them together.

Narratives play a critical part in the devotional activities pilgrims and resident practitioners engage in, even on non-festival days. Ordinary pilgrims are either already disciples of Nadia's different resident Vaishnavas, or in search of appropriate gurus, or simply semi-tourists. Poorer pilgrims travel by trains and buses, and richer ones visiting ISKCON often travel in personal cars. Pilgrims moving between Navadvip and Mayapur use ferry-boats, and cycle-vans and rickshaws take them around Navadvip and Mayapur. Storytelling sessions begin right with the cycle-van or rickshaw-pullers, who, when asked by their pilgrim-clients about the temples they visit, give semi-spontaneous narrative accounts. Fellow pilgrims who have visited the places earlier narrate stories to first-timers. Also, on hot, lazy afternoons pilgrims sit under shades and discuss these storied landscapes, while at other times local shopkeepers narrate them to willing listeners. The most common and structured narrative occasions of public recitation are in the temples, where specialist temple attendants greet pilgrims and give exegetical commentaries on Chaitanya's life-events which their particular temple represents and other stories associated with the temples. Thus, the stories circulate through both formal occasions of public recitation and traditions of oral knowledge. As pilgrims travel, stories travel with them, establishing bonds among "travel, territory and text" (Dubow 2001, 241), and in walking through the landscape, the stories sediment as knowledge (Legat 2008).

The circulating stories reflect Vaishnava practitioners' debates over Nadia's landscape. These debates are eventually regarding notions of true Vaishnava subjectivities—with *subjectivity* defined, borrowing from Luhrmann (2006), as the emotional experience of a political, and in this case more aptly, a religio-political subject. In every instance of the plural modes of narrating Nadia's emotional landscape, different Vaishnava groups claim to discover the true essence of the sacred topography, asserting their multiform practices of devotional self-experience and place-experience as authentic representations of religion. ISKCON, for instance, experiences and constitutes its devotional self and landscape through modern religious principles of historical accuracy of sites and stories; householder *goswamis,* through familial principles of attachment; and renouncer *babajis,* through miraculous realizations of strict asceticism. Fernandez (2003) similarly argues regarding the formation and experience of sacred places that people constitute their identities in relation to the environment and that its qualities are projected onto buildings as part of a larger architectonic space.

Thus, the ways of experiencing, consolidating, and asserting contested devotional selves are in intimate and necessary relations with the ways in which sacred places are experienced. These contested experiences of belonging to and assertions of authority over Nadia's physical geography make the contrasted and consecrated landscape, and embody differentiated religious identities.

However, it is also interesting to compare the inhabitants' experiences of the landscape with that of the traveller-pilgrims, who as active, intelligent listeners recast the stories they hear, overriding concerns with specific sites in favor of a passionate engagement with the entire

landscape. Thus, the devotional landscape unveils itself through countless stories both to those who narrate them and to those who listen,
and the practices of the foregrounded contested physical landscape echo
the background of an aesthetics of embodied belonging.[5] So devotees
experience the landscape both affectively, in terms of their belonging,
and discursively through socially constructed stories which reflect their
contested senses of belonging and constitute the landscape in turn.

Both Navadvip and Mayapur are famous as Chaitanya's birthplace(s).
They are ardent competitors in the sacred-political map of Bengal.
Both places commemorate Chaitanya's pre-renunciation life-events.
The imagined landscapes of the towns are thus "knit together by . . .
repetitions and homologies" (Eck 1999, 29), though each disputes the
temple-histories and religious dispositions of the other. The towns are
separated by a massive bridge named after Chaitanya. Pilgrims crossing the bridge cannot miss his big statues. The bridge is a symbolic
connection in the contested region, the statues being an immediate
invitation to pilgrims to sacred lands on either side.

The historical-mythical space enveloped by Navadvip-Mayapur presents a unique situation wherein the pilgrimage places cannot be thought
of together as a single place (being fraught with myriad tensions), nor
can they embody disjointed spatial identities (since they symbolize the
same life-events of Chaitanya). Thus, I ethnographically focus on both
the particular pilgrimage places—their temples/ashrams and the stories
narrated about them—and pilgrims' journeys within and between them.
This strategy also helps us understand how pilgrims relate to the entire
sacred landscape despite immense contestations over individual places
and sites.

My ethnography of the contested relation between the twin towns
thereby contributes to theoretical insights and debates in the anthropology of place. While Appadurai (1986, 356) argues that categories of
locality and place should be in the foreground of anthropology, Bowen
(1995) criticizes studies of "intense localness" since they overlook
translocal experiences. "Interplaces," or journeys undertaken between
locations, are also effective ways to sense places (Casey 1996, 39).
Thus, dimensions of both individual places and journeys to and within
them are important to conceptualize. Casey additionally also suggests
that we think of places with similarities and draw the connections as a
"region" (30). The reflexivity of journeying then remains within a similar ethnogeography. Yet, Bowen (2002, 226) points out that pilgrimage
ethnographies have only focused on either particular pilgrimage places

or the journeys to the same. My ethnography is an exception to these one-sided approaches, and Nadia's devotional topography approximates Casey's definition of a region, and what Gold (1988, 307) calls a "dialogic locality."

THE BIRTHPLACE CONTROVERSY

One major controversy in Nadia's devotional life revolves around Chaitanya's birthplace. Claims to the birthplace by different practitioners constitute their claims to *gupta*-Vrindavan. The chief debaters are *goswamis*, a group of Navadvip's *babajis*, and the modern religious institutions of Mayapur: the Gaudiya Math and ISKCON. Gaudiya Math was established in 1918 as a monastic institution professing reformist Vaishnava ideals, and ISKCON began as its offshoot in the late 1960s. Chaitanya's birthplace controversy was shaped by a complex history involving campaigns by these institutions to develop a positivistic, historical account of sacred sites, to which they were committed in ways that reflected the concerns of revivalist organizations of the nineteenth and early twentieth centuries, in which religion had to be culturally rationalized yet also connected with spiritual truth and heritage. The myriad debates and stories circulated by religious practitioners in the contemporary period regard issues of toponymic and archaeological exactitudes of temples, and historical and mythical claims to cultural memory.

Being a Bengali, I had always known that Chaitanya's birthplace is a matter of enduring dispute, but I first became aware of extreme place-name contestations in connection with the birthplace debate while chatting with pilgrims from north Bengal during a festival in November 2009. We were waiting in a queue before ISKCON's main temple in Mayapur to watch the evening *arati* (light-offering). I asked, "Where do you think is Chaitanya's birthplace?" This simple question opened up a Pandora's Box.

Pilgrim A: From childhood we have heard it is in Navadvip—

B: No, as far as I know it is in Mayapur.

C: Yes, Navadvip means "nine islands" around this place. Mahaprabhu was born in Mayapur, in Navadvip.

Local rickshaw-puller: But this is not Mayapur—it is Miyapur. God was born in Navadvip, because Navadvip is Nadia. As they say, "Nader Nimai" [Nadia's Chaitanya].

A: Also, Prachin [old] Mayapur is in the Navadvip town—

C: No, but Mayapur is Prachin Navadvip.

Place-names are put to different semantic uses by religious actors in Navadvip-Mayapur, since, as Casey (1993, 23) points out, place-names, despite their brevity, embody a "complex collective concreteness." They transform the geographical into the experiential and act as mnemonics for historical interventions (Tilley 1994, 18).

Bengalis grow up hearing that Chaitanya was born in Navadvip, while ISKCON devotees know for sure that his birthplace is in Mayapur. This contradiction has a century-long history. I came to know of these debates mostly from cheap books and pamphlets sold in the respective birthplace-temples, and many of the details of these debates are also a part of the common knowledge of Vaishnava practitioners. I also obtained some important historical information about the birthplace controversy (from the perspective of claimants of Navadvip's birth-site) during official meetings with members of Navadvip's municipal office and archaeological society. These town societies are small institutions, but their influence among the town's intellectuals is substantial. Most Vaishnava practitioners and townspeople were very vocal in their opinions regarding the controversy, and despite intense debates there were overlaps in their discourses.

Mayapur received its name in 1894 from Kedarnath Datta, a renowned Vaishnava (renunciate name, Bhaktivinode Thakur). He was a leading intellectual of the Bengal Renaissance, who served as a district magistrate for the colonial government, retired in 1892, and dedicated the rest of his life to reforming and modernizing Vaishnavism.[6] His conceptualization of modern Vaishnavism influenced his son, the founder of Gaudiya Math, and later, his son's disciple, the founder of ISKCON.

Toponymic obsessions reigned supreme among scholars and Sanskritists during the colonial period. Tracing linguistic roots, unpacking semantic contents, fixing phonetic correctness and territorializing names in the true places of tradition became significant concerns of an etymologically charged toponymic discourse (Kar 2007, 215).

In 1894, Kedarnath Datta claimed to have a vision of Chaitanya's true birthplace, which had been submerged by flood-waters about a hundred years before that. This, he said, was in the town that was then called Meyapur (literally, "land of Muslims"), and which he renamed Mayapur.

This declaration faced severe opposition from the traditional Vaishnava authorities—Navadvip's *goswamis* and *babajis*. A significant group of *babajis* claimed that they had been able to locate the birth-place in the northern part of Navadvip, which was earlier called Ramchandrapur, and which they in turn renamed Prachin (old/original) Mayapur.

Datta had to deal with the place-name issue from a twofold perspective: his discovery was in contrast to a long-held idea among Bengalis, and Meyapur was a Muslim fishermen's village. He floated two spiritual-historical ideas, which also constitute the official discourse of Gaudiya Math and ISKCON in the contemporary period. He said, following an older Vaishnava text, that Mahaprabhu's birthplace was in "Mayapur," the term having been mispronounced and altered to "Meyapur" by the local Muslim populace (Fuller 2005, 234). Mayapur, the true *gupta*-Vrindavan, would thus have to be reclaimed, and this toponymic shift would be its crucial symbol. He suggested that Mayapur was the Prachin (old/original) Navadvip, the present-day town of Navadvip having been formed only in the mid-eighteenth century. He argued that Mayapur was one of *nava* (nine) *dvips* (islands) around the Ganga in which Chaitanya carries out his divine activities, and visualized Mayapur as the central island (210–40).

As an ISKCON devotee told me: "So much confusion about Sri Chaitanya's birthplace arises because people conflate the present-day town, Navadvip, with *navadvip*—the nine islands. Navadvip is the birthplace only insofar as Mayapur is its center."

The *babajis* of Navadvip's Prachin Mayapur birthplace-temple also pilfer from the same scriptural evidence and keep intact the cartographic and toponymic constructions circulated by Mayapur ideologues. They maintain the birthplace-name as Mayapur and the meaning of Navadvip as "nine islands." They claim, however, that their temple in the town of Navadvip was built in the original birthplace location, and that Mayapur was originally Miyapur, a Muslim habitat since the thirteenth century. Thus they invert the logic of linguistic-homophonic misrepresentation and suggest that Datta distorted the original name, Miyapur.

Thus, toponymic debates between advocates of both birthplaces and the consequent consolidation of their territories are based on reading similar texts and argued on the basis of similar assumptions. However, the place-name politics and cartographic imaginings of *gupta*-Vrindavan are rendered more complicated by a third ideological position, which is shared by Navadvip's *goswamis*. They argue that the birthplace was lost in floods and that the supporters of both birthplaces are mistaken in their claims. An elderly *goswami*, Krishnagopal, one of my first and closest friends in the field, had done independent scriptural research on the birthplace issue and come to his own conclusions. He was a senior *goswami* of Chaitanya's brother-in-law's lineage, and his views have influenced others of his extended *goswami* family. He said emphatically, "None of Mahaprabhu's biographies mention Mayapur. The *Bhaktiratnakara* mentioned it for the first time.[7] But there, the meanings of Navadvip or the idea of Mayapur, . . . are simply poetic referents, claiming no correspondence with any real geographical space".[8]

Goswamis construe the meaning of Navadvip as *nava* (new) *dvip* (island) (Majumdar 1995; Mondol 2002, 73; Radi 2004).[9] Toponymic imaginings and topographic constellations have a connection. Every alternate year newspapers report the considerable losses Nadia undergoes due to floods. I myself was once caught in torrential rainfall while crossing the Ganga with other pilgrims on a small boat, and the situation was so daunting that the ferryman too began to lose hope. Nadia's distinctive waterscape and insecure geography are such that its people and temples are repeatedly threatened by annual floods. So, for those who claim to have discovered the birthplace(s), Navadvip's meaning "nine islands" is a more comforting assumption than the island's constant "newness," which corresponds to the irresoluteness of being able to rediscover birth-sites after they have drowned. *Goswamis*, however, who do not have any stake in either of the birthplace-temples, emphasize the newness of the island and correspondingly the impossibility of reclaiming lost lands.

In an interesting parallel, Paul Carter mentions that Cook named an Australian island New Island. Carter (1987, 8–9) remarks of this name that "it precisely delimits the conditions under which it came to be known. . . . It is a subtle critique of those who might think a name with a history ('Old Island', perhaps) is somehow more appropriate." Thus, while the material topography impacts upon naming imaginations, place-name semantics in turn justify the persistence of contrasting ideologies. In airing their myriad claims, religious actors also solidify the cases for their own temples and authority positions in the pilgrimage scene.

However, toponymic stories during the nineteenth century were complemented by archaeological and literary proofs. A material culture permeated with a history of naming, mythmaking, and landscaping confers a *longue durée* aura on the face of religion (Casey 1993, 32), a "chronotopic" significance to its life-world (277).

The renaming of places was just one component of the historical ventures carried out to discover the true *gupta*-Vrindavan. The birthplace

FIGURE 5. Chaitanya's birthplace temple in Mayapur.

controversy shook Bengali intellectual circles beginning in the 1880s (Bhatia 2009, 5; Chakrabarty 1985, 396; Majumdar 1992). This was the time of the neo-Krishna movement, when there was a massive change in the public redefinition of Krishna/Chaitanya's image. Krishna was now the *Mahabharata*'s warrior, not only Vrindavan's lover (Kaviraj 1995, 72–106; Lutt 1995, 147). He could defend his religion and territory. This reformist tradition gave rise to a public culture of debating sacred places and reclaiming lost sites.

When pilgrims visit the birthplace temples in Navadvip/Mayapur in the contemporary period, they express confusion and ask temple attendants why there are two birthplaces. Despite this rare phenomenon of twin birth-sites, however, pilgrims generally visit both and carry back *mati* (soil) from them as mark of reverence for the sacred lands. Hayden (2002) argues that the tolerance claimants have with respect to spatial clashes may actually be because concerned groups are unable to replace one another due to differential resources. The situation is similar among Nadia's contestants.

Claimants of both Navadvip and Mayapur birthplace-temples have produced innumerable documents to establish their findings as "historical facts," a crucial modernist way to deal with "mythical" narratives. From within a discursive apparatus of proofs and counter-proofs about spatial layouts in the past, readings of Chaitanya's biographies, and

divine revelations, the life-histories of the places were shaped and contestations crystallized.

I had initially imagined that controversies regarding the saint's birthplace would be sensitive matters to discuss with informants. But on
hindsight, listening to people discuss the real-world geographies of the
pilgrimage places and the debates over them were the easiest aspects of
my fieldwork. Practitioners and temple attendants were very willing to
tell me stories and discuss temple histories, both because they are used
to discussing these issues with pilgrims, storytelling being the prime
mode of publicity during pilgrimage, and also because they felt that the
right histories of *gupta*-Vrindavan must be publicized.

Two recent works (Bhatia 2009; Fuller 2005) have discussed the
birthplace controversy between Mayapur and Navadvip. Both conceptualize the issue from Kedarnath Datta's perspective: his recovery
of Vaishnavism in the late nineteenth century and the discovery of
Chaitanya's birthplace in Mayapur as a crucial landmark in the process.
Their historical premises, I argue, are one-sided, when judged in light of
contemporary receptions of the controversy.

The primacy given to Mayapur's story by Fuller and Bhatia fails to
recognize alternative cultural memories. They view the birthplace controversy led by Mayapur as resulting in the "wresting of spiritual authority from the traditional establishment" of Navadvip (Fuller 2005, 210).
They characterize Mayapur proponents as the colonial, middle-class,
Western-educated elite, armed with the weapon of disciplinary history
and archaeology, and narrate the story of their victory over the traditional habitus, custom, and faith of Navadvip's *goswamis* and *babajis*.
My ethnography revealed, however, that the other Vaishnavas have not
only survived the influence of ISKCON but have an insistent influence
in people's lives.

Moreover, Navadvip's *babajis* were also using historical and archaeological sources to claim a history of recovering the birthplace twice before
Kedarnath. Both versions of history use the same sources to substantiate
their claims. Datta, since 1887, and Navadvip's *babajis*, from shortly
afterwards, referred to the *Calcutta Review* (1846), Hunter's statistical
accounts of Bengal (1875), Rennel's map (1779), geological survey documents, land settlement reports, revenue surveys, historical texts, and
scriptural/biographical and other archaeological evidence, to corrobo-
rate their arguments (Fuller 2005, 210).

Both contesting parties also foreground mythical recollections of
past geographies, for instance dreams and other divine revelations

famous Vaishnava personalities have had about the sanctity of these places; divine lights seen by Datta flashing from the Mayapur birth-site; people feeling devotional vibrations when walking through or visiting these sites; and discoveries of sacred objects and idols under the temple grounds. These stories are written up in pamphlets about the temples' histories and sold in the temples, and narrated by temple attendants with equal conviction, every time pilgrims raise questions about the birthplaces. Standing before the nim tree under which Chaitanya was supposedly born, the attendant of Navadvip's birthplace-temple for instance repeats the same stories every day to willing listeners, for whom the stories are indispensable parts of their pilgrimage.

Chaitanya's birthplace controversy has resonances with the famous debate over Ram's birthplace in Ayodhya. An inter-religious milieu, in the case of Ayodhya, takes similar discursive forms in the intra-religious debate in Vaishnava Bengal. However, while in Ayodhya it is the immutability of the monument which is of prime significance (Pandey 1995, 378); in Nadia it is the sacred landscape—the importance of discovering *gupta*-Vrindavan.

Debates over the sacred landscape in contemporary Nadia are also debates about the best way to be a Vaishnava. Both birthplace temples embody what Upton (1985, quoted in Winer 2001, 261) calls "vernacular architecture": "the visual embodiment of a social process, in which available architectural ideas from many sources . . . are shaped into buildings answering the special requirements of a . . . local or ethnic community."

The birthplace debate, which crystallized over time within similar historical-mythical discourses, influences the contemporary circulating stories and identity assertions. Historicity in its pure form is always difficult to grapple with in the context of religious imaginings (Tedlock 2002, 398). The past is available for thinking about from within the lens of presentism, which involves reflective cultural processes of debating about the contemporary with respect to the community's own (religious) past (Bayly 2004, 112). History is thereby used as a resource in identity formation (van der Veer 1988, 48). Thus, Nadia's religious actors use the landscape stories in ways appropriate to their contrasting self-fashionings.

ISKCON promulgates a modern culture of Vaishnavism based on the primary ideals of scientific *prachar* (preaching), service to *gupta*-Vrindavan conceptualized as working toward the physical lands, and a democratic, exoteric model of religiosity, a significant component of which is to spread awareness about the true birthplace. Renouncer-*babajis*, on the other hand, stress the need to focus on *achar* (private ritual discipline) and share with *goswamis* a strong suspicion of the kind of Vaishnavism propagated by ISKCON and of the overriding importance ISKCON ascribes to preaching and publicizing. It seems paradoxical, then, for *babajis* to enter into the public birthplace debate with ISKCON and Gaudiya Math. The caretaker *babaji* of Navadvip's birthplace-temple eased my confusion.

On about three occasions, I had waited for him in the heat, sitting in the open outside his little room adjoining the birthplace-temple for a long time. He had been busy doing *puja* and meditating. When we finally met, I asked hesitantly about their religious contradiction, about why they were at all interested in debating with ISKCON and establishing their truth before pilgrims, when they emphasized that they cared most about their private spirituality. He said, "ISKCON is superficial about religion. . . . Their spiritual spuriousness is reflected in their claimed birth-site as well. Now, every year, a number of pilgrims come to Nadia. Many come to find gurus for themselves. Most immediately get attracted to Mayapur because it has a newer look as compared to Navadvip, and these days cleaner-looking religions sell better! If we did not enter into this debate with Mayapur, did not defend our discovery of *gupta*-Vrindavan, then pilgrims would not consider our assertion of the sect authentic. . . . They would follow false Vaishnavism."

Similarly, ISKCON devotees are aware of what other Vaishnavas feel about them. Once during a lunch-invitation in his house, a sophisticated, middle-aged devotee from Bangalore, who had been a science student himself, commented with a disapproving look, "*Babajis*' disciples mainly come from lower, uneducated classes. . . . They do not need scientific explanations of religion. But our members are educated Indians and international devotees. Thus, our religion is scientific, and democratic, and we spread its rationality, also about the birthplace, to people. . . . This is what *babajis* criticize as inauthentic!"

ISKCON's imagining of religion as scientific, exoteric, and clarified for public appraisal, and of their devotional self-experiences as preachers of this "rationality to people," is also evident in their modes of preaching about other temples in Mayapur.

THE MAYAPUR LANDSCAPE

All Mayapur temples commemorating Chaitanya's life-events belong to the Gaudiya Math trust, which collects the revenue generated from pilgrimage.

Devotees of Gaudiya Math predominantly come from the urban population, while ISKCON also caters to international devotees. Middle-class devotees visit Mayapur in groups, especially during holidays and weekends. Their visits are a mix of pilgrimage and tourism. Mayapur, with its beautiful rural ambience, solitude, open fields, and the vast stretch of the river, appeals to these people with otherwise busy, urban lives. And along with the feeling of idyllic village Bengal, inside ISKCON's headquarters enclosure pilgrims get all urban comforts they are used to, from pizzas and comfortable guest-house rooms, to sophisticated English-speaking tour guides and disciplined, punctual services from devotees. The massive inflow of urban pilgrims to Mayapur is because no other pilgrimage place in Bengal offers any comparable service. Also, the arrangement of temples, in a syntactical chain along the well-developed main road which cuts across the village and which has open fields on the other side, creates a topographical impact such that pilgrims do not need to exert themselves physically and can visit all the temples one after the other. As Mack (2004, 71) observes, in addition to spiritual senses of a place, pilgrimage landscapes are also "engineered to enhance such effects."

The narrative neatness temple attendants invoke in retelling stories of Chaitanya's life provides pilgrims with the ideal opportunity to satisfy their religious-touristy trips. The ideological focus of the stories rests on establishing Chaitanya's and Mayapur's divinity. Bhatia (2011) mentions that since the nineteenth century Chaitanya's biographies have been used to assert "historical" accuracies of his life to draw the attention of "historically-determined" urban devotees. Similarly, before narrating any story, temple attendants tell pilgrim-listeners that the narratives are strictly historical, insofar as they are based on Chaitanya's biographies. They assert that their versions of landscape-stories are reliable since they are the right mix of *tathya* (evidence) and *tattva* (theory).

Pilgrims often ask temple attendants and tour guides about miracles they may have personally experienced at these temple-sites. Attendants resolutely stress that miracles were only experienced by Chaitanya, his associates, and the founding figures of Gaudiya Math and ISKCON. Given the hierarchical structure of these modern religious institutions, it is heretical for individual members to claim spiritual ascendancy in experiencing divine miracles.

However, once pilgrims complete their round of Mayapur, *gupta*-Vrindavan, they are able to form a consistent, standardized story of Chaitanya's life and the institutions' history in sanctifying and preserving Vaishnava heritage. On visiting each of these temples the pilgrim is given a uniform narrative with proper space-time (historical) correlates. All temple-attendants say, "This is the *exact* spot where Sri Chaitanya's *lila* took place. Bhaktivinode Thakur discovered these places in and after 1894. Later, Gaudiya Math devotees constructed temples here." Temple attendants narrate stories of not only the particular temple they look after but also other Mayapur temples owned by Gaudiya Math, following which they ask pilgrims to visit them. The temples, being a part of the same economic-monopolistic establishment, construct a historical narrative syntax among themselves as embodiments of Chaitanya's serially instructive life.

Richer pilgrims visit these temples in their cars, while others travel by rickshaws and cycle-vans. All day, except for an hour during lunchtime, there are temple attendants waiting to narrate stories to pilgrims. These temples are modernized and spanking clean. They are strictly policed such that pilgrims cannot sit with their backs to deities, talk loudly, or loiter in temple-compounds. They have marble floors, and fans; when pilgrims walk in out of the heat, they get a quiet, cool, and serene atmosphere in which to listen to stories.

The temple known as Advaita Bhavan commemorates the meditation place of Advaita, an elder associate of Chaitanya, due to whose prayers Krishna/Chaitanya was born in *gupta*-Vrindavan. Devotee-attendants tell pilgrims that Chaitanya's birth was divine, not natural. The story goes that by Advaita's prayers, one morning, while Sachi Devi (Chaitanya's mother) was bathing in the Ganga, a basil leaf touched her stomach, and she conceived him. At the time of my fieldwork, the attendant of this temple was an old, enthusiastic man, who narrated this story in great detail and then sent pilgrims to the other temples.

From here pilgrims visit the birthplace temple, where attendants tell them the history of the discovery of the place, and stories of Chaitanya's childhood, which will strike any listener as similar to Krishna's. The attendant narrates the stories loudly and stresses that people must not believe in any other birthplace.

Two or three kilometers from there is the Gaudiya Math headquarters, popularly referred to as Abhinna (indistinguishable from) Vrindavan or Vrajapattan (Vrindavan's descent). The story goes that Chaitanya and his associates had theatrically enacted Krishna's activities in Vrindavan in this place for a whole night, and astounded the audience with their real emotions. This was his way to establish before them the sanctity of this place as authentic *gupta*-Vrindavan.

The headquarters were established at this site in 1918. Very often I have seen pilgrims listen to these stories, raise their hands and shout Krishna, Radha, and Chaitanya's names in the same breath, indicating the saint's sameness with deities.

Temple attendants then take pilgrims to visit Shyamkunda (Krishna's bathing-pond) and Radhakunda (Radha's bathing-pond), inside the temple premises. The whole compound is called Govardhan (hill considered to be an embodiment of Krishna's powers). These three structures are sacred centers of prime spiritual importance in Vrindavan's pilgrimage (Case 2000, 13; Ghosh 2005, 192; Haberman 1994; Hawley 1981). Devotees then head toward an exhibition of beautiful paintings depicting Chaitanya's life-events performed in *gupta*-Vrindavan.

Two central affective tenets of Bengal-Vaishnavism lie in Radha's love for Krishna and in this mood's finesse as experienced in Chaitanya's persona. These emotional states, embodied in idols of Radha-Krishna and Chaitanya, are kept in the central temple-altar. Temple attendants guide pilgrims to take *darshan* (spiritual gaze) of the idols and tell them that the idols encapsulate treasures of Vaishnava *bhakti* and that therefore their *darshan* will render their pilgrimage fruitful. In the same breath, attendants say that this temple is where Gaudiya Math renunciates receive their training and their roles to become ideal preachers. Narratives employed in Chaitanya Math thus reveal simultaneous assertions about Chaitanya's divinity, the indistinguishability of *gupta*-Vrindavan from Vrindavan, and an exoteric model of worship wherein idols become the sole mode of apprehending *bhakti*.

Apart from the birthplace temple and Chaitanya Math, two other important pilgrimage sites in Mayapur are Srivas Angan and Chand *qazi samadhi* (Chakrabarty 1985, 54–63; Kennedy 1925, 27–28). The chronicles of the two places are intrinsically connected. On several occasions I travelled with pilgrims to these two temples consecutively. Every time, the attendant of Srivas Angan firmly urged us to sit and listen to the story of the place. As we sat huddled close to him, he said, "This was the house of Srivas Pandit, Mahaprabhu's important associate. He was the god of music in heavens. Every night Mahaprabhu would chant here with devotees. A beautiful tree blossomed at this place; it started bearing flowers the same day as the music started, and died when god left for Puri. . . .

One day when Mahaprabhu was not there, the *qazi* [legal officer of the medieval Islamic ruler] sent his people to cause havoc at this place. . . . Hearing this, Mahaprabhu was very angry. He arranged for a procession to the *qazi's* house. . . . On seeing the large numbers that Mahaprabhu had mobilized, the *qazi* realized his divinity and became a devotee. . . . Later, Mahaprabhu planted a *goloka-chapa* [flower] tree on the *qazi's* grave. That tree is still there. Please go and visit the place after this."

We then proceeded to the *qazi's* *samadhi* (grave), around 5 km from there. Rather than any temple, a gigantic tree is worshipped at the site, which is considered sacred by both local Vaishnavas and Muslims. Local Muslim boys sell incense sticks and flowers to pilgrims, which they place before the tree on the grave. The attendant asked us to circumambulate the tree four times and come back to hear the grave's story. As we stood before the huge tree, he went on: "Mahaprabhu planted this tree. It has miraculously lived for five hundred years. Since he promised the *qazi* that every day a flower would offer itself to the grave, the tree has continued to blossom! The *qazi* was grateful to Sri Chaitanya and left all these lands to him, and that is why they now belong to us. The tree as an emblem of *gupta*-Vrindavan is scripted with god's deeds."

So, Mayapur's practitioners ground the primary theological tenets of Bengal-Vaishnavism and their affective dispositions toward the lands in markers of physical geography, such that they become embodied in the form of temples and trees, and democratize this sense of place for all who visit the lands. The prerogative of explaining these precepts, of discovering and preserving *gupta*-Vrindavan, remains with the modern institutions, however.

THE NAVADVIP LANDSCAPE

Chaitanya's pre-renunciation life and *gupta*-Vrindavan's inviolability are narrated in other contested ways as well. The emotional landscape configuration in contemporary Navadvip exhibits networks of power, assertions of authority, and corresponding "cultural biographies" (Kopytoff 1986, cited in Peabody 1991, 727) of temples and idols to be foregrounded by Navadvip's *goswamis*. Their devotional self-experience and sense of place differ markedly from Mayapur institutions.

Navadvip's atmosphere is very different from Mayapur. It is a chaotic, noisy town, and its lanes and vehicles are not as ordered as Mayapur. This leads to a lot of confusion whenever there are large pilgrim inflows. The temples are also not ordered in any syntax but rather scattered across the entire town-space. *Goswamis* who own big temples generally live in adjoining houses. A few *goswamis* who can afford it maintain their century-old temples, while many more temples are relatively unrestored. There are attendants who narrate temple-stories, but they are not always as punctual and disciplined as in Mayapur.

Although they are full-time devotees, like *babajis* and ISKCON devotees, *goswamis* have marital households. Thus, apart from knowing them as temple attendants I was also happily allowed into their personal domestic spaces. I know *goswamis'* wives, children, and even few distant relatives. Thus, in addition to reading books and pamphlets written about their temples by learned *goswamis* and hearing them narrate stories to pilgrims, I was privy to many familial sentimental associations they have with the landscape.

Goswamis claim biological descent from Chaitanya's brother-in-law and other important associates. Thus, the ways in which they carry out their daily domestic devotional commitments, and relate to the saint and his lands, are articulated through familial rhetorics of attachment. For instance, they celebrate Mahaprabhu's birthday not in the way one worships deities but as a Bengali mother celebrates her son's birthday: bathing him affectionately, serving him his favorite food, and putting on his best adornments. In this Bengali Hindu way of indulging in familial love, they celebrate Chaitanya's first birthday, every year.

Goswamis uphold Hindu familial values by wearing their Brahmanical sacred threads, and holding landed property in Navadvip. Case (2000, 44) mentions, however, that *goswamis'* orientation to the family is spiritual, such that "they are good to the family, because they love god" and not vice versa, thus exemplifying the classic South Asian phenomenon Lynch (1990, 190–91) calls "this worldly mysticism."

To keep the family tradition intact they generally do not marry outside *goswami* families, and never outside the Brahmin caste. The children are initiated by their mothers, and only *goswami* women are allowed to cook for their temples. They fast after the morning, and cook for a large number of family members and pilgrims every day. In one important temple, Dhameswar Mahaprabhu Mandir, the women cook in a huge antechamber for hours together, and no one is allowed to see or talk to them during this time.

Unlike *babajis* or ISKCON devotees, who are strict vegetarians, some *goswamis* eat fish. Once, in a *goswami's* house, I smelled cooked fish in the kitchen. Surprised, I looked at the *goswami* man. Slightly embarrassed, he said, "Vaishnavas are meant to be vegetarians, and so are most of our family. We do not allow non-vegetarian cooking in the

FIGURE 6. Wooden idol of Dhameswar Mahaprabhu.

temple. But, you know, Bengali married women must have some fish, since they need to bear strong children."

In the same way that ISKCON's professionalism and *babajis*' asceticism attract initiates, it is *goswamis*' ancestral spiritual heritage which makes them gurus of utmost importance in Bengal. In many cases they give initiation following family lines, such that over the generations a Bengali family may take initiation from members of a *goswami* family. *Goswamis* make a distinction between *bongsho* (lineage, referring to their line of *goswamis*) and *parivar* (family, referring to disciples of that lineage). This indicates the extension of familial idioms to their intimate relations with the initiated. Disciples in turn claim to love and respect their gurus as much as their parents. So in addition to their regular contributions to *goswami* temples and support of *goswami* households, it is common to find well-off disciples sponsoring their gurus' surgeries, travel, and so on.

The most frequented temple in Navadvip is Dhameswar (Lord of the Land) Mahaprabhu Mandir. It is a big temple, with a large courtyard used for devotee congregations, evening scripture readings, and musical gatherings, and it houses a most famous wooden Chaitanya idol.

The Dhameswar temple is owned by *goswamis* claiming descent from Chaitanya's brother-in-law. The temple's service schedules are passed on through lineage-logic such that if one does not have a son, it passes down through daughters or adopted children considered to be deserving future gurus. The temple services comprise looking after the regular needs of Chaitanya's idol: serving him his favorite food and other items five times a day, knowledge of which has come down through the family's oral tradition. This is similar to devotional orders like Pustimargis, who draw a distinction between *murtis*, ordinary idols, which depend on Brahmanical rites, and *svarupas*, Krishna's eternal embodied expressions, which require familial emotional attention (Bennett 1990, 182–83).

Goswamis' authority in Nadia's landscape solidified with the settlement of Chaitanya's idol in this temple. I recollect widely circulated mythical narratives about the temple's origins. These stories are known to most people in Navadvip, and whether or not they are *goswamis'* disciples, all relish the chronicles, and many repeated them to me several times during fieldwork. The stories, like the narratives accompanying Mayapur temples, do not retell a finished past but are ever-new, itinerant iterations (Lund 2008) of Chaitanya's eternal manifestation in *gupta*-Vrindavan.

Mahaprabhu, in 1510, took renunciation vows (*sannyas*) and left Navadvip for Puri. He left behind his mother and his sixteen-year-old wife, Vishnupriya. This incident is considered an epic tragic event among Bengalis. There are countless literary renditions of it, popularly referred to as Nimai *sannyas*. A popular soulful song among them says:

> O Vishnupriya,
> I leave, as you sleep in the early hours of dawn.
> . . .
> In those tender moments you held me in your slender arms
> But when you wake in the morning, I will be gone
> You will break your bangles and shout to everyone
> That cruel is Nadia's Nimai, I know you will
> O Vishnupriya, but I must go.
> . . .
> Listen, O people of Nadia,
> I am Krishna's lover and I leave to search for Krishna's touch.
> O Vishnupriya I leave.

As a *goswami's* wife explained, "Mahaprabhu is not a distant god to us, as he is to others [implying ISKCON]. He was married into our family, and we treat him as we treat our brothers-in-law. While others [referring to ISKCON and *babaji* renouncers] celebrate his renunciation, we mourn it. We do not even look at pictures depicting him as a *sannyasi* [renouncer]. Navadvip cries for Nimai, as Vrindavan cries for Krishna."

There are mythical representations of this anguished landscape among *goswamis*. It is said that Chaitanya left very early in the morning. When his mother woke up, shocked and angry, she cursed the Navadvip's banks which he had crossed, and the crows which did not call long enough for her to wake up. Those riverbanks are still known as the *nidoya-r ghat* (pitiless banks), and it is said that crows cannot reside in Navadvip. The entire landscape and natural habitat are believed to respond to the *goswamis'* affect. Since devotees worship Chaitanya as Radha's and Krishna's incarnation, and Navadvip as *gupta*-Vrindavan, they thus conceptualize Chaitanya's taking up renunciation and leaving Navadvip as the mirror-*lila* of Krishna's leaving Vrindavan to become Mathura's warrior-king, bereaving his devotees and lovers.

Chaitanya came back one last time to meet his mother in a town close to Navadvip. Vishnupriya was at home, desperate to meet him. At this point he appeared before her and asked her to make an idol of him from the wood of the nim tree under which he was born. Other devotees say the idol appeared before her miraculously; some others, that he appeared and gave her the idol; while others remember that she received orders from her husband/god in her dreams.

Vishnupriya served the idol for the rest of her life. Chaitanya also left his pair of sandals for her service; like the idol, it is a most venerated object in Bengal's devotional world. *Goswamis* touch them to pilgrims' heads to bless them. *Goswamis* say that Vishnupriya, at the age of 96, eventually merged into the same idol, on Mahaprabhu's birthday. She asked her brother's son to worship her in the same idol. Thus, this 500-year-old idol is sometimes dressed in a *sari,* and at other times in a *dhoti.* Her pearl nose-ring is still attached to it as a mark of their merging. For *goswamis* the idol is the simultaneous embodiment of Mahaprabhu and Vishnupriya—the vehicle of their ever-presence in Navadvip.

Thus, while the prime mode of devotional self-expression, pilgrimage organization, and narrative employment about temples among Mayapur practitioners lies in the ideology of rational, historical, and exoteric preaching, for *goswamis* it lies in intimate service toward family heritage and affective mythical representations of the landscape.

However, apart from the mythical significance this idol carries, the idol's and temple's position in the pilgrimage landscape can also be mapped through the power positions of those who claim the temple. As the story goes, this idol was kept in Chaitanya's birthplace till floods were about to destroy it. *Goswamis* then took it away from the birth-place and served it in hiding, since the public worship of a god-saint-like figure was forbidden by the mother-goddess-worshipping rulers of the time. The idol was then rotated amongst *goswami* descendants.[10]

In 1798, Manipur's king received Mahaprabhu's orders in his dreams to arrange his public worship, and under the instruction of Manipur's king the Nadia rulers finally allowed public veneration of Chaitanya (Goswami 2007, 37). The *goswamis* had waited to establish their own position of authority within the devotional topography with this idol in the fore-ground. Finally, a west-facing temple was constructed, and a large stone brought from the birthplace-temple was placed on its main door, which still signifies its authenticity to devotees (Goswami 2007; Mondol 2002).

In 1803, public worship of Chaitanya began in Nadia (Goswami 2007, 38), marking the onset of Chaitanya-idol-worship on a large scale in Bengal, and it was from the beginning of twentieth century that the impetus to build temples increased in Navadvip. In 2006–07 the central government awarded the Dhameswar temple the status of a her-itage building. Thus, Dhameswar temple is relatively well-maintained as compared to other temples in Navadvip, but still not glossy like the Mayapur temples.

Gradually, after the mid-eighteenth century, *goswami* families shifted to the locality around the temple, and a busy pilgrimage center developed. This area is known as Mahaprabhu-*para* (neighborhood). This prominent neighborhood is bustling with pilgrims, shops selling *puja* items, and loudspeakers blaring devotional songs. Devotees flock the temple for *arati* five times a day, from four in the morning to nine at night, and for evening sermons and *kirtan*. No family occasion in the town, such as a wedding, initiation, funeral, or birthday, is celebrated without blessings from Dhameswar-Mahaprabhu.

This temple's establishment marked a significant transformative moment in the history and aesthetics of Bengal-Vaishnavism. *Goswamis* came to assume a very important position in the hierarchy of religious specialists in Navadvip.

Mayapur practitioners find this idol's centrality, and the *goswamis'* parallel familial, anti-renunciatory rhetoric, difficult to grapple with. The attendant of Mayapur's birthplace-temple suggested that Vishnupriya never served any idol at all, but rather Chaitanya's painting, which she had made herself. He added, "You must never hear stories of biological descent from saints/gods. Chaitanya was a preacher of religion, and his marriage was not important. Scriptures say that Chaitanya never met his wife after taking renunciation vows. And these vows are a matter of pride, not lament."

Goswamis' claims of consanguinity and spiritual ascendance in serving *gupta*-Vrindavan are not limited to the Dhameswar temple, however. There are several small temples in Navadvip's sacred topography in and around Mahaprabhu-*para,* carrying 50–200 years of history.

Many of these are popularly known as *lila-smarak-mandirs* (temples commemorating divine plays). While Navadvip has temples venerating all the events that the temples in Mayapur do (the ones mentioned in Chaitanya's biographies), there are also others with no exact historical reference. The purpose of these temples is not mere "occupation" but active "inhabitation" of the consecrated landscape (Wedlock 2008). Their stories thus order the emotional sensorium of *goswamis' gupta-*Vrindavan through Hindu familial principles.

For instance, there are temples commemorating Chaitanya's mother's consoling Vishnupriya after his renunciation—symbolizing an affective bond between the mother and daughter-in-law—as well as one known as Upanayan-lila, celebrating the saint's initiation into Brahmanism, and one called Bibaho-lila, depicting a Hindu marriage ceremony between Chaitanya and Vishnupriya. In the Upanayan *mandir* attendants also sell sacred threads and vermilion considered holy by Hindu married women, and say that prayers in this temple for good marriages and children are answered. Navadvip's rickshaw-pullers are interested parties in the pilgrimage and insist on taking pilgrims to some of these temples over others, since their attendants reserve revenue shares for them. They convince pilgrims by telling them these temple-stories on the way.

Most temples, including Dhameswar, claim to have miracles associated with them. *Goswamis* say that temple courtyards resound with Radha's/Mahaprabhu's anklets; that people have witnessed deities before the early morning *arati*; that attendants find the deity-consort's bed disheveled in the morning; that deities keep *goswamis* from locking the temple if some devotee desperately needs to visit it after prescribed hours; and that at festival times Mahaprabhu participates in the celebration and devotees feel his presence through an unidentifiable sweet smell in the air. However, they also insist that there are stories about temple-deities and personal experiences which one must not mention to outsiders. Thus, unlike at ISKCON, there are stories not meant for public democratic appraisal.

The *goswamis* serving these temples are also attendants of the Dhameswar temple. Their portion of the Dhameswar revenue is not always sufficient. Thus, some of them have also constructed these small personal temples. They pay taxes for their ownership, and revenues collected from pilgrims' offerings constitute their personal income. So, although they are part of the same family, there is a sense of economic competition among *goswamis*.

Most *goswamis* claim no exactitude in the space-time coordinates of their respective temples and candidly confess that their temple-constructions only relive Chaitanya's times and *lilas*. Some do claim, however, that their temple is on the exact spot of one of Chaitanya's historical incidents. But the economic competition is such that other *goswamis* immediately dismantle their claims by providing alternative stories. Thus, unlike in Mayapur, there is generally no narrative syntax among *goswamis'* temple-stories.

For instance, Srivas-Angan temple's attendant shows a tree which Mahaprabhu planted and which miraculously stands despite having no solid roots. This temple compares in size and popularity to the Dhameswar temple. However, another *goswami* belonging to Chaitanya's brother-in-law's lineage commented, "Not only are those claims false, but their identities also distorted. Srivas-Angan's *goswamis* claim descent from Nityananda [Chaitanya's most important associate in Navadvip]. Yet the scriptures say that Nityananda's son had no children!" However, the different lineages of Navadvip's *goswamis* otherwise share cordial everyday relations. Contestations among them are not matters of enmity or as stark as with Mayapur's Vaishnavas.

Apart from Chaitanya's brother-in-law's family, the other major *goswami* lineage in Navadvip claims descent from Nityananda. They are aware of skepticism regarding their authenticity and keep diagrammatic representations of their family tree to show to devotees. A *goswami* of their family took me to an old, shabby room adjoining the Srivas Angan temple, in which he kept pictures, books, scriptures, furniture, clothes, manuscripts, and so on, all belonging to his ancestors. He took out a parchment scroll with details of the family tree extending back fourteen generations. *Goswamis'* spiritual heritage is largely familial, and they put utmost emphasis on asserting it.

Since *goswamis* of Nityananda's lineage are important participants in *gupta*-Vrindavan, their temple also bears inscriptions of Chaitanya's divinity. In the temple premises a stone said to bear his footprints is worshipped. The temple attendant said, "When Krishna plays his flute even stone melts; so also, one night as Mahaprabhu was doing *kirtan*, the stone slab on which he was dancing melted, and retained the god's footprints."

So, from the perspective of historical-mythical thinking, the Mayapur-Navadvip sacred topography poses interesting problematics, somewhat corresponding to Tilley's (1994, 20) distinction between controlled "disciplinary spaces," where "architectural forms resemble each other," and architecture as embodiment of myth and cosmology. If historical thought is defined as having unambiguous space-time chronologies (Pandey 1995, 372), and mythical imaginings as being partially about such claims, then a spatial conditioning of community histories and mythical connections can be imagined such that Mayapur practitioners, that is, Gaudiya Math and ISKCON, adopt a clear-cut historical stance with respect to their temples and their own religious selves, while Navadvip exhibits a more diffused relation with its past. In Mayapur, places are fixed in scripture, while in Navadvip, stories respond to familial-emotional contours. Historical syntax and economic monopoly in Mayapur, and economic competition and mythical fractures in Navadvip, have also been demonstrated to have a connection.

Goswamis, in their roles as temple owners, embody religious mnemonics which are relatively independent of historical reckonings. Unlike history's fixation with remembering what actually happened, cultural memory involves a sifting of remembering and forgetting. This dialectical "memory work" is of crucial importance in the formation of cultural identities and the understanding of "popular historiology" (Fabian 2003, 489).

However, the above description of narratives employed in Mayapur and Navadvip temples does not suggest a neat division between historical and mythical thinking, either. Myths make use of available historical common sense while forming alternative stories, while historical attempts remain partial and invoke the sense of miracles just as mythical operations.

THE *BABAJIS' AKHRAS*

Gupta-Vrindavan's landscape is also home to reveried mythemes experienced by Navadvip's *babajis*. Generally far from bustle of the town center, *babajis* live in ashrams or *akhras*. They wear white loincloths and follow the strict ritual discipline demanded of Vaishnava renouncers. While a *goswami*, after dedicating adequate time to his temple and spiritual practices, also has personal time for his family, friends, and other regular town activities, *babajis'* lives are largely confined to ashrams. In addition to dedicating most of their waking hours to *sadhana* (spiritual discipline) and scripture reading, *babajis*, unlike *goswamis*, cannot afford servants and thus do all the cleaning, cooking, and other chores in the ashrams. *Babaji* temples and ashrams are often modest in size and appearance, but kept very clean by the resident *babajis*.

Ordinary pilgrims do not generally visit *babajis'* ashrams as their locations in town interiors do not fall on the main pilgrimage routes in the town center.[11] Rickshaw-pullers also do not tell pilgrims about them. However, *babajis'* initiates stay in ashrams, especially during festival times, both to spend valuable time with their gurus and because all the hotels, temples, and even street corners are overflowing with pilgrims then, while *babaji*-gurus give first priority for residence to their disciples. Also, since *babajis'* abstinence and scriptural knowledge are famous all over Bengal, many others come in search of appropriate gurus. Devotees who wish to be renunciate gurus themselves choose to be initiated by *babajis* rather than *goswamis*, who only allow lineage-members to be gurus.

In popular Bengali imagination, archetypal *babajis* are remembered for feats of spiritual discipline—the enormous numbers of times they chanted daily, the number of days they kept fasts, the long hours (sometimes days) during which they meditated, the extraordinary lengths of their lives, or their ability to predict the time of their death. This corresponds to Horstmann's (2001, 175) idea of the renouncer's exemplary figure as one revealing what becomes of a devotee who exercises his devotion to its "radical end."

Babajis are celibate renouncers. Thus, unlike *goswamis* they are not as comfortable chatting with women. However, most *babajis* are very humble and helpful since they consider these to be important Vaishnava values, and a major part of my fieldwork benefitted from sustained relations with them. Older *babajis* are relatively more relaxed about mixing with women. However, we would generally sit in temple/ashram courtyards and avoid *babajis'* rooms, lest they be misunderstood by others. Sitting on a bench in his ashram's courtyard, one *babaji* friend started weeping as he recounted his guru's miraculous powers and how his guru once saved his life. *Babajis* are not miracle-men, however. They consider senior *babaji* gurus' powers to be mere derivatives of spiritual integrity, not ends in themselves.

Babajis' principal modes of asserting Vaishnava authority, ashram-stories and claims to *gupta*-Vrindavan are through idioms of ascetic excellence and scriptural knowledge derived from austere ritual correctness and training interiorized from paradigmatic renunciate gurus of Bengal-Vaishnavism. People hear stories of famous *babajis*, miracles experienced by them, and how *akhras* embody their commemoration, during evening sermons in ashrams and also through a vibrant culture of oral lore.

Babajis also come into direct contact with townspeople on important festival occasions. During Ras, in early November, when devotees celebrate Krishna's circular dance with his lovers in the Vrindavan forests on an autumn full-moon night, Chaitanya's idol, which Vaishnavas consider Krishna's embodiment, is taken on a round of Navadvip, *gupta*-Vrindavan, from Samajbari, one of the most important *babaji* temples. Similarly, during Holi, the idol is taken to devotees' houses, accompanied by *kirtans*, which Samajbari is very famous for.

In their renunciation, *babajis* forsake everything to do with earthly life. Renunciation is considered ritual death in the ordinary world and birth in Krishna's. Thus, when *babajis* die, their bodies are not cremated (like ordinary Hindus') but buried. Their *samadhis* are preserved and worshipped in *akhras*. Many ashrams have also preserved hundreds of scriptures which *babajis* consulted, *jap-malas* with which they chanted, and their clothes, sandals, and paintings, which hold tremendous spiritual value for present generations of ascetics and devotees. These material belongings embodying renunciates' hallowed sobriety permeate the mythopoetic atmosphere of *akhras* with the sacrality of the lands, of *gupta*-Vrindavan, in which *babajis* lived, learned, practiced devotion, and were blessed by Chaitanya's grace.

Most *babaji* temples are known for phenomenal miracles accompanying them. As Tilley (1994, 33) argues, when stories are sedimented in landscapes, they dialectically reproduce each other; so while the landscape is narrativized, stories derive their life force from being associated with materialities people can touch and see.

The Harisabha Mandir, built around 200 years ago, is known for its founding *babaji,* Vrajamohan Vidyaratna. The story goes that one night as he was coming back from a nearby town, he lost his way. A little boy took him to his house to stay overnight. In his dreams, the boy appeared in the form of Natua (dancing) Gour (Chaitanya). He then established this temple with an idol depicting the figure of his dreams. Then, as days passed, local boys began complaining of a madman called Nehal Khyapa, who slept in the temple compounds and shouted every night, "My deities have been stolen!" Then after a few hours he would shout, "They have come back!" One night the *babaji* stayed with him to solve the mystery. He saw that the man carried a sack with idols of Radha-Raman (Radha-Krishna). Late in the night the idols united into

Chaitanya's figure, embodying their night-time intimate encounters, and by early morning, reassumed their separate forms. The Radha-Raman idols, along with Natua Gour, are still worshipped in the temple.

In another of these stories, a wandering ascetic used to wear his Gopal (child Krishna) idol around his neck (*kontho*). One day, as many times as he served Gopal food, a little boy snatched it away. Finally he realized that this was baby Chaitanya, identical with baby Krishna. Commemorating this incident, a temple was established with the Kontho-Gopal idol.

Not all *akhras* are temples, however; that is, some do not house idols but are simply residential places for *babajis*, built in memory of famous ascetics. The *babajis* living in these *akhras* are proud that rather than converting ashrams into temples, which automatically draw more pilgrims and donations, they dedicate their time to spiritual discipline, remaining indifferent to economic prospects.

The Boro *akhra*, an ashram built in the seventeenth century, was founded by Ramdas *babaji*, still famous for his immense grasp of scriptures. Popular lore recounts how one day while he was meditating on the Ganga shore, some boys hung a pair of shoes around his neck. Because they carry dust, a polluting substance, shoes are held in deep disdain by Hindus. Tying shoes around someone's neck is thus a most disrespectful act. But the *babaji* was so engrossed that he did not realize. During this time the *dewan* (native treasurer) of East India Company, Gangagovinda Singha, was crossing the Ganga. Watching this incident he was deeply in awe of the *babaji*. On completing his meditation, rather than being angry, Ramdas *babaji* kissed the shoes, because they carried *gupta*-Vrindavan's dust. Commemorating this incident, the festival of Dhulot was initiated in Navadvip.

The famous Haribol *kutir* (hut) was established in memory of an ascetic who used to wake the people of Navadvip before dawn, crying out "Haribol" ("take Krishna's name"). One of his disciples, Haridas Das, is one of the most renowned Vaishnava scholars. He travelled all over India in the early twentieth century to recover lost scriptures. He produced the most thorough, widely acclaimed and influential *avidhan* (dictionary) of Gaudiya Vaishnavism, which documents the history, literature, and practices of the tradition. The underground room in which he meditated is still revered by devotees.

There are many more *akhras* with exemplary *"milieux de memoire"* (Nelson and Olin 2003, 74), which devotees venerate with affection. *Akhras* are indispensable elements of *gupta*-Vrindavan, embodying

Chaitanya's grace in the paradigmatic virtues of renunciate Vaishnavas, which in turn constitute the impact of ashram-chronicles.

PILGRIMS OF THE REGION

This chapter has documented the multiple contested public faces of Vaishnava groups and the inherent relationships between their religious self-experiences and the physical landscape which is inhabited and constituted simultaneously. With an abundance of temples, discourses, and debates, there is a unique situation wherein differences over the multiform landscape become visible as sites. What then is the nature of popular "nomadic discourse" (Carter 1987, 28) in the pilgrimage geography, and how do pilgrims negotiate this chaotic space?

Thousands of pilgrims come to Nadia year-round, leaving behind their agricultural work, struggling in local trains and buses, sleeping at night on railway platforms, and spending hard-earned money on pilgrimage. It became perplexing to me to comprehend the inspiration behind such passions.

I was most intrigued by the utter uncertainty of public response to the splintered religious discourses in circulation. It was common to find pilgrims with divergent Vaishnava affiliations and gurus sitting and chatting together. Until they were brought up, the predicaments of toponymy, the exactitudes of Chaitanya's birthplace, the hierarchy of various specialists in the preference for a guru, the respective ratings of Navadvip and Mayapur in the run for authentic Vaishnavism, did not evoke anxiety. But once open to discussion, the anguish of skepticism and the violent disparities, as well as the contrary response of decisive rejection of the issues, were obvious. It was a complicated interlock of emotions toward the storied landscape. After one such conversation with devotees in a Mayapur roadside hotel during Ras, I began to make sense of the logic of this uncertainty.

> A (in search of a good guru): It is difficult to say which of the places has the birthplace. The original and imitation are impossible to distinguish. New things are given old looks and old things polished anew these days!
>
> B (initiated with a *goswami* family): Different scriptures say different things. . . . We dress the same god in different clothes. . . . For some people, advertising the birthplace is important; for someone else, simply seeing Mahaprabhu is [implying the Dhameswar-Mahaprabu idol].
>
> A: How does it make a difference? These days people have two sets of parents—a set of birthplaces won't make a difference! [Laughter from all.]

> C (wants to be initiated in Gaudiya Math, Mayapur): See, in foreign places, safety is more important than authenticity. . . . So we go where we are safer [implying Mayapur]. . . .
>
> A: But it's more expensive in Mayapur.

At this point some others who had overheard our conversation pointed out, "During Dol you will find people following their gurus or institutions in traversing the region. But once it is over, most of them, barring the city people who leave from Mayapur, will go around all the places." Confused, I asked them whether the sacrality of places per se has no importance during pilgrimage.

> B: Of course it does! But sacredness cannot be measured in historical and economic terms. As long as we can remember Mahaprabhu emotionally, historical detail does not matter. The whole landscape around this region is sacred because Mahaprabhu's *lilas* will be apparent wherever a devotee searches. . . . The stories we hear in different temples create an orientation with which we taste the landscape.[12]
>
> A: In this process, we do watch the lifestyles of different Vaishnavas, and might choose gurus for ourselves from among them, but that never stops us from traversing all the places associated with Nimai.

It is thus evident that devotees structure their pilgrimage despite controversies, but not independent of them. A conceptual question, then, is whether the believer can act on the basis of critical cognitive capacities, or whether she is bound by "unthinking" traps of affective belief; in other words, whether belief itself can be a source of critical thinking. The solution to this problematic lies in a careful hearing of pilgrims' creative "chorus of idle footsteps" (de Certeau 1984, 107).

Clearly, it is from within the belief for the landscape that some invoke further belief in historical specificities of sites, while others practice their affective orientations alongside a critical sidestepping of history. This active exercise of critical choice, or "historical surplus," constitutes popular "creativity" (Hastrup 2007, 204). So I argue that the structures of affective belief might themselves give rise to conditions of further belief or unbelief.

Thus, the decision to avoid historical considerations is a choice some devotees employ to emotionally relate to the materiality of the entire sacred landscape. The landscape stories unveil the multiplicity and passionate sacrality of the entire region to pilgrims. Similarly, Ratnagar (2004) demonstrates that despite the presence of multiple competitive shrines in Ayodhya claiming to be Ram's birth-site, ardent devotees do not hold any particular reverence for individual sites but rather for the entire place. Brosius (2004, 350, cited in Ratnagar 2004) argues that therefore historicity does not matter to devotees, who continue to reserve their affection for the places. However, following this argument, she suggests a lack of criticality on the part of ordinary devotees. As I have argued above, while I agree that people may not delve into the historicity of claims, this is not due to unreasoning acceptance. It rather follows from the philosophy of pilgrims' itinerant embodied devotions, which spell out Casey's (1996, 26) conviction that individual sites cannot exhaust the ontological possibilities of places; that senses of place precede (and in this case supersede) sites (1993, 143). Casey's argument in turn is influenced by Heidegger's (1975, 154) assertion about buildings and sites following from senses of prior dwelling.

For every kind of devotee, therefore, it is the relation between religious self-experience and the sense of belonging in an emotional landscape which defines different physical spatial practices in Bengal-Vaishnavism. However, just as pilgrims find ways of negotiating the sacred region without being confined by (contested) sites, there are Vaishnava practitioners who dwell in Vrindavan without relating solely to the physical landscape.

OTHER SENSES OF PLACE

While the description of the physical landscape and analysis of debates over it might appear both the obvious and also the only way to understand sacred geography in Hinduism generally and Vaishnavism specifically, it is only the beginning of what's significant about experiencing the sacred place in the life of Bengal-Vaishnavas.

After spending the first three or four months of fieldwork studying the varying social meanings of Nadia's topography, clues and meanings of a simultaneous retreat from it began to emerge. It was evident, for instance, that the vigor which accompanied Mayapur's defense and advertisement of temples was relatively bleaker in the case of Navadvip's *babajis*. And this was definitely not because of any comparative lack of mobilization but because religious actors exhibit both attachment to and detachment from the physical landscape in important ways.

In many *babaji* ashrams and *goswami* temples there were stories that were told in the pilgrimage-market and others that were not. And these were stories I was now interested in.

A *goswami* elder of Srivas Angan temple put it beautifully: "As long as smell is blind and cries inside the bud, it is good. The moment the bud blooms, the smell will die. Everything is not for everyone. Vaishnavas should ideally avoid preaching in the final instance. Of course we need to engage publicly and have disciples. But just like material reasons, there are spiritual reasons to have disciples. This *gupta*-Vrindavan that you see is there for everyone to experience. . . . But there are higher places, and after their initiation, we take them there!"

By this time I had made quite a number of *goswami* friends who insisted that I think about issues "more significant" to their spiritual lives, not only about historical controversies. This agentive suspension of concrete historicism was equally asserted by *babajis*. Surprisingly, the attendant *babaji* in charge of Navadvip's birthplace-temple, who spent a great part of the day defending the "true" birthplace-site to pilgrims, spoke a somewhat different language in a later meeting. "An ascetic is one who has everything and then leaves it, not one who does not have anything. The strength of our ashrams increases by the day, but material concerns can't bog us down. Debates and clashes are inevitable in the material world. But beyond a certain point we leave these issues to ISKCON and concentrate on our *bhajan* [spiritual discipline]. Debate and talk are hindrances to our spiritual life."

This paradox of maintaining social stances vis-à-vis the physical *gupta*-Vrindavan and simultaneously professing a retreat from public spheres gradually made sense when I realized that the withdrawal itself is a mode of Vaishnava subjectivation. A number of parallel stories and archetypes establish this. A most popular recollection among *goswamis* and *babajis* dates back to seventeenth century. The story goes that once, in Vrindavan, a famous Sanskrit scholar came to debate with Rupa Goswami and Sanatan Goswami, Chaitanya's most trusted disciples and famous Vaishnava scholars. Surprisingly, they signed a blank paper and said that the scholar was free to add that he had won the debate. Elated, the man went away. He lost, however, to their nephew, Jiva Goswami. Rupa later instructed Jiva that a Vaishnava must not sacrifice spiritual time for anything unnecessary (in this case implying the scholarly debate) and rebuked him, saying that his ideal place was a proud king's throne, not Krishna's Vrindavan.

The *babaji* at Navadvip's birthplace-temple narrated the story and added, "ISKCON can have the king's throne, but we will stay in Vrindavan."

By extolling an ideal of withdrawal from the physical aspect of the sacred place, these Vaishnavas do not mean that it is futile to engage with the place's physicality but rather that for a Vaishnava there can never be only a single exclusive means of apprehending the sacred place. Cort's (1999, 89) rethinking of renunciation is apt in this case, where it is not about leaving everything of the past life, but a mode of "psychological renunciation," where "the person renounces aspects of his or her socially-constructed personality in pursuit of a transcendent goal."

One *babaji* of a certain Baladev *akhra* made a radical revelation which only strengthened my sense of the importance of Vrindavan to Vaishnavas' lives. He was a musician and played the sacred drum (*khol*). He was playing the *khol* for me as we sat in his room, since it was raining heavily outside. He sang a song describing how Krishna's lovers in Vrindavan were running to meet him in the forest and how their jewelry fell off in the process. When the song was over, I asked the *babaji* why he thought that Vrindavan is so essential to every Vaishnava song. He said, "Vaishnavas and Vrindavan cannot be separated. If one is a pure devotee, Vrindavan will be apparent to him in *gupta*-Vrindavan. Just as Nadia lands can make Vrindavan apparent, so can other *gupta*-Vrindavans. Bless me that I can go there."

Thus, for *goswamis* and *babajis,* there are sacred places of greater spiritual significance than is necessarily experienced in physical geographies. Since for ISKCON religion is a public expression, they emphasize the centrality of the physical landscape as *gupta*-Vrindavan, so that it can be manifest to all. It is in terms of this idea of the democratic public that *babajis* engage in the birthplace debate. But their sense of place is extended further. There is a shift from a debating culture to silent withdrawal—from the domain of warrior Krishna to a search for the lover god.

Thus, another famous seventeenth-century chronicle recollects how a poor man went to Sanatan Goswami, since he was known to have a lot of treasures. Sanatan gave him the jewels that were in his possession. The man, contented, was leaving, when something struck him. He thought the saint must have something much more precious if he was willing to sacrifice the jewels. He went back to him. Sanatan then gave him the clue to Vaishnava spiritual life.

This "treasure," for *goswamis* and *babajis,* lies in another veiled-Vrindavan, another experience of the sacred place, another Vaishnavism. It is to the analysis of that experience of Vrindavan we will now turn.

CHAPTER 3

Imagining in *Gupta*-Vrindavan: Experiencing the Self and Emotions in the Mind-Heart Landscape

INTRODUCTION: PLACING IMAGINATION

The exact moment when the field becomes engraved in the anthropologist's flesh and dream escapes her. It can only be recalled in reactions, much later. On a fortunate day in Cambridge, I woke up before dawn. Sipping my morning tea I looked out at the sky. The golden sun had just started to brighten the cloud lines. I could immediately "see" that Radha was being woken up by her friends after her nocturnal tryst with Krishna in a Vrindavan forest and quickly sent back home, lest her all-night absence from the house be discovered by her in-laws.[1] But before I could enjoy the sight of their waking embraces, my objective self kicked in. I realized I was *imagining*. Yet, just as I was beginning to feel distressed by the clash between professional objectivity and an enraptured spiritual self, I remembered what a *babaji* had told me: "Only when one is blessed with divine grace are one's subtle senses able to feel Vrindavan *lilas* in the *manas* [mind-heart]. This is not to be confused with *kolpona* [unreal]. It is as true as perception. The *manas gupta*-Vrindavan has manifested the simultaneous events of Vrindavan, right there and right then."

While the previous chapter dealt with the visible, historicized, articulated and publicly accessible face of Bengal-Vaishnavism in discussing debates on Nadia's geography, here I document another dimension of the experience of place: the practices of an imaginative landscape in the interiorized affective space of the mind. I analyze the key devotional practice known as *manjari sadhana* performed by Navadvip's *goswamis* and *babajis*, in which the devotee's *manas*, is deemed to be a veiled-Vrindavan, which unveils or manifests Radha-Krishna's erotic activities in Vrindavan through practices of imagination.[2] Thus, the main aim of this discussion is to document techniques and experiences of transportation to an imaginative sense of unveiled Vrindavan. The way in which this transportation is effectuated is quite specific: it is a process of placing the practitioner's imagined body and self as a handmaiden of the deities' erotic *lilas* in a particular kind of imagined space. Radha and Krishna enact their sexual plays in celestial Vrindavan. *Goswamis* and *babajis* claim that through their spiritual practices, these sexual plays manifest in their imagination, or simply that their *manas* or imagination then becomes Vrindavan. Shifting from public narratives of places in historical time-space, this chapter thus analyzes the dimensions of the spiritual place experienced by practitioners as an intensely imagined space of the deities' divine play as lovers and dispensers of erotic bliss, and a radical form of gendered devotion in which practitioners focus on cultivating feminine subjectivities in order to experience the deities' *lilas* in imagination.

While Navadvip's *babajis* and *goswamis* have differences in their daily lives, primarily because *babajis* live in monastic ashrams and *goswamis* in familial householder settings, they both practice this form of imaginative devotion. I have discussed *goswamis'* and *babajis'* different ways of engaging with the pilgrimage industry. But the way they treat pilgrims and aspects of physical landscape, and the way they practice imagination, are completely separate realms of life. This chapter is about their inner spirituality as opposed to their relations with pilgrims. Although the details of their esoteric practices are unknown to ordinary pilgrims, it is a part of pilgrims' devotional common sense that *goswamis* and *babajis* as full-time committed practitioners are extremely knowledgeable about sophisticated Vaishnava practices. *Goswamis* and *babajis* say that their spiritual genealogies date back to the sixteenth and seventeenth centuries and that their long-standing tradition of practices and distinctive way of being Vaishnavite were taught by Chaitanya.

In my conversations with them, *goswamis* and *babajis* explained that the physical town of Navadvip is of course most significant since this is where Chaitanya was born, where their gurus lived, and where they practice devotion, but that philosophically there is another equally important if not greater way of understanding and experiencing the spiritual place: their *manas* as Vrindavan. Thus, a *goswami* sitting in his individual worship-room in his house, and a *babaji* in his personal ashram room, may equally be, in their imagination, in Vrindavan.

However, while the English *imagination* would usually be translated into colloquial Bengali as *kolpona,* my interlocutors never used this term to describe their practices, since they associate *kolpona* with unreality, and their own practice with a true experience of Vrindavan. What they typically say is *"manas-e Vrindavan prakat hoy",* "Vrindavan is apparent in the mind-heart," a process still best captured by the English term *imagination.* A lot of philosophical and experiential detail is packed into this phrase. It refers to a cultivated spirituality which transforms the mind-heart as veiled-Vrindavan into an unveiled Vrindavan. Practitioners use this phrase to indicate that an entire ensemble which would be called a place, that is, the deities, the celestial space in which they are located, and the devotees' selves as handmaidens serving them during their erotic moments, together becomes manifest or present in the mind-heart. Thus, while there is a definite aspect of visualization or formation of mental pictures involved here, the word *imagination* in this case also needs to be readjusted, since the practice is not just about attaining a glimpse of Vrindavan but about bringing the whole place into being, a process which involves not only vision but the entire body's affective capacities.[3] Thus, in this case the sense of place is intimately connected with imagination's capacity of making Vrindavan experienced as real. The sense of reality is evident in the term *prakat,* which means "shining forth" or real or true, rather than unreal in the sense of an illusion or falsity. I therefore argue that in *goswamis'* and *babajis'* practices, not only is the place imagined but also imagination *itself* is experienced as the place. So the word *imagining* in the chapter's title does not imply the commonsensical idea of "making up" but rather "making apparent" the place—Vrindavan.

Also, therefore, while Basso (1996, 53) says that sensations of the physical landscape are interpolated by imagination, and while "toposemantic" studies imply that an archaeology of landscape will always correspond to an archaeology of imagination (Whitridge 2004, 228), Bengal-Vaishnava practices of imagination are distinctive, in that they do not simply imply a connection between senses of place and imagination but rather show how imagination itself is experienced as the place.

I also analyze the devotee's experience while journeying to and emplacing herself in imagination, and her emotions as she becomes both a participant and a spectator of her own body-mind practices. Such impersonality of emotions constitutes the domain of poetic *rasa* (Haberman 2003, xl), and Haberman (1988, 3) deftly argues that practices of emotional *bhakti* in Bengal-Vaishnavism generally, and *manjari sadhana* specifically, depend on the techniques and philosophies of Indian aesthetic theory, especially dramatic experiences and role-playing. *Goswamis* and *babajis* claim an exalted form of imaginative participation in divine activities such that sexual dalliance itself is reserved to deities, while they imagine their spiritual selves as the deities' handmaidens, witnessing and serving them during their sexual play in imagination-Vrindavan and deriving the utmost sensual pleasures therefrom.

The devotee's imagination follows a predetermined script given by his guru, which describes his perfected spiritual body and personhood in Vrindavan (Haberman 1988, 1–7). My interlocutors referred to this body as the *antash-chintita deha* (inner-felt-thought body).[4] Irrespective of the practitioner's gender and age, the self which inhabits the mind-heart is cultivated and imagined as an ego-effaced, subservient, young girl, who remains enraptured in serving the deities' sexuality. The self's chief predicament is that it must never desire divine sexuality for itself, while its imagination-as-Vrindavan must manifest the most intensely intimate divine sensuous activities.[5]

Celestial Vrindavan, which manifests in their imagination, is a place of the utmost spiritual beauty, devotees say—with dense forested groves cut across by the rippling river Yamuna; where spring is the eternal season, where spring birds sing melodies and spring flowers are tasted by humming bees; where devotees' eternally perfected selves as attractive young girls wander and savor the lands and where they serve the divine couple during their passionate love-plays.

Thus, there are three simultaneous senses of place experienced by *goswamis* and *babajis*: Navadvip, where they live physically; celestial Vrindavan; and imagination.[6] Devotees consider all these places, and their activities there, equally real. Imagination presents the sense of place in two ways: as a journey and as a destination. Thus, practitioners argue that those whose imagined selves as deities' handmaidens influence their ordinary selves completely, travel after death to celestial Vrindavan, their after-life destination. Otherwise, even for the temporal span that they imagine intensely, they are transported there. The felt reality of their mind-heart can however be ascribed to the experience of imagination itself as a "somatic mode of attention" (Csordas 1993, 1994, 80), which brings the place into bodily being at every instance of performative utterance.

My interpretations follow closely from devotees' narrativized practice, since neither participation in nor observation of solitary imagination is possible. Devotees' interpretations are, however, intensely embodied. Thus, although my analysis is not an exercise in phenomenology, it is influenced by phenomenological approaches to imagination. My anthropological role also involved sympathetic imagination to soften the boundaries of alterity, to travel into an-other's body-mind and render the believer's world in its "sensory richness, philosophical depth, emotional range and moral complexity" (Lambek 2002, 5).

Imagination has received less anthropological attention than other mental processes such as memory, and other categories of affect such as the senses. Influenced by Csordas's (1994, 74–108) study of charismatic healing in North America, where "imaginal performance" as an embodied process is intimately related to the "autobiographical self process," I seek to provide a fine-grained analytical account of the synesthetic imaginations which form a central part of Bengal-Vaishnava *sadhana*. Since I refer to the explanations practitioners themselves offer to narrate emotions of their imaginative landscape, my position comes close to that of Halliburton (2000, 1123), who says in her ethnography of possession experiences in Kerala that locally informed phenomenological philosophies are useful theoretical tools.

Goswamis' and *babajis'* practice of imagination involves prior meditation. While meditation practices are common in other religions, practices of imagination in this case use meditation as a step toward further spiritual goals of emplacement and emotion. Thus, while Buddhist meditative practices aim at cultivating a sense of non-self, and yogic meditation seeks to dissolve the self in the Universal Self or *atman*,[7] both sharing the premise that practitioners must forego their sexuality, my interlocutors assert their difference from such religions which stress meditation, dissolution of the self, and corresponding purging of the sensory body as ends in themselves. A common saying among them goes, "Our *sadhana* begins where yoga stops." Vaishnavas emphasize the importance of retaining a qualified self without an ego, whose sexual desire and volition are not eradicated but refashioned to be directed toward Vrindavan deities.

Vaishnavism is indeed a religion of passions, and it celebrates the body's feeling capacities. It asserts that without intense emotions neither Krishna nor Vrindavan can be apprehended. In general, *bhakti* traditions do not view renunciation as final detachment from the world but rather as definite attachment to one's devotional object (Horstmann

2001, 175). Thus, Bengal-Vaishnavas practice meditation and other physical routines as necessary but not sufficient conditions, to cultivate the senses and their creative potential. These constitute the journey toward an embodied imaginative space.

The *manas,* which means both mind and heart, is *gupta* (veiled) Vrindavan in this case, and imagination the process through which it manifests the sacred place.[8] So I analyze the mind's capacity to imagine the place in detail and experience it as real. Thus, developing from anthropological-philosophical debates which question the Cartesian dualism of mind and body (see Scheper-Hughes and Lock 1987) and those which foreground the notion of body-in-place (Casey 1993), I argue for an understanding of the mind-in-place, and indeed, the mind-*as*-place.[9] However, in the Vaishnava context, imagination is thoroughly embodied and not an abstract mental process. It is not merely a matter of consciousness, as in Bachelard's (1994) analysis of interiorized imaginative senses of place, but equally corporeal. The term *manas* itself points to the equal importance of mind and body, cognition and emotion, in imagination. Thus, I use the word *mind* as shorthand, in line with Ingold's (2000, 171) idea of the "embodied mind," which both develops through practices of and impacts upon the Vaishnava "enminded body." As Casey (2000, xi) argues, imagination is intimately associated with both emplacement and embodiment.

This then leads to the question: Is embodied imagination emotional—in the sense of being discursively constituted through social and bodily practices—or affectively experienced? In the Vaishnava case, it is both. Imagination is systematically scripted. First, there are detailed bodily practices the practitioner learns from his guru, which cultivate ego-effacement and hone sensory intensities, only after which the devotee is allowed to imagine. Second, there are prescribed rules regarding how and what to imagine, including the devotee's feminized form of the self and her service to the deity-couple. Third, what practitioners cultivate as embodied spiritual practice is connected with long-standing philosophical discourses which are discussed in sermons and taught by gurus. Vaishnava imagination is therefore a "hypercognised emotion" (Levy 1984, 30) and thoroughly discursive.

However, imagination also has its autonomy and indeterminacy (Sneath, Holbraad, and Pederson 2009, 19; Stephen 1995, 98–99), such that, while governed by strict religious practices, it also has affective creativity which impacts the imaginer's experience.[10] First, the precise moment when imagination is effective, that is, when exactly the devotee is able to visualize the sacred place and his aspired form in it, and moments when she experiences novel sights which were not mentioned in the script, are always experienced as totally sudden, and therefore not immediately grasped by her consciousness. This incalculable, unexpected nature of imagination is affective since it overwhelms the sense of subjective sovereignty. Second, imagination deeply impacts the entire physical sensory body in unanticipated ways. In both its pre- or supra-conscious and its visceral aspects, imagination is an affective experience. Thus, *goswamis'* and *babajis'* interiorized sense of place experienced through imagination is thoroughly embodied and both socially constructed and affectively sensed.

This imaginative sense of place, practitioners assert, is a real experience. This reality is asserted in the sense of both spiritual truth and clarified experience. I made sense of my interlocutors' interiorized experiences of the mind-heart as place and imagination's real or apodictic qualities through established studies of imagination.

When viewed as a phenomenological performance, imagination mediates between body and mind, percept and concept, senses and cognition (Casey 2000, 16, 17; Csordas 1993, 148). It also dissolves the boundaries between self and other, subject and object, inside and outside, and unreal and real. As an "inner enactment," it reconciles experience and performance (Palmer and Jankowiak 1996, 242). Also, its inherent performativity ensures incessant potential for "eidetic" creativity (Saso 1997, 236). My analysis of Vaishnava imagination will engage with all these different aspects of imagination-as-experience.

Philosophers have often debated imagination's potential in motivating action (Currie 2002; Funkhouser and Spaulding 2009). However, I concur with Sneath, Holbraad, and Pederson (2009) that imagination must be studied in a non-instrumental way. Thus, I build on the idea of imagination itself as an action, in this case manifesting the place in the devotee's heart-mind.

Studies of imagination conceptualize it as either recollecting previous perceptions or imagining situations not perceived before (Nichols 2007, 232; Sadoski 1992, 271). Dreamlike in its attributes, its reality or real impact in both cases is asserted in terms of effects it has on the imaginer/dreamer.[11] Indeed, some Vaishnavas say that they were able to witness their feminine selves in Vrindavan for the first time not during *sadhana,* but in dreams. Neither *sadhana* imaginations nor dreams, however, are hallucinatory realms. They are considered spiritual experiences which are more real than ordinary life-experiences. Thus, the Vaishnava sense of reality cannot only be addressed through phenomenological ideas of real effects on the imaginer's body-mind.

Bengal-Vaishnavas articulate a unique conceptual position wherein imagination's reality is affirmed in terms of its material effects on the body *and* its simultaneous occurrence. Every manifestation moment, they insist, reveals what is then actually happening in eternal Vrindavan. Thus, studies which talk of imagination's intrinsic sense of reality and real sensory impact on the body, and those which theorize cultural framings of cosmological reality, are both important in this case. So Casey's (2000, 98, 169) phenomenology is useful insofar as it demonstrates that the element of manifestation or 'appearing' that accompanies imagination implies its 'total transparency' and affective 'certainty' (see also Csordas 1994, 162, 2002, 34). And Mittermaier's (2011, 12) arguments are particularly useful, since in her study of Egyptian dreams she argues that the conventional divisions between reality and imagination must be rethought. Much like Vaishnavas, Sufis conceptualize imagination as not constructing but perceiving, that is, making present and "tuning in" the divinity that is already present (19). Mittermaier therefore asserts that the anthropology of imagination must pay close attention to how it is conceptualized in different contexts (15).

The Bengali verb *mon-e kora* used by my interlocutors to describe higher spiritual stages reveals the simultaneous senses this chapter analyzes: to practice in the mind-heart, to remember, and to imagine oneself (in Vrindavan).

GLIMPSES OF THE PLACE AND FEMININE SELVES

After the heavy monsoon, the onset of winter in October allowed me to spend some relaxed time in Navadvip's sun-bathed temples and *akhras,* and to accept several lunch and evening invitations from *goswamis* and *babajis.* Some very intriguing discoveries engaged me for most of my time for the next few months. These discoveries began as glimpses, initially. My notebooks were full of these glimpses, and they frustrated me deeply till I made sense of them.

By then I had learned to identify Bengal-Vaishnavas by their adornments—*tulsi malas, tulsi* being a sacred plant considered Krishna's favorite, and different vertical designs of white or black forehead *tilaks.* *Tilaks* are made from a blend of sandalwood and Vrindavan soil. This soil is distributed among all major Vaishnava pilgrimage-markets by Vrindavan's shop owners. Devotees explained that Krishna's lovers walked on Vrindavan lands and their foot-dust (*pada-dhuli*) was desired by Krishna himself, since his lovers were embodiments of finest feminine love.[12] The soil for a white variety of *tilak* known as *gopichandan* is collected from a Vrindavan pond's bank, where some lovers of Krishna sacrificed their lives, unable to bear their separation from him when he left Vrindavan. Black *tilaks* are made from another Vrindavan pond's soil, which is said to have been carved out with Radha's bangle. The fragrant *tilaks*, sanctified by Krishna's different names, are used to mark twelve different parts of the Vaishnava's body as symbols of the erotic Vrindavan lands.

I recognized the *tilak's* significance during a young *goswami's* evening sermon. While reading from the *Bhagavatam* to a large group of devotees, he stopped to offer an explanation of a verse and said softly, "*Gopis* [Krishna-lovers] are those who tasted Krishna with all their senses. His name danced on their tongues, their ears heard his flute, their eyes saw those beautiful curls and they smelled lovely flowers on his neck. Like shadows they followed Radha all day and night and arranged her trysts with the dark lord. Keeping their blessings, their foot-dust, on our bodies, we hope to some day taste Vrindavan's *lilas*." As he spoke, there was a marked change from how he spoke when discussing mundane matters: his voice and hand gestures were distinctly more womanly. This is not specific to him. Many practitioners, when narrating divine *lilas,* speak softly with calm, shy smiles, and their body language becomes more feminine. This is a significant dimension of their imagining a female persona for themselves. Also, while they ordinarily speak in colloquial Bengali, when discussing Vrindavan they carefully choose their words, trying to approximate the *Bhagavatam's* sophisticated and finely detailed descriptions.

The forehead *tilak* is shaped like a U extending from the top of the forehead to the middle of the eyebrows. This is to indicate that devotees' imaginative experience must always be directed "above" to Krishna's dwelling and never come "down" to earthly matters. The U also symbolizes a mythological river, crossing which, one travels to Vrindavan. Thus, the devotee's corporeality is bounded and marked as Vrindavan's shell. It contains, and waits to manifest, the sacred place.

Similar to all other Hindu temples, *aratis* are offered to the deity-consort in all the hundreds of temples in Navadvip. Navadvip's *arati* times mirror Radha-Krishna's *lila* times in eternal Vrindavan. For instance, the first *arati* is performed at around four A.M. to wake the consort; another at six P.M., when the deities sneak out of their houses for a short tryst; similarly, through the day's other *aratis,* devotees participate as onlookers in Vrindavan's cosmic dramas (Hawley 1981, 11). During these *aratis* all Navadvip resounds with cacophonous temple bells, and devotees know immediately what Vrindavan is then experiencing.

In the temple belonging to Manipuri Vaishnavas, before the morning ritual itself, the head priest recites verses commemorating the entire day's *lilas* in celestial Vrindavan.[13] Samajbari is the only temple in Bengal, however, which commemorates every activity of the deities at appropriate times as mentioned in the *Bhagavatam*.[14] Samajbari's *aratis* are accompanied by ecstatic devotional singing, the lyrics of which describe the corresponding *lilas.* The more detailed the lyrics, the finer is the listener's imagination of the divine sensuality being described. Over time I learned that Samajbari's *babajis* are much respected among *goswamis* and *babajis* since they are very particular about following the correct procedures of commemorating Vrindavan in both temple rituals and imagination.

One time, during the last of these *aratis,* held at midnight, very intimate songs narrating the consort's entry into Vrindavan's bowers for their passionate encounter were being sung. The songs described how Radha sneaked out of her house, how along with her friends she dressed up and went to the forest, how Krishna was waiting impatiently for her, and what Radha-Krishna felt and did when they finally met. I was trying to follow the lyrics carefully, when a *babaji* said, "Shut your eyes and try to feel the *lilas.* The songs' meanings will reveal themselves to you. Feeling these songs helps us participate in Vrindavan's daily life. Our material bodies are here then, but we are with Radharani." Radharani, or "dearest Radha," is an affectionate way that *goswamis* and *babajis* often refer to Radha, as if she is someone known personally to them, not only a distant deity. Some devotees, almost unconsciously, also refer to her or Krishna as "*amar* Radharani/Shyam", "my dearest" Radha or Dark Lord, thus even acknowledging a personal claim (*mamata*) over them.

On my first visit to Samajbari, the same *babaji* took me to a *samadhi* within the temple compound. The *samadhi* has a *sari* draped over it. Over the next few months I came to learn that the deceased is one of the most celebrated Vaishnava personalities. Once, during a festival in their ashram, after enacting a play with other *babajis* in the role of a lover of Krishna in an episode of Krishna's life in Vrindavan, he became completely engrossed in that mood, and remained thus for the rest of his life. He adopted the *sari* as his permanent attire, and led a woman's life.

She always covered her head with the *sari* like modest Hindu women, followed her guru's instructions, and never left the temple. She dedicated all her time to reading scriptures and composing innumerable songs in the mood of a lover of Krishna. His voice too is said to have changed to that of a woman's, and some devotees believe that she even menstruated. She is fondly remembered as Lalita Sakhi, Lalita being the spiritual name given by her guru, and *sakhi* meaning Radha-Krishna's handmaiden-friend.[15] *Babajis* revere her as an ideal devotee, and her songs are still sung during daily Samajbari rituals.

Once, while showing me his deity-idols, a *goswami,* immensely famous as knowledgeable in Vaishnava scriptures and a teacher to many younger *goswamis,* mentioned with moist eyes how he pampers and scolds them and takes them to his bed at night so that they can sleep soundly. He is otherwise a stern person, and I was taken aback at how easily he cried when talking about his idols. When I expressed surprise at his serving me *prasad* (food offered to and tasted by deities) without uttering mantras, one of his women disciples said, "You must accept that this is the best form of food-offering. She is always in Vrindavan, and therefore the food comes directly from that wondrous place." She implied that the food needs no added efficacious utterance to impart power and meaning to it, simply because the devotee-*goswami* is always in his imagination, in Vrindavan.

On another occasion I saw an elderly man sitting in a temple corner, chanting with basil beads, with eyes shut, and having what would strike an external observer as convulsions. Thinking he was ill, I approached to help, when other temple-residents rushed to stop me. They told me he was in his imagination then in Vrindavan, and the spasms were only external manifestations of that affective state.[16]

During a lunch-invitation at a *babaji's* disciple's house, he allowed me to take photographs of his altar-deities but asked me to stop when he went in to give them *bhog* (the food-offering). Some time later, as he was about to go into the altar room again to serve dessert, he stood before the door and clapped his hands, as if to let them know he was coming inside, then went in and shut the door. His wife, sensing my confusion, said, "He is in a different place now. She is acting in a mood which suits her."

In some ashrams it is common to find *babajis* wearing bangles, *bindis*, and/or *alta*.[17] Samajbari has a tradition of priests wearing *saris* and covering their heads with *sari*-ends while performing the evening *arati*. If asked why they do this, they say they are intensely involved in serving (*seva*) deities during those moments.

During Holi, in the midst of a huge crowd, a *babaji* stared at the idol of Chaitanya in the Dhameswar temple and shouted, "Why can't I see my own *svarup* [essential self]?" I was the only one who found this notable. Other devotees seemed to find his lament both normal and common.

On the main day of Ras, I was distressed because I could not make it in time for a particular temple's celebrations. A senior *goswami*, on hearing this, said, "Your own heart is a potential *gupta*-Vrindavan, a Ras-stage. Devotees taste the full-moon Ras within themselves! They serve Krishna's lovers before their dance begins."

I was most impressed that almost all religious practitioners, some highly educated and some barely so, were thoroughly fluent in the *Bhagavatam*, *Chaitanya Charitamrta*, and other Vaishnava literature. They would quote instances from texts and sing songs during our conversations. Often they would choke with emotion or weep outright when describing *lilas*. A *goswami's* wife explained, "Please do not feel uncomfortable. These are tears of joy. We feel *lilas* so intimately in our mind-hearts that it becomes difficult to maintain public composure at times."

Thus, there were consistent allusions to intense relationships with Vrindavan's deities experienced by devotees in a feminine mood in their imagination. The next obvious question was about the exact relationship between embodying femininity and imagining Vrindavan.

MANJARI SADHANA AND THE ANTHROPOLOGICAL JOURNEY

As my devotee friends became more accustomed to my interest in their religiosity, they gradually discussed how Vrindavan manifests its intensity in their heart-minds through a practice called *manjari sadhana*. I first encountered the term when on learning that he was unwell I went to meet a *goswami* in his house. Before then we had always sat in his home's outer reception room. This time he was lying on his bed, and his wife escorted me to their bedroom. I noticed two large framed sketches on the wall, realizing only later that they were not meant for the public drawing-room. The sketches were shaped as lotuses with intricate designs. One of them, captioned "Navadvip *yogapitha*" (place of union), had male Vaishnavas' names and corresponding female *sakhi* and *manjari* (Radha's handmaiden-friends') names, written in tiny Bengali characters in every petal and sub-petal. The other, captioned "Vrindavan *yogapitha*," had women-Vaishnavas' names, each with a

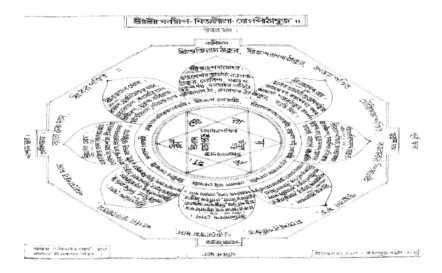

FIGURE 7. Sketch of Navadvip *yogapitha*.

Picture credit: Tony K. Stewart, reproduced from: Stewart, T.K. 2011. Replicating Vaisnava worlds: organizing devotional space through the architectonics of the mandala. *South Asian History and Culture* 2/2, 300-36, page 311, Figure 6. Copyright year: 2011.

FIGURE 8. Sketch of Vrindavan *yogapitha*.

Picture credit: Tony K. Stewart, reproduced from: Stewart, T.K. 2011. Replicating Vaisnava worlds: organizing devotional space through the architectonics of the mandala. *South Asian History and Culture* 2/2, 300-36, page 308, Figure 5. Copyright year: 2011.

suffix of *sakhi* or *manjari* and detailed descriptions of their physical forms. Since childhood I had heard that celestial Vrindavan is imagined by Vaishnavas as a hundred-petalled lotus, but I had always thought that this was merely metaphorical. I understood during my fieldwork that these pictorial representations of the sacred place facilitate concrete imagination.[18]

The *goswami* and his wife were elated that I asked about these pictures. Pointing to them, she said, "*Now* you are asking about the most significant aspect of our lives. These are sketches of celestial Navadvip and Vrindavan. All of us have a place here." I later found similar charts in some books given to me by *babajis,* and other practitioners' private altars, distributed to them in printed or written forms by their gurus.

However, practitioners were not equally welcoming in discussions of *manjari sadhana*. Generally, *goswamis* were more comfortable discussing it. The practice involves imagining passionate erotic details of Radha-Krishna's relationship and practitioners' relations with them, and since both the *goswamis* and I were married, they felt more comfortable; renouncer *babajis* found it hard to chat with a woman. Also, while I was always welcome in *goswamis'* houses, I never sat in a *babaji's* personal room but in public spaces such as ashram-compounds. However, with time, I developed very personal relations with both. I never "conducted interviews." We preferred long, intense conversations which went in unanticipated but most creative directions. Occasionally, some *babajis* would decide to give short lectures on a question I had. I avoided taking notes, as the atmosphere tended to become emotional, and scribbling intermittently would definitely have been inappropriate. Instead, I used a little recorder, which I could set discreetly to one side.

I came to know *goswamis* and *babajis* of over thirty temples/*akhras*. However, some relationships were more personal, and without intimacy, discussions of erotic imaginations would never be possible. Krishnagopal was an elderly, respected, moderately well-off *goswami*; he had been a school-teacher and a *kirtan* singer in his younger days.[19] He was a jovial, intelligent man and we grew very close. He said I must have been his mother in our past life, or else we would not have been so compatible. The large age gap between us also helped alleviate shyness about erotic matters. Kunjabihari, on the other hand, was a very serious, scholarly, middle-aged *goswami* who spent most of his time sitting in his temple and reading religious books. He was my most important interlocutor in more complex Vaishnava understandings. Despite his gravity, he was extremely welcoming and visibly enjoyed our spiritual discussions. Haribandhu was the only *goswami* who said he never practiced *manjari sadhana,* but he was well-read and knew a lot of people who did. Thus, his objectivity was helpful. Shyamsundar and his parental affection hold a special place in my memory. An elderly, knowledgeable, soft-spoken *babaji,* he did not have much of a social circle and spent a lot of time reading and writing. Like many other *babajis,* he was not economically comfortable. He had written four volumes on Vaishnavism, but despite insufficient money to run his ashram, did not do much to publicize them. He said that it would eat up his *sadhana* time. We had some of the longest conversations sitting in his quiet ashram. Charandas, an energetic and sincere ashram worker, was my youngest *babaji* friend. We never discussed the practice per se, but he often provided significant clarifications. My comprehension progressed in conversation with these Vaishnavas.

Manjari sadhana is passed from gurus to disciples as a practiced tradition. It is the main devotional practice of *goswamis* and *babajis,* the claimants of mainstream Vaishnavism. This claim stems from their lineage affiliations, exact guru-sequences given to them during initiation and mastery over *manjari sadhana.* These groups compose what Persson (2007, 47) calls a "community of practice" and Jordt (2006, 193) calls "knowledge communities," who constitute, justify, and share a particular knowledge system and perpetuate social relations on that basis.

Although practitioners insist that both householders and renouncers can cultivate the imaginative spiritual discipline, my sense is that *babajis,* since they have no householder duties, devote more time to the elaborate practices.

Goswamis generally restrict teaching *manjari sadhana* to their family members, and *babajis* allow only ashram residents to practice it. In rare instances, depending on devotional capacity or the devotee's desire, the practice is taught to other disciples. Also, most practitioners are men, although potentially both men and women (*goswamis*) may practice.

Being largely an esoteric practice, there is no source material on how individual practitioners perform(ed) it. Also, it was possible neither to directly participate, since I am not initiated, nor to observe, as it is a solitary affair carried out in individual worship rooms. Thus, some important ways to learn about it were to read relevant philosophical texts and local literature produced in Navadvip,[20] hear innumerable songs composed for deities in the lover-mood, and sit through evening sermons in Navadvip's temples/ashrams. The most important way, however, was to hold sustained, intensive conversations with practitioners. Knowledge of the practice constitutes *goswamis'* and *babajis'* proud distinction from other sects and religions, and although the details of personal practice are concealed, they appreciated that I was not being precocious by only reading books but trying to understand its lived dimensions. Also, as Charandas emphasized repeatedly, "One would imagine modern people like you to only be attracted to ISKCON. . . . But . . . ISKCON does not understand any bit of this traditional practice."

My interpretations of embodied imagination follow from my interlocutors' interpreted practice. Both their own and my interpretations themselves are also embodied. My interlocutors reflected on intensely visceral aspects of their rituals and imagination, and my analyses of narrativized experiences try to remain close to their fleshy descriptions. The narrative strategy I explore, accordingly, is one of close-grained descriptions and metaphors which form their vocabulary. Also, their acts of narration themselves were very alive—the ways they spoke, the content, postures, and our conversations' moods, together created an aura that transported us to Vrindavan every time.

However, our conversations intersected and deflected at thorny points of secrecy. Their main problem was how I could study the practice without experiencing it as an initiate. Understanding without the possibility of participation was met with ambivalent responses from devotees.

Practitioners have an aptitude for philosophical discourse, which they are socialized into from childhood through sustained discussions at daily sermons and informal dialogues among fellow Vaishnavas. Thus, I did not have difficulty receiving ample "native exegesis" (Csordas 1994, xi). But there were ethical issues to deal with.

The theoretical/methodological problems they posed were: How, without initiation, would I know the *sadhana*'s essence? How, without practicing and thereby feeling their intimate imagination of the sacred place, would I write about it? And if I did manage to feel their devotion, how would I return to ordinary life? By only partially resolving these troubling questions, I traced the anthropologist's emotional interfaces with the field and its self-transforming potentials. As Cook (2010a, 239) puts it, "Rather than reducing emotion to an unfortunate impediment, such an approach allows the anthropologist to understand her field experiences in ways that provide insight into the conditions of the field."

Secrecy is not an absence but a mode of communication (Fabian 2003, 490). Bellman's (1981, 4) distinction between *private* and *secret* is useful here. Practitioners' knowledge is not private. It is a secret which may be shared if one finds an appropriate aesthete. Also, linguistically speaking, "*mythological* discourse must itself be *mythomorphic*. It must have the form of that of which it speaks" (Derrida 1978, 286). So esoteric issues were spoken about in ways that pertained to the content of the discourse. The basic problems associated with esoteric understandings are of two kinds: how to know (epistemological) and how to say (ethical) (Price 1983, 23; Urban 1998, 211). Sharing knowledge with the non-*rasika* (non-feeler), they say, is like pouring water into a broken vessel, one that will bleed out its essential experiences, retaining only dry knowledge. While it is sufficient to feel Vaishnava aesthetics in order to know it, the reverse is not true. Vaishnavas insist that knowledge (*gyan*) follows from emotional devotion (*bhakti*) and not the other way round.

However, after sustained efforts, practitioners made way for my knowledge. For instance, on many occasions, sitting on his small bed, Krishnagopal sang beautiful songs describing Radha-Krishna's love-acts, while I sat at his feet and recorded them. Except for the bed-space his small room was full of old religious books, from which he gave me a number of Bengali books, asking me to memorize Radha-Krishna's daily activities in Vrindavan. Sometimes he would explain the songs' meanings, and sometimes ask me to describe what I felt while listening to the songs or reading the books. Gradually he started saying that I could sympathize with his feminine sensibilities as a witness of the deities' *lilas,* since I was a woman myself. Many others attributed my research to divine grace. They said it was Radha-Krishna's wish that I write about them.

However, the practice is dependent on accompanying mantras.[21] Thus, without initiation from authorized gurus who teach these mantras, one will understand but never be able to practice. So I was gradually introduced to their emotional world, but without their making me an insider.

Manjari sadhana is primarily an exercise in ego-effacement, an intense affective imagination without a desire for self-gratification. Yet these imaginings are often of the most erotic sort, bordering on sexual arousal. To intuit the deities' sexual intimacy without experiencing personal carnal desire is the most delicate paradox of practitioners' imagination. Their constant fear is that there will be disparagement and sensationalization of the transgendered and erotic dimensions of their imagined place sense. Thus, their initial concern was that I would misread their imaginations as being of an ego-gratifying, voyeuristic kind. Consistent dialogue, however, gradually convinced them that my association with practicing Vaishnavas was introducing in me the appropriate temperament to comprehend the complexities of their in-depth discipline.

Manjari may be translated as "bud." Since not buds but only flowers are offered to the passion-taster, Krishna, the term signifies the devotee's affective state—a girl's liminal adolescent age, when her innocence and emotional intensity combine in measures appropriate for adoration through intimate service toward the deity-couple's desires, without ever engaging in direct sexual activity with Krishna. Siegel (1983, 17) argues that in Indian aesthetic philosophies, a young girl's dilemmas between innocence and passion, and her chastity, are imagined as ornaments enhancing her sexual appeal. Thus, this state is an eternally budding one, its incompleteness and youth celebrated as the aspired status of the "devotional connoisseur" (Rosen 1992, v). Irrespective of age and gender, in his or her imagination the practitioner is a *manjari* who finds her existential essence in the role of a passionate handmaiden, Radha's and Krishna's pleasures in Vrindavan being her only occupying engagement.

Manjari sadhana forms the essence of the Bengal-Vaishnava devotional paradigm known as *raganuga bhakti* (Das 2014, Part 1, 650–51; Haberman 1988, 2003, 270–352). *Raga,* meaning "passion," and *anuga*, "the feminine subservient one," together point to the devotee's aspired personhood. *Raganuga* may be translated as a devotional form of tracking traces of the passion trail left by the lovers of Krishna. This points to a genre of devotion, a poetics of femininity, which far surpasses simple deity-allegiance. A crucial conceptual problem then becomes one of theorizing subservience as a form of passionate selfhood.

TRANSFORMATION OF DISCIPLINE TO PASSION

Vaishnava experiences of feminine personhood and the sacred place in imagination begin only after rigorous physical discipline.

Devotional practices are classified into two types: those followed as agentive corporeal-psychological discipline (*vaidhi bhakti*), and passionate realizations which descend relatively spontaneously (*raganuga bhakti*). The former, evoked by Krishna's opulent *aishwarya* form, arises from fear; the latter, inspired by Krishna's *madhurya*, develops as the greed to serve him (Haberman 1988, 118, 2003, lix; Klostermaier 1974, 102). Fear must ultimately be subordinated to greed and love. Humility and passion form the axiological ethical core of Bengal-Vaishnavism

(Schweig 2002). The formality of *vaidhi bhakti,* devotees argue, engenders a taste for loving service and prepares the mind-heart for spontaneous desire.[22]

Devotees agree that not everyone can experience either perfection in discipline or transformation from discipline to passion, and that these are not considered failures. Since the practice demands spiritual perfection, devotees believe that one's progress will count toward efforts in the following life. They conceptualize rebirths as progressive steps toward reaching perfection such that finally the karmic cycle stops and one travels to celestial Vrindavan.

Devotees are divided in their views of the relationship between these two devotional forms. Some say rules are inimical to affective development, while most argue that spontaneity or devotional excess develops only through self-flagellating rigor.[23] Exacting discipline invokes the sense of something more permanent than oneself. This in turn is the base upon which spontaneous love feeds. A devotee, invoking cultural stereotypes, said, "From . . . discipline to passion is the journey from being a man to a woman."

The best ritual example of this process is *kartik vrata* (October, a month of severe austerities). During this time every Vaishnava performs strict regimented routines, including long fasts followed by simple food, little sleep, concentrated chanting, regular temple rituals, and intensive scripture-reading. Some Vaishnavas practice these for a month, and some others, for four months. It ends in November, just before the Ras festival. Once during this period I went to Krishnagopal's house. He was tired after the day's fast and asked me to come back later. He said, "This is a difficult month for us. But among those who do the rituals well, some lucky ones will experience Ras in their heart-minds."

Without discipline, adequate conceptualization is not possible, and without understanding, aesthetic imagination impossible. Intense discipline also embodies ritual suffering and engenders the sense of subservience toward rules and deities. In Hindu imaginings this disposition is especially exemplified by women (Trawick 1991, 19, cited in Hanssen 2006, 115). Thus, the idealized Vaishnava self is a young girl in a mood of enraptured attendance to the deities.

Discipline's productive capacity has been extensively analyzed by Asad. He argues that medieval Christian practices generated virtues of humility and subservience, or what he calls "the desire for subjectivation," among practitioners (1987, 187). Ritual pain, including fasts, austerities, and less sleep, was the chief embodied means of establishing religious Truth in this context (Asad 1983). Influenced by Asad, van der Veer (1989, 459–60) also demonstrates how the Ramanandi spirit of submission to religion is generated through disciplinary practices. Bengal-Vaishnavas embody similar religious virtues of ritual pain and subservience. However, I argue that it is equally important to think about religious practices and the affective experiences they engender, since religious subjects allude to both.

In Bengal-Vaishnavas' vocabulary, the term *raga* in *raga-nuga* refers to pleasurable emotions which have lasting traces in memory. The word also means "color," implying that the devotee's heart is gradually colored with passion. Following the linguistic and ritual clues of *manjari sadhana* it may therefore be argued that there is a necessary association among repeated disciplinary practice (*vaidhi*), (awakening of) mnemonics, and sensuous desire, wherein "Emotion *is* memory, feelings *are* cognition" (Mitchell 1997, 84).

To explicate the affective transformation from discipline to passion, devotees commonly use "embodied metaphors" (Low 1994, 143) of gnawing visceral activities. For instance, it is through careful mastication that one hones the taste-buds, and only after sustained chafing that one can smell sandalwood. Similarly, after having borne the prolonged burning sensation, the incense engenders its perfume. Thus, devotees say that ritual inflictions on the external body automatically alter the internal mentality; disciplined devotion reminds the devotee of his perfected passionate self in celestial Vrindavan.

Vaishnavas associate their pre-*sadhana* lives with a spiritual forgetting. Shyamsundar said during an evening sermon, "We have forgotten our eternal beautiful selves and place. . . . Just as sometimes when we know but have forgotten something, it comes back in dreams, so also in *sadhana*. Spiritual essence lies in this remembering [*smaran*]".[24] In the Buddhist context, similarly, recollective memory is part of repetitive mindfulness (Cox 1992). Its mnemonics consist in "recognizing" forgotten truths and existential delusions (Kapstein 1992).

The act of remembering entailed in Vaishnava devotion falls between what Whitehouse describes as "semantic" and "episodic" modes of memory (discussed in Laidlaw 2004b, 1–3). It is doctrinal insofar as it is prescribed and repeated many times through practices, and imagistic insofar as it is simultaneously also experienced as emotionally intense and spontaneous (see also Laidlaw 2004a, 99). However, the remembering, the anamnetic moment or "flashbulb memory" entailed in *sadhana*, is part of imagining. After repeated enactment of a script (of divine plays in the sacred place) in imagination, the memory is gradually reawakened.

While the *vaidhi bhakti* stage corresponds to a "voluntary ethical project" (Laidlaw 2005), the transformation to *raga* is also dependent on divine grace. When exactly discipline will stimulate passion is unknown. This is a complex situation, in which, while there is an element of unanticipated temporal spontaneity, the believer also has an informed idea about what to expect. This situation approximates a "double agency of imagination"—the interplay of human and divine will (Hedley 2008, 7).[25] Also, while *raga* develops through strict discursive practices, its relative autonomy may be ascribed to the psychology of affect.

The spontaneous sacred self which develops from the ritual habitus, the oxymoronic phenomenon of "rehearsed spontaneity" (Csordas 1994, 95), is felt as a sudden achievement. A *babaji,* to make it clear to me in an everyday language, said, "Think of a sportsperson, who after sustained practice is suddenly able to clear a high-jump hurdle, or a scholar able to crack a mathematical puzzle. But for us it is not something novel, but only a manifestation of the hidden. It is like those children's drawing books where by simply rubbing the pencil constantly, the paper itself reveals the form."

In this case, the paper is veiled-Vrindavan or *manas,* the hidden form is the eternal feminine self-in-Vrindavan, and the total act of "bodying forth" (Hedley 2008, 6) or manifesting is *sadhana* imagination. Also, one will have to learn the proper technique of rubbing (*vaidhi bhakti,* preparing the self, or the journey), for instance sharpening the pencil, setting it at the proper angle, and so on, only after which the imaginative potentials of "making apparent" (*raganuga bhakti,* or remembering the destination) comes about.

Practitioners were always very willing to discuss the affective orientations of transformation from discipline to passion. It was the practice itself that took longer to learn about and understand.

I had gone to meet a *babaji* one afternoon. This is a relatively free time for them, when after the day's ashram-work they rest in their shabby rooms, read, or chat with fellow *babajis* in the quiet midday milieu, before waking the temple-deities from their siesta. It was the beginning of winter, and the days were shorter and cold. So we sat in a semi-official ashram-room. We were discussing very mundane matters, and the conversation flowed in ample directions. I don't at all remember the context, but he suddenly started telling me how he is a teenage girl in Vrindavan, that she is fair, walks slowly, is dressed in blue, is moody, serves

Radha-Krishna betel leaves, and so on. His voice had softened, and he had a coy smile. His description was in complete contrast to his ordinary self—he was middle-aged, dark, and spoke in a rough, hasty manner. I was completely taken aback and about to ask him what he meant, when suddenly his senior *babaji* friend, overhearing our conversation from the next room, came in and stopped him, saying, "You must never discuss your personal *sadhana* with anyone." My interlocutor then changed his narrative technique and continued the discussion by invoking anecdotal references of others' *sadhana* instances, without mentioning names.

Striking this sensitive balance between familiarity and distance, practitioners advised me to think about paradigmatic spiritual imaginations.[26] This involves an ethical strategy which avoids utter generality of otherness, yet allows non-attached, unabashed frankness about sensuous effects of imagination, while maintaining a distance from the individual.

PREPARING TO IMAGINE

The practitioner's journey begins with the initiation process, *diksha,* when the initiated is given a Krishna-mantra by the guru. Following *diksha,* the Vaishnava is given *shiksha* (elaborate training) and engages himself in a number of daily rituals which form the sixty-four tenets of spiritual discipline (*vaidhi bhakti*). Of these sixty-four, nine are compulsory:[27]

> *sravan*—hearing about gods' *lilas*
> *kirtan*—repeating gods' names and *lilas*
> *smaran*—remembering/memorizing Radha-Krishna's daily *lilas* by
>   reading scriptures, performing commemorative temple rituals, and
>   learning to practice this remembrance in meditation
> *vandan*—singing praises of deities
> *padasevan*—serving deities' feet
> *dasya*—developing subservience
> *archan*—learning intricate worship rules
> *sakhya*—developing friendship with deities
> *atmanivedan*—surrendering oneself completely to the deity-couple's service

In Bengal-Vaishnavism, self-abnegating submission is a complex emotion. Subservience must be guided not by fear or reverence but by love and attachment. The conceptual paradox regarding how discipline can effectuate desire is concomitant with how servitude can engender a lover's longing.

These nine disciplining practices form the practitioner's ritual body (*sadhak deha*). When they have mastered these rituals, some *babajis* receive a second initiation. This might be given even after up to twenty years of service in the first initiation stage.

As a sign of abstinence, they then give up their *desh* (old residence), *besh* (old dress), and *kesh* (hair). Leaving the old residence symbolizes that they now seek to place themselves in Vrindavan. *Babajis* refer to this as receiving *bhek* from the guru. *Bhek* refers both to the renouncer's external features, such as loincloth, and to his mental state. He then renounces the material world and attaches himself completely to Radha-Krishna's thoughts. Ideally, *babajis* should then beg for their daily food, but these days many *babajis* who live in ashrams don't. However, I knew one *babaji* in Navadvip who lived in a small hut, wore simple jute clothes, had no shoes, slept on rugs, and begged every day.

This ambivalent state of renouncing everything for another form of everything is exemplified especially by a man devotee. He gives up his masculine pride for the mood of a feminine handmaiden-lover. Sanderson (1985, 201) argues, with respect to Kashmiri Brahmins, that the shift from asceticism to excess is embodied by a move from the male domain to female. Khandelwal (1997) questions the general assumption that Hindu renunciation is ungendered or unequivocally masculine. *Goswamis* and *babajis* embody a most radical form of gendered devotion such that their essential selves (*siddha deha*) in Vrindavan, which they realize in imagination, are of young girls.

The *goswami* couple in whose house I saw the lotus-pictures for the first time mentioned that they practice imagination sitting side by side in their worship room. They said that in their eternal roles they are both women and serve Radha-Krishna. I asked whether this complex sexuality does not become a hindrance to their marital life. The man said, "This is not about our material bodies/minds. Why should it create a problem? It brings us closer as we feel like equals and understand each other better."

However, all agree that the feminine mood must be confined to private imagination moments, and not brought openly to public attention, in order to avoid undeserved criticism.[28] For instance, only one among the senior *babajis* of Samajbari wears the *sari*, and only during the evening-*arati* (rather than during all the eight *aratis* carried out in the temple), to perform the light-offering in the mood of Radha's handmaiden.[29] He carefully pulls the *sari*-end well over his head so that the many devotees who gather in the temple then don't see his face or know who he is.

Practitioners want to keep their spiritual identities hidden from ordinary people. One of the *babajis* who conducts the evening-*arati* told me

FIGURE 9. Samajbari *arati* performed by a *babaji*.

later, "Many *babajis* want to do this. I tell them, do it in your mind-heart. In any case it is as real. Why risk criticism from modern people who won't see its significance?"

However, the guru allows one to embody one's feminine self only after he masters ego-effacement, or else there is the fear that in imagination she may want sexual union with Krishna. One afternoon I arrived early at Shyamsundar's ashram and was waiting to share *prasad* with him. It was already two P.M. and the other *babajis* said that Shyamsundar had only had some milk since the morning. Yet he did a lot of work before eating. He cleaned the ashram compound, watered plants, did *puja*, and served stray dogs, all the while repeating Radha-Krishna's names softly. I suggested that he should have younger *babajis* do these chores. But he stressed the importance of hard work and said, "Just as sustained comfort creates an attachment to the body, rigor inflicted by discipline generates the sense of a belittled ego—that we're all the same and essentially Radha-Krishna's servants."

When the disciple exhibits this kind of temperament, and after sustained practice of *vaidhi bhakti* when suddenly an intense pining (*lobh/sadh*) develops in the devotee's heart to visualize her essential self in Vrindavan, his guru, through developed intuitive/imaginative powers, and on basis of the devotee's natural propensities, helps him approximate her essential feminine form and service. Those devotees of Krishna who have acquired a location in Vrindavan forever are known as *ragatmika bhaktas* (devotees with passionate selves). The devotee ought to emulate and serve as handmaiden those friends of Radha-Krishna who perform that particular service, without expecting that she will *become* them. This is the crux of selfhood formation in *raganuga bhakti* (the practice that *follows* the *ragatmika*).[30] Thus for instance if the disciple loves to dress up in his ordinary life, then in her role as the deity-couple's handmaiden, she may be given the service of emulating and following Radha's friends who dress her before her nocturnal meeting with Krishna.

The *sadhana* is an introspective journey, turning from one's given self, through the disciplined ritual self, to finally the eternal, essential, forgotten self. On reaching the required level of spiritual-emotional maturity, the practitioner is taught the most difficult element of *sadhana*: memorizing the deity-couple's daily pastimes in Vrindavan. It is an intensive temporal engagement with the sacred place, a meditation technique known as *asta-kaliya-lila-smaran* (remembering the pastimes of the eight daily periods).[31] Some do this in their timely temple rituals, some in imagination, some in both. A Samajbari *babaji* said, "We translate our *manas*-service into temple-service. Say, while we do the incense-rounds during the evening *arati,* we think in detail of what Radha-Krishna are doing then in Vrindavan and services we are offering." Even as he spoke to me, he smiled and rotated his hands most gracefully, as if he were in Vrindavan letting deities smell the incense.

Although ideally one performs this meditation at least once in every three-hour period, most people meditate at night since the intense concentration required might disrupt a person's external senses and social duties. Kunjabihari said, for instance, that his grandfather would meditate for twelve hours at a stretch. On returning to his ordinary senses he would forget his temporary absence from the social world. This implies that *sadhana*-time, although simultaneous with ordinary time, is an absorbed temporality of complete detachment. Others say that practitioners often have a trace of their concentrated imagination in their ordinary bodies and lives, such that they may cry, laugh, and exhibit all sorts of socially inappropriate behavior. Lalita Sakhi, Samajbari's *babaji,* whose imagination of her handmaiden-self in Vrindavan overwhelmed her ordinary life completely and who decided to live a woman's life, was therefore urged by her guru to always stay within the ashram, to avoid ordinary people's disdain.

Thus, through practiced remembering, the devotee sharpens his imagination which will transport him to the always-simultaneous times of Vrindavan. Repeated remembering augments perceptual attentiveness to the object of remembrance, hones "imagination inflation" (Beuke, Garry, and Sharman 2004), and enhances the sense of imaginative reality.

The practitioner now performs daily rituals with his *sthul-deha* (physical, acting body-mind) and practices cognitive translocations with his *shukhho-deha* (subtle, dreaming/imagining body-mind). Those who master these practices are said to develop special cognitive powers. Devotees refer to practitioners who foretold their own deaths, talked to dead people, changed real situations in dreams, and witnessed far-off things invisible to the naked eye. It is difficult to tell whether people claim to possess these powers these days, for even if they do, they will not talk about it. Only once did a *goswami* secretly mention to me his guru's powers. Yogic powers are however not the aim but a by-product of the imagination process.

However, the mnemonic technique is dependent on yogic discipline, especially breathing routines which affectively pacify the mind.[32] Without this, the calm concentration required for imagination is impossible. Psychologists refer to these meditative conditions as "low-stress" states (Willis 1979, 93). Through deep-breathing practices the basic instincts (including sexual ones) are brought under control. Without that the emotion/taste (*rasa*), basic to all others, the peaceful one (*santa rasa*) is not stimulated. Emotions become self-directed unless an ego-effacing perfection is achieved through *santa rasa*.

After weeks of visits, Kunjabihari explained the phenomenology of breathing. Unlike many others he was not emotionally driven when talking about the practice; he treated it as a sophisticated knowledge system. He sat in his *dhoti*, poised under the huge tree in his temple compound where he spent most of his day reading, shut his eyes, recreating the meditative mood, and with a proud air of knowledge, clarified clinically:

> The aim of discipline is to reduce the sense of ego, yet increase sensory intensity. . . . Disciplined breathing helps in this process. . . . If I continually concentrate and decrease my breathing succession, then four things happen. . . .
> My concentration increases tremendously; epidermal sensitivity sharpens (just as a flash of light blinds more after darkness); and the temporal sense extends, as I am putting utmost attention on greater breath retention-times. The extended time-sense aids in intuiting the simultaneous cosmic time of Vrindavan. Most important, with sustained practice, my sense of I-hood [*ami-tva*] decreases. Since it is on breathing's involuntariness that I-hood depends, the more I am attentive to my not-breathing, the more I am able

to cultivate . . . egolessness. The aim is to belong to Vrindavan with a self/
identity [abhiman] but without an ego [ahamkar].[33]

After speaking a little he asked me what I understood, went on,
stopped again, and so on. My conversations with Vaishnavas were
deeply dialogic.

One of his disciples was present as we conversed. Unlike Kunjabihari,
these matters were not merely intellectual for him. Leaning toward me
with his pupils dilated, he added about sensory heightening, "During
these exercises, breath-air circulates in the body. This creates an undula-
tion inside. At higher stages of yogic perfection, practitioners hear different sounds in their inner [manas] ear. The perfected breathing transforms
into sacred sounds. The deities' grace may manifest in the form of the loud
tinkling anklet sounds of Radha/Krishna/Mahaprabhu, for instance."
From the urgency in his voice it seemed he was recalling his own imaginative experience. But practitioners never acknowledge their own spiritual
experiences and may even ascribe them to others. They believe that telling
another about one's own spirituality decreases its potency.

The stylistics of manjari sadhana begin however only after the devotee's egolessness is confirmed.

Practitioners speak of three embodied states which are active during sadhana: sthul-deha or sthul-sharir, which performs bodily rituals, sukkho-sharir which meditates and imagines, and the causal body
(karan-sharir) which witnesses these activities as overseer. This approximates Merleau-Ponty's description of the body which "simultaneously
sees and is seen. That which looks at all things can also look at itself
and recognize, in what it sees, the 'other side' of its power of looking. It
sees itself seeing; it touches itself touching" (Merleau-Ponty 1993, 124,
cited in Tilley 2008, 25).

Most practitioners explain metaphorically that the gross sthul-deha,
heavy with unreflective materiality, is like ice, which through breathing practices and yogic contemplations transforms into lightweight
vapor-like clarity, and passes through the causal body into Vrindavan's
essential self. This metaphor implies the abandonment of components
which clog the imagination's pores and cause amnesia of the essential
self. The subtle and causal bodies have a paradoxical ontological status. Although they are not primarily sensory, they can be grasped only
through intuitive affective perception.

The final dissolution of the causal body confirms the suspension of
egohood.

Once again, Kunjabihari clarified with a calm confidence. Although I could never witness his imaginative experience, his clear exegesis always proved his perfection as a practitioner. He said:

> The causal body is the most imperceptible one. Its ontology comes closest to dreamless slumber. After waking from sleep one says, "I've had such a good sleep!" How can he know, if he was sleeping? The sense of self which stays awake at all times to tell us about our sensations is the causal self. Thus, it is the most insistent part of our ego. During rituals of *vaidhi bhakti,* this observer-self watches over the acting and meditating body. Thus, there is still a false distinction between an active sense of ego as observer and imagined as observed. There is then the unmanifest sense of the mind-heart as Vrindavan's container. Through sustained breathing practices and scripture readings, as the causal body is dissolved, the difference between subject and object disappears, the potentiality of the container gives way to the essence of the contained and what is left is imagination as occurrence, and the pure self in Vrindavan.[34]

Through these rarified affective processes of the body and mind, the thinking ego/imaginer as subject, the process of imagination, and the imagined merge, and what is left is imagination as indistinguishable from the place—Vrindavan.

THE *MANJARI* IN IMAGINATION-AS-VRINDAVAN

Vaishnava imagination follows a strict script, and the *manjari's* location is mapped. The devotee is given an exact narrative of divine activities of which she is to be a part, a "canon" modeling affective relationships (Horstmann 2001, 177). It is in the devotee's being able to partake in the narrative's *rasa* that the questions Hardy (1983, 559) raises from the perspective of Sanskrit poetics can be answered; that is, how a man can embody a woman's emotions, and how one travels from ordinary to cosmic reality.

However, imagination's pure possibilities and the spontaneity of divine grace also ensure personal creative moments in the *manjari's* psychosomatic role-playing. Personal experiences in the *manas*-Vrindavan are deemed to be real in two senses. First, they impact both the body-mind's inner senses and the physical body. Second, all imaginative experiences are recognized by Vaishnavas as present occurrences. Summarizing imagination's apodictic qualities, Krishnagopal said, "If you and I as *manjaris* are seeing two different things at the same time in our respective mind-hearts, then both are equally true and occurring simultaneously in celestial Vrindavan(s). Proper *sadhana* cannot be wrong." What this implies is that a celestial Vrindavan, in all its reality, is effectuated or manifested with every proper devotional imagination in the space of the *manas*.

In the Bengal-Vaishnava script, the deity-couple's intimate activities are very difficult since they have an extramarital relationship. Radha has eight dear friends (*sakhis*) who make all necessary arrangements for her daily secret trysts with Krishna. Each of these friends has eight assistants, called *manjaris*.

These characters are represented in an elaborate pictorial chart shaped as a lotus, known as Vrindavan *yogapitha*, or "place of union" (Haberman 1988, 122).[35] The lotus center houses the deity-couple; the eight *sakhis* are placed in the main petals, and the *manjaris* in sub-petals. However, a few sub-petals (*manjaris*) are closer to the center than the main petals (*sakhis*) are.

Sakhis are the same age as Radha or older, and married. Thus, they have experienced sexual satisfaction. Some *sakhis* therefore develop desire for self-gratification while arranging for Radha-Krishna's sensual pleasures. *Manjaris* however are all younger than Radha, and unmarried. Without the memory of active sexuality, they never desire any form of selfish sexual gratification. Vaishnavas argue that the complete lack of possibilities of sexual possession, paradoxically, multiplies *manjaris'* sensory empathy, while exemplifying the best case of ego-effacement.

Some *babajis* confessed, however, that during early stages of imagination, there might be moments when they as *manjaris* develop personal sexual desire to unite with Krishna. But through discussions with the guru and repeated practice, the aim is to abide by the script of egolessness. As Hedley (2008, 65) suggests, practiced imagination itself is responsible for the crystallization of new affects.

Also, *sakhis* have their households to look after, while *manjaris* stay with Radha all the time. Thus, *manjaris* are allowed even in the closest quarters of the couple's nocturnal pastimes in Vrindavan's forest bowers, while *sakhis* are not.[36] This implies that in imagination *manjaris* can directly witness the deities' sexual activities. *Sakhis* can intuit these pastimes, while *manjaris* directly feel them. *Sakhis* arouse reverence and inhibition in Radha; *manjaris,* pure unabashed affection.

Haribandhu cited an instance of a *manjari's* eidetic imagination, for instance, where she suddenly had a vision of Radha-Krishna quarrelling and parting. Later, both felt the urge to meet. Radha sent a friend-handmaiden to fetch Krishna. Then, when Radha and Krishna came close, they started calling out each other's names, and the *manjari's* ears filled with the chants of and by the deities themselves. This is considered the highest possible affective bliss. In another similar instance, when Radha was upset with Krishna, a *sakhi* prayed and the sky roared with lightning. Scared, Radha forgot her anger and rushed to embrace Krishna, and the *sakhi* savored the tastes of this sight. Thus, handmaidens' main engagement consists in staging situations, arranging for the couple's meeting, and deriving incomparable delight in the process.

Each of the *sakhis* has particular services which she performs, assisted by her *manjaris*. These include braiding Radha's hair, putting *alta* (red paint) on her feet, fanning the couple when they rest, serving betel nut or perfumed water before they go into the bowers at night, making necklaces for them out of flowers, massaging their feet before and after their erotic activities, dressing Radha for the night, preparing sandalwood for their adornments, and so on. All these services aim at arousing the couple's senses.

However, there are other very intimate services reserved for Radha's most cherished handmaidens, her favourite *manjaris,* which are generally performed during the deities' late-night sexual dalliance. There is a *manjari,* for instance, who performs a delicate little service as the keeper of Radha's anklets, so their sound is silenced when she keeps her tryst with Krishna. Others have responsibilities of waking them in the morning, or collecting the flower petals and pearls that fall from their bodies and garlands during intense lovemaking, and distributing them among *manjaris* for their savoring.

Once, a *manjari,* while performing her daily service in her mind-heart-Vrindavan, suddenly saw that Radha's tightly bound hair was at odds with the ecstasy of Radha-Krishna's sexual abandon. So she crept into their bedchamber and released the hairpins, with the couple still locked in an unseeing embrace. Another had a vision of Radha's head slipping off the pillow, and of finding, when she crept to her side to see to her comfort, that she was snugly nestled on her divine lover's arm. She withdrew in blissful satisfaction. These anecdotes convey the claim that the divine couple take special pleasure in the virginal *manjari*-handmaidens' youthful innocence and sexual inexperience. They don't indulge in voyeuristic participation in the lovers' bliss and serve in a truly egoless state of non-desiring rapture. Their services remain non-auto-referential.[37]

The *manjaris*' self-experience is paradigmatic for *goswamis* and *babajis* for three reasons. First, *manjaris* witness the most intimate activities, which give the devotee the finest taste of divine love. Second, they exemplify a most inexplicable embodied state, which even though participating in sexually charged activities never develops a desire for personal gratification. Third, *manjaris* are role models of perfect subservience, since they are completely controlled by their senior *sakhis*.

Given this "paradigmatic" model (Haberman 1988, 8), the devotee is given an exact imagination technique by his guru. First he is given his *manjari svarup* (eternal form), consisting of eleven components: her age (11–13 years generally), name, dress, complexion, group, relation, command, specialty, residence, the *sakhi* under whom she serves, and service (see also Haberman 1988, 90). These are basic criteria of emplacement in Vrindavan.[38] Next he is given the *guru-pranali* (names of gurus in his spiritual lineage) and *siddha-pranali* (the names of the corresponding *manjari* or "perfected" forms of these gurus, experienced by them in their respective mind-hearts).

After perfecting the knowledge and visualization of deities' daily activities, the devotee has to practice imagining her own eternal form, get an overwhelming sense of her "real" body, identity, moods, demeanor, and service, and then proceed to imagining the forms and services of her guru lineage.

Practitioners told me that each of these progressions in imagination is equally difficult and takes years to achieve. In fact most stick to only imagining their own and their gurus' essential forms, and then proceed to performing their services in imagination. Ideally, however, the devotee's imagination of the guru-lineage goes up to the point of the first guru whose *manjari* self is an eternally perfected one, such that she has received a permanent place in celestial Vrindavan. She is one of the eight main *manjaris* in the lotus-imagining, under the tutelage of one of the eight *sakhis*. The devotee-*manjari* is thus placed in a chained subservience to guru-*manjaris*.

Along with the *manjari* form, the devotee is also given a picture of the lotus-shaped Vrindavan and an exact location in it. A particular route is marked out for her (similar to her guru's other disciples), traversing various petals and sub-petals, to follow her guru, via the guru-*manjari*-lineage and their senior *sakhis,* to the deities in the lotus-center, and perform her daily services.[39] There is a particular time in the day, which the guru reveals to the devotee, when Radha-Krishna find time out of their daily schedules to gather near a *gupta kunda* (secret lake) in Vrindavan and stand with their friends and handmaidens in the order specified in the pictorial charts, such that devotees, following the scripted route, can offer ritual worship to them in imagination. Their imagination is then the exact counterpart of the lotus-shaped celestial Vrindavan.

Practitioners compulsorily follow this routine at the given time. However, each devotee may also perform her personal service at other times of the day. Depending on her spiritual mentality, one who gets the taste of these services may want to perform them for extended hours through the day.

However, after imagining oneself repeatedly within a prefigured normative discursive plot, an experienced practitioner suddenly senses extra-script innovative acts in it. Like the leap from discipline to passion, this move from the grammatical to the excessive is a moment of grace. It cannot be intentionally captured. Despite being provided with an "exemplary script" (Haberman 1988, 45), she may encounter an untainted space in her cognition such that she can experience a mythopoetic patchwork, new every time, and unknown to the mediations of her guru and to her own previous imaginations. The infinitely variant, playful possibilities of imagination constitute its domain of autonomy, the domain of affect. Imagination's affective autonomy also impacts the physical body in unanticipated ways.

Every time the devotee begins *sadhana,* she hopes for real but unfelt-before *lilas* of which she is a part. What one experiences then is "neither a suspension of spontaneous emotion, nor a cathartic release of unsocialised elements" (Mahmood 2001, 828). Imagination therefore is precisely this middle ground between the social or discursive and the asocial or affective. This presents "a genre of being with respect to which the subject is not sovereign, but without his being imprisoned in it" (Merleau-Ponty 1945, 66, cited in Krell 1982, 503). A practitioner said, summarizing this, "We would not have the incentive to sit for *sadhana* every day if we had to only do the same things. In repeating the routine, we still have ample hope for tasting *lilas* anew, every time." Thus, following Casey's (2000, 66) theorization of imagination, the Vaishnava case demonstrates that controlledness is a feature of the "act phase" of imagination, and spontaneity, of the "object phase." I attribute the former to socially constructed emotion, and the latter to affect.

Devotees assert that intense imagination often impacts the body, the cognized self transforming the physical self. Krishnagopal's nephew, Radheshyam, cited a beautiful metaphor to explicate these transformative processes. There is an insect known as *kumor-poka* in Bengali. They hunt in swarms. Once they get hold of some other insect, they encircle it and buzz around, although not attacking it. The other insect is, however, consumed with fear of being attacked any moment. Due to this constant thought about *kumor-poka,* it is changed into one. Radheshyam said, "The relation between the essential self, the hunter, and the ritual body, the hunted, is similar. Constant thought leads to physical transformation." He shivered mildly and had goose bumps while describing this, and his eyes flooded with tears.[40]

Once, a devotee in *sadhana* imagination learned that her guru-*man-jari* could not be found in Vrindavan. Desperately looking for her, she discovered that Radha had lost her anklet and that their lineage had been given the responsibility to look for it. Thus, all the gurus in her line were under Radhakunda (Radha's bathing lake), searching. Getting permission from them, she too started looking for it. In some time she found the anklet. However, she could not go and directly give it to Radha. So she passed it on to her guru, she to hers, and so on, up to the first *manjari,* who handed it over to Radha through her guru-*sakhi.*

In one version of this celebrated anecdote, Radha, pleased with the *manjari,* graced her by striking her on the head with her anklets (*nupur*), right at the point where the main *tilak* is drawn. When the devotee returned to his ordinary senses, he found a new anklet-*tilak* drawn on his forehead. The practitioner's subsequent initiated generations wear the same *tilak* to this day.

In another version of the story, the *manjari* told the main *sakhi* that she needed proof that the anklets belonged to Radha. Radha then showed her the bottoms of her beautiful feet, seeing which she immediately fainted. In his real body, too, he experienced a swoon and then a blissful awakening.

Another *manjari* has the service of warming milk for Krishna, which Radha takes to him in the evening. Once, while performing it in her *manas*-Vrindavan, she let her mind wander off to the thought of the deities' divine activities which were taking place then, and burnt her finger. He was immediately shaken to consciousness, and found that he really had a burnt finger.

Once, an ascetic told another to cook some rice pudding for their altar-deities. Then, in her imagination, a beautiful young girl came and gave her the milk and she cooked the pudding. After he returned to his ordinary senses and tasted the pudding, it turned out to be tastier than ever before. He reported the experience to his ascetic friend, who immediately recognized the young girl as Radha herself.[41]

Once, a devotee and his guru were worshipping together when, in their respective imaginative revelations, they together found for Radha her lost nose-ring, which had fallen off during her love-encounter with Krishna. Pleased, Radha called them close to her and stuffed betel leaves in their mouths. The handmaiden-practitioners came back to their ordinary senses and, chewing on their betel leaves, exchanged aware smiles.

There are other celebrated paradigmatic narratives which reveal the translations among celestial Vrindavan, *manas*-Vrindavan, and physical lands where practitioners reside. Thus, one time, a practitioner using his yogic powers dipped under the (physical) Radhakunda in Vrindavan to look for Radha's earrings, which she discovered in imagination were lost in celestial Radhakunda; he got up crying after seven days, saying he had found them.

Certain deductions may be inferred from the preceding exploration of practices of imagination. First, higher stages of rumination effect bodily transformations (McDaniel 1995, 45). Affective and cognitive spaces are co-constituted and intermediated by imagination. No longer does imagination remain confined to visualization. Its synesthetic appeal urges us to take a "methodological step away from an empiricist conception of imagination as abstract representation to a phenomenological conception of imagination as a feature of the bodily synthesis" (Csordas 1993, 147–48).

Second, subservience is the main logic of selfhood here. At no point during *sadhana* can the *manjari* outdo her gurus' primacy. She depends on their orders in imagination/Vrindavan. Yet this is no way hinders but rather augments her pleasures. It is in assisting her guru in facilitating the deities' eros that her pleasures rest completely.

However, practitioners assert that such is the empathic connection between Radha and the *manjari* by virtue of being completely engrossed in her loyalties, that she is bound to feel Radha's pleasure in lovemaking. A *babaji* explained the nature of this empathy: "Unless one feels what Radha feels, how will she understand what Radha wants? How will she serve her? When you burn a piece of iron, it gradually becomes bright red. It acquires the qualities of fire; but it never *becomes* the fire. Similarly, both a lamp and a forest fire emit heat. But when wind comes, one dies out, the other spreads. So, both the part and the whole have similar characteristics, but the whole has qualities which supersede the part, and which the latter can hope to embody but not emulate."

Almost challenging him humorously, I asked Krishnagopal what need there is to empathize with someone else's sexuality so intensely. Unperturbed by my arrogance, he said with a coy smile, almost as if he could visualize what he was describing, "*Manjaris* are of impressionable ages. Their hearts are as soft as clay. Thus, the imprints of Radha's emotions are distinct. If Krishna kisses or bites or embraces her, then the pain or pleasure that Radha feels will also impact the *manjari's* body. The greater the sensitivity, greater is the reception of empathy." The paradox is that another's erotic pleasures can be felt in the body without desires developing for ego-gratification.

Practitioners offer interesting explanations for such experiences of submissiveness. At the earliest stages of *sadhana*, Krishna is imagined to be Vrindavan's only subject (*visaya*); all the rest, objects (*asraya*) of his pleasure. *Asraya* literally means "vessel." Devotees explain that if one confines one's embodied experiences to one's own body-vessel, then a limited sense of pleasurable empathy is attained. The gurus are spiritually more developed, and thus their senses more refined than the devotee's. Thus, their capacities to indulge in Vrindavan's pleasures are multiplied exponentially. When one submits to the powers of the pyramidal guru-lineage, the gurus' body-vessels, one also apprehends and resonates with the tastes of such (interlocked and exponentially increasing) pleasures. They can then transfer their body-minds onto a realm of infinite affective possibilities. This is literally a model of a vessel, taking as its subject another vessel, and it continues ad infinitum (Haberman 1988, 112).

The weaker the sense of bounded agentive egohood, the greater are the chances of tasting Vrindavan's aesthetic delights. The only autonomy is thus in accepting and enjoying one's essential subservience. Ego-effacement is thus cognized in terms of chained subservience. The devotee tries to be like Vrindavan's eternal participants, without aspiring to equal them.

However, the paradigm of extreme emotional possibility is contained in Radha. She embodies a grammar of affective concentration of sweet-tasting emotions toward Krishna: pure devotion, dalliance, love, attraction, jealousy, romance, passion, and finally, the concentrated form of all these emotions (*mahabhava*).[42] To explicate this point, many devotees invoke a metaphor of crystallization: from sweet syrup, to jaggery, to sugar, and finally sugar cubes. The greater the emotive congealment, the greater its permanence, and therefore its capacity to be tasted by Krishna. In Bengal-Vaishnava aesthetics, Radha derives more pleasure in serving and loving Krishna than Krishna himself. Thus, the pleasures of the vessel/lover/servant are greater than those of the object/loved/served. For practitioners, therefore, not Krishna but Radha becomes the primary paradigm of worship.[43] The *manjari's* true devotion thus becomes a matter of being able to apprehend Radha's intense sensuous needs and desires.

In the ego-dissolved state, all *manjaris* are subservient to and share in the emotional intensity of the sacred place, Vrindavan. Devotees emphasize that their pleasures are then not self-directed (*kama*) but always focused on the deities (*prem*).[44] The self thus remains, but with an idea of the affective body and senses mediated by Vaishnava discourses. The affects belong to imagination-Vrindavan, and are heightened without being ego-directed.

As explained above, rigorous bodily practices aim at stifling notions of corporeal autonomy, and practiced contemplations place *manjaris* in relation to many others, thus placing their independent relationships within an economy of other actors without belittling the importance of each. The egoless appraisal of emotions enables a *manjari*, as a non-agentive feeler, to taste Radha's pleasures without authoring them. An "ordinary emotion" is limited to an ego's pains and pleasures. But *manjaris'* experiences are shared and impersonal, and there is therefore an aesthetic "artistic distance" between the spectator and her emotions (Haberman 1988, 17).

Arindam Chakrabarti (2009) makes similar observations in his analysis of rasaesthetics. He argues that "unbelonging" (2009, 190–91) depersonalized affects or "ownerless emotions" (198) are capable of forging impersonal subjectivities. Precisely because there is then no centered ego, no "unsharable individuality," (190) that perfect empathic possibility is offered. What remains is a pure, self-contained aftertaste of shared, distilled sentiments (*rasa*).[45] These sentiments are never felt less intensely by actors, however. In fact, they impact the epidermal/cognitive worlds of co-feelers with an even more passionate wrap, for the shame/fear/limits of the bounded egos are now absent. The *rasika* (aesthete/connoisseur) is defined as a person who through years of practice derives pleasure from the universality of sentiments, as both participant and observer (Siegel 1983, 3).

Although the infinite stylistics of the *manjari's* imagination affect her visceral body, imagination as such cannot be exactly located. It is the entire transformative space of the mind-heart geography where Vrindavan is felt. It is also that exercise which dissolves the boundaries between subject and object, inner and outer, knower and known, journey and place. The limits of bodily and subjective sovereignty are automatically released. Imagination is therefore not only embodied but also intensely affective.

The perspectivist position of a thinker-feeler thus gets challenged, in feeling with the same subterranean shared "flesh" (Carman 2008, 1, 133). There is an analogical perception in her, a simultaneity of emotional identification. An elderly *babaji* summed this up for me: "Since I do not have a sense of *my own* body, thus, every time my *manjari* self feels something, she knows this is because she is located in Vrindavan, and that the pleasure belongs to all in Vrindavan." He maintained an objective distance from his true/essential self by referring to it in the third person.

Ethnographies reveal the translatable potentials of synesthetic experiences, kinesthetics of the body (Csordas 1990, 22), and cognitive and ethical faculties of the mind (Debes 2009; Lutz 1988, 224–25). In this case, similarly, through bodily and mental practices one is able to cultivate ethical ego-effacement and taste the sacred place in one's heart-mind with all one's physical and inner sensory capacities: eyes witnessing divine *lilas,* clairaudience resonating with Krishna's flute, clairaroma enjoying the smell of wild Vrindavan forest flowers, and skin sensing Radha's.

This complete sensory absorption is augmented when the bud-like *manjari's* devotion is tasted by Krishna. Devotees, comparing him to the taster-bee, explain this beautifully when they say that a bee is attracted with all senses—it sees, smells, touches, and tastes the flower, and only after that emits its *gunjan*—pleasure sounds. Both the attractor and the attracted indulge in sensory excess because their location, Vrindavan, is the embodiment of visceral bliss. In this case, the embodied place is the mind-heart, and the process of manifesting it, imagination.

OTHER SENSES OF PLACE

So the *goswamis'* and *babajis' manas* as *gupta*-Vrindavan is unveiled as the spiritual place through perceptive and fine-tuned imagination. Three components of imagination have been discussed in this regard. The first are practices through which the mind-heart is prepared for imagination. This involves the cultivation of an ego-effaced feminine sensibility in the devotee. Second, Vaishnava imagination follows a strict discursive script defining the location and emotions of the devotee's spiritual self. These emotions are of egolessness and empathy. Third, imagination's affective autonomy manifests itself in its unanticipated, creative moments, and also its intense sensory impact on the practitioner's body. The imaginative sense of place thus operates as an intermediary between socially constructed emotions and the autonomous domain of affect.

Manas-Vrindavan has egoless selves experiencing inter-self empathic continuity. This self exemplifies a paradoxical status of savoring divine sensuality through heightened senses, yet not desiring ego-gratification. The egoless feminine self relishes Vrindavan's passions; in other words, the emotive body delights in imagination.

However, the politics of placing Vrindavan in imagination has far-reaching consequences for the sect's consolidation (see also Case 2000, 71). The relation between the *goswami* or *babaji* guru and his disciples practicing *manjari sadhana* is not only a material one based on providing initiation and receiving sectarian loyalty. The perpetuation of their relationship and therefore the strong organization of their Vaishnavism are also conceptualized as spiritual. Even after his physical death, the guru literally continues to hold a crucial location in the disciple's imagination. The disciple in turn is indispensable for the guru-*manjari,* in providing her requisite assistance in her services in imagination. All potential disciples are therefore literally promised a place in Vaishnavism, and their spiritual subservience provides the deference necessary for community maintenance. Thus, although imagination is commonly understood as a solitary internal act, imagination here is also inherently social, due to both the embodied socialization the disciple undergoes from his guru as preparation for subsequent imagination, and the reciprocity engendered between guru and disciple in their respective imaginations. These social articulations constitute the basis of the perpetuation of *goswamis'* and *babajis'* kind of Vaishnavism.

Any "social," however, thrives on its distinction from others. Imagination experienced as place exerts its power through corresponding social exclusions. *Goswamis* and *babajis* assert their difference from ISKCON on the basis that the latter do not have appropriate spiritual lineages through which *manjari sadhana* is imparted. The persistent discourse is that although ISKCON may have tons of money, temples, and rich international devotees, they will never know or be able to teach their disciples the essence of traditional Vaishnavism, which is *manjari sadhana.*

However, there is another Vaishnava group against which *goswamis* and *babajis* position their practices. They are the *sahajiyas* who live in Navadvip's outskirts. While *goswamis* and *babajis* think of ISKCON as improper Vaishnavas, they call *sahajiyas* members of an *apasampraday,* literally "outcastes," and not Vaishnavas at all. Spiritual practices involving imagination are clean and respectable, they assert, because although intensely sensuous they reserve the sexual act itself for the deities, their own selves being imagined as only serving them during the process. Their chosen site to experience the spiritual place is the sanitized mind-heart and not the body. Thus, although practitioners admit both the corporeal basis (bodily practices preparing for imagination) and bodily receptions of imagination (imagination's impact upon the senses), their experience of the place in imagination is intimately related to the avoidance of carnal possibilities.

This is the prime factor which distinguishes *goswamis* and *babajis* and their sense of place from *sahajiyas,* who site veiled-Vrindavan within their physical body, which unveils the spiritual place through direct sexual relationships. Indeed, *goswamis'* and *babajis'* practice of *manjari sadhana* began as a response to the frequent associations of Bengal-Vaishnavism with *sahajiya* sexual practices (see also Klaiman 198, 39).

One morning, Krishnagopal was checking whether my work in Navadvip was progressing well. He mentioned a number of *goswamis'* temples and *babajis'* ashrams and asked whether I had visited them. At one point I told him that I had read books about *sahajiya* Vaishnavas and asked whether he knew if they live in Navadvip, since I would like to meet them. My jovial friend turned grim, stiffened his lips and said, "Don't call them Vaishnavas. They are most dirty. I don't think they deserve a place in your work on Vaishnavism." Although I sensed what problems he had with the *sahajiyas,* I still asked why he reacted that way. He raised his voice and continued, "They have random sex, keep unmarried girls as partners, have illicit relations with gurus, and say they are sensing Vrindavan. What more is there to say? . . . They *imitate* [*anukaran*] Radha and Krishna, we only *follow* [*anusaran*] them!"

Despite similar reactions from a number of *goswamis* and *babajis,* I now desperately wanted to meet Navadvip's *sahajiyas.* It is to the analysis of the kind of Vaishnavism and sense of place *sahajiyas* embody that we now turn.

CHAPTER 4

Bodying *Gupta*-Vrindavan: Experiencing the Self and Emotions in the Corporeal Space

INTRODUCTION: THE PLACE IN THE BODY

Throughout my fieldwork all the other Vaishnavas unequivocally emphasized that I must not include the *sahajiyas* in my research. They insisted that although *sahajiyas* claim to be Vaishnavas, they are actually not Vaishnavas at all, and have disgusting practices such as non-marital sex and illicit relationships with gurus.

For some months I was unable to locate a recognizable group of *sahajiyas* in Navadvip, since they own no major temple/ashram. Then one afternoon I was travelling with a *goswami's* woman disciple on a rickshaw to attend a *kirtan* recital in Navadvip's outskirts. We happened to pass by the main rail-lines. A group of women were crossing over to the other side. My friend remarked, with disdain written all over her face, "They are the *sahajiyas* you asked me about. See how they are wearing white *saris* and carrying *aslas* [begging cloth-bags]. Only *sannyasis* carry them. Who but *sahajiyas* would allow women renunciation! They live near the railroad tracks." Despite other Vaishnavas' hostility toward them, getting to know *sahajiyas* was a most fortunate turning point of my research, since the next few months were spent making sense of another experience of place, another *gupta* (veiled) Vrindavan, another Vaishnavism.

Sahajiyas are very poor and of the lowest Bengali castes.[1] They live far from the town center in clusters of cramped huts along

FIGURE 10. *Sahajiya* huts along Navadvip's railway lines.

Navadvip's railroad tracks, both because they cannot afford to build houses in the main town and because they are despised by *goswamis* and *babajis*.

Sahajiya settlements extend from Navadvip's outskirts to Bardhamman, the district adjacent to Nadia. I initially thought *sahajiyas* to be relatively fewer than other Vaishnavas, but later realized that hundreds reside all along the Nadia–Bardhamman border. Although many *babajis* are also poor, their daily needs are met by the ashrams they live in. But *sahajiyas* have no temple/ashram within which they reside; they work hard to earn their daily meals, mostly by doing farm labor and odd jobs.[2] Renouncer *sahajiyas* mostly beg, both to sustain themselves and as a mark of detachment from worldly concerns. Mostly illiterate or barely educated, with rustic Bengali pronunciation and shabby clothes, with money just sufficient for sustenance, living in thatched-roof huts, *sahajiyas* are simply like other poor Bengali villagers. It is therefore impossible to identify them from their external demeanor. It is their practices involving the body's interior which make them distinctive.

In terms of their levels of education, occupational backgrounds, and cultural manners, although these people of humble rural circumstances are substantially different from other Vaishnavas, including the sophisticated, metropolitan ISKCON devotees and the educated, small-town *goswamis* leading comfortable lives, *sahajiyas* do not however live in situations of desperate deprivation, and resources exist for them to be able to commit to their rigorous spiritual lives. Also, despite their modest education, their informed conceptual understanding of their religion, like that of other Vaishnavas, reflects their sincere commitment to a Vaishnavite life.

While all Vaishnavas receive *diksha* mantras, the easiest way I learned to identify a *sahajiya* was when someone said in the same breath that he or she had received *diksha* and *shiksha* (esoteric training) mantras from their guru(s). *Sahajiya* gurus, mostly men but also women, have disciples all over rural Bengal, and through association with gurus and their disciples, villagers get initiated into *sahajiya*-Vaishnavism. Other Vaishnavas had told me early on in my fieldwork that I should avoid people who mention *shiksha*-mantras. I later realized that this is because *sahajiyas'* *shiksha* refers to their gurus' teaching them techniques of sexual arousal, which they venerate as ideal means of experiencing Vaishnava religiosity. The term *sahajiya* refers to a person who experiences the state of being *sahaja*, which means both "natural" and "easy" or "spontaneous," implying an affective disposition of savoring the primeval state of man (Krishna)–woman (Radha) union through sexual heightening.[3]

Some *sahajiyas* are married, with children; some among them take renunciation when their children are older; some live with partners without being married, and often take renunciation while young. Once renouncers, *sahajiyas* are instructed by their gurus to stop having children. Partnerships are also not always permanent, and instances of *sahajiya* men and women taking on other partners are not uncommon. This diversity in partnership models is possible since being unmarried, married, or renouncers does not make a difference to *sahajiyas'* sexual practices. Sexual pleasure, according to them, is the chief means of realizing Radha-Krishna's pleasures in Vrindavan, regardless of marriage. *Sahajiyas'* living together without marriage, their conjugal fluidity, and particularly their renunciation practices are detested by other Vaishnavas. This is because among other Vaishnavas (*babajis* and ISKCON renouncers) only men take renunciation, and associate it with celibacy, while *sahajiyas* emphasize the importance of sexual relationships even after renunciation, and observe the distinctive practice of *yukta-vairagya* (renunciation of both partners together).

Goswamis and *babajis* claim an exalted form of participation in Radha-Krishna's *lilas* through practices of imagination. They use terms like *nongra* (dirty) or *ghrinya* (disgusting) when referring to *sahajiyas'* practices. These terms have both physical and moral implications, since they despise the fact that *sahajiyas* define their religion not in terms of the sanitized space of spiritual imagination but through the direct use of their physical bodies and sexual ecstasy.

However, while other Vaishnavas refer to *sahajiyas* as *apa-sampradaya* (not-Vaishnavas), *sahajiyas* claim not only that they are Vaishnavas but (as they told me repeatedly) that they are the best kind of Vaishnavas. They say that Chaitanya was a major practitioner of their tradition, and therefore claim to be the best representatives of what the saint taught. They say that while *goswami* and *babaji* practices rest merely on *anu-man* (indirect inference/imagination) of Radha-Krishna's *lilas,* theirs exemplify the path of *bartaman* (presentness/corporeal sensuality/car-nal immediacy). In ordinary Bengali, *bartaman* means "the present." In this context it carries the qualified sense of immediacy, clarity, and efficacy of corporeal experiences in making Radha-Krishna's sexual play in Vrindavan apparent in *sahajiyas'* bodies. Thus, while chapter 3 was about techniques of imagination cultivated by *goswamis* and *babajis* to experience Vrindavan in their *manas,* here I document the practices of *sahajiya*-Vaishnavas, who make an even more radical claim of experiencing Radha-Krishna's sexual pleasures within their own physical bodies, through their own cultivated sexual lives. Thus, the crucial distinction is that *goswamis* and *babajis* claim to witness but not to directly participate in the deities' sexuality, while *sahajiyas* claim to directly physically feel divine sexual heights in the most intimate affective levels of their interiorized body-spaces.

My main concerns here are to document and analyze *sahajiyas'* sexual practices through which their bodies manifest the deities' erotic passions in Vrindavan, that is, how the body is experienced as the sacred place, and practitioners' emotions while affectively emplaced in the internal corporeal space of the spiritually cultivated body. Thus, I extend Casey's (1993, xiii) idea of "implacement" from the body-in-place to body-as-place. This approximates the state Csordas (1994, 4) calls "proprioception," or the senses of being in a body and being oriented toward external space—the distinctiveness in this case being the orientation toward the body-space itself through a turn toward interiority. As in my analyses of *goswamis'* and *babajis'* embodied experience of the mind-as-place as being an interiorized place-experience, I seek to demonstrate that *sahajiyas'* practices are also a cultivation of interiorized bodily spaces. However, while for *goswamis* and *babajis* the body is the preparatory ground for and recipient of effects of imagination, for *sahajiyas* it is itself the vessel with which to experience place. The critical thing about *sahajiyas'* religion is that they cultivate and conceptualize sacred geography in terms of the body as a tool to manifest the pleasures of Vrindavan through yogic techniques of specified movement of breath and body-fluids in the corporeal interior. Thus, the dimensions of place and journey in this chapter are about the internal body-space and flows of body-fluids, respectively. This is particularly important for me since it adds a further layer of complexity to the theoretical interface between place-experience and affect. As in chapter 3, I argue here that interiorized experiences of place, unlike what has been predominantly stressed in the anthropology of place and affect, may be intensely embodied and affective rather than only being prerogatives of abstract consciousness.

Sahajiyas conceptualize their practices within an established Vaishnava discourse. This, I argue below, serves two purposes. It helps maintain their claims to Vaishnavism and also conceals the details of their practices from outsiders. Although other Vaishnavas have a vague idea of *sahajiyas'* practices, they don't know the ritual details or the philosophies undergirding them. *Sahajiyas* define their religiosity in terms of passionate love for Radha-Krishna, intense desire to experience their love-play in Vrindavan, cultivating egolessness and femininity as prerequisites for the purpose, and their sensuous experiences of the deities' sexual arousal within their own selves. These devotional principles would hardly seem different from *goswamis'* and *babajis'* practices, till one comprehends *sahajiyas'* interpretations of these tenets.

Sahajiya practices focus on five bodily emissions, referred to throughout this chapter alternatively as body-substances or fluids— semen, feces, urine, menstrual blood, and female sexual fluid—which the devotee learns through instruction and practice either to hold back within the body through yogic techniques of interrupted flow and non-emission, or to take back into the body after release. Body-substances, along with the practitioner's breath and cranium, are venerated as cosmic equivalents of natural elements: earth, water, fire, air, and sky.[4] A common *sahajiya* proverb proclaims, "What is not there in the body, is not there in the universe," and in a practice known as *pancha ras-er upasana* (worship of five fluids), *sahajiyas* ingest these excreta, their consumption associated with maintenance of cosmic rhythm.

Sahajiyas learn breathing techniques of controlling the fluids' flow and release within their bodies, and the body-space manifests Vrindavan, they say, when they master these fluid journeys. *Sahajiyas* deify body-fluids as embodiments of Vaishnava deities. The male principle, Krishna, is embodied in semen, and Radha, in menstrual blood and/or female sexual fluid. Thus *sahajiyas* conceptualize these fluids' unification in the body, through consuming them together during ingestion practices and retaining or pulling them up through yogic practices, as the union of Radha-Krishna and thus the preservation of Vrindavan's pleasures within the body. The man's head, where he meditates from and where he claims to be able to pull up sexual fluids through urethral suction, and the woman's vagina, are understood to be *gupta*-Vrindavans, which unveil the sacred place when the fluids, Radha and Krishna, unite there. Hayes (2005, 20) refers to this as the "indwelling" of male and female powers within the physical body-space.

Sahajiyas equate ejaculation with self-seeking pleasure or ego-gratification and thus conceptualize egolessness as non-ejaculatory spiritual practices. They say that a body in lust (*kama*) ejaculates but a body in love (*prem*) retains Vrindavan (body-fluids) inside. Thus, *sahajiya* practices of ingestion and fluid-retention thrive on paradigms of internal absorption. Most *sahajiyas* explained that since penetration is the hallmark of male pride (*purushabhiman*), and absorption the symbol of femininity (*naritva*), both male and female practitioners embody feminine subjectivities by retaining or consuming fluids. By cultivating these feminine sensibilities, both partners imagine themselves as Krishna's egoless lovers.

Semen retention is a common practice in many religious contexts, especially tantric ones. What is significant in the case of *sahajiyas* is that fluid retention is associated by them with the experience of their bodies-as-Vrindavan. Vrindavan is imagined by all Vaishnavas as the site of heightened divine pleasure. *Sahajiyas* say that retention of sexual fluids indicates longer duration of the sexual activity and pleasure, and thus the manifestation of the body as the site of intensified pleasure, Vrindavan. However, this pleasure is different from ordinary sexual pleasure since it does not aim at self-seeking ejaculation but at understanding the continuous but egoless nature of divine love. While *goswamis* and *babajis* say, "manas-e Vrindavan prakat hoy" (Vrindavan is apparent in the mind-heart), *sahajiyas* simply say, "ei deha Vrindavan": the body is Vrindavan.

Many of the practices I document in this chapter have similarities with what has been documented in the literature on *sahajiya*-Vaishnavism and tantric religiosities generally.[5] I had for instance read about semen retention and other sexual-yogic practices before beginning fieldwork.

What is particularly important to note in the light of the literature, what has not been fully explored, and what I had rare access to through *sahajiyas'* narrativized experiences, is the affective dimension of how the interior of the *sahajiya's* body and movement of body-fluids within are cultivated and conceptualized by them as experiencing a sense of place.

Sahajiyas use a distinctive geographical vocabulary to refer to their bodies and spiritual practices. As McDaniel (1995, 51) argues, Bengali devotional emotions are expressed through metaphors of substance and space. For instance, during their conversations with me, *sahajiyas* often referred to their spiritual goal as the place to get to, their gurus as boatmen guiding them through stormy seas, and so on. A common poem learned from their gurus and known by heart by many *sahajiyas* is known as the Eighteen-Place Theory. It refers to the body as the "sacred house" and mentions eighteen sites within it, sanctified by different deities' names. Most importantly, *sahajiyas* refer to their spiritual progressions as cultivated lands (*desh*) in the body. Although in ordinary Bengali the word *desh* carries connotations of one's country or native land of birth, intimate inhabitation, or more generally an abode or sanctified terrain, *sahajiyas* use it to signify stages of their spiritual journey toward emplacement in the body-place.

Are *sahajiyas'* experiences of their bodies-as-places emotional in the sense of being discursively constituted, or affectively perceived? I show that it is both. The body-space, body-parts, body-substances, and practices of retention or absorption of fluids, as well as the physical sensations of sexual pleasure, are thoroughly conceptualized by *sahajiyas* within an established Vaishnava discourse. This helps them verbalize their experiences of physical sensations, which might otherwise appear antithetical to articulated exegesis. The emotions practitioners embody at various stages of spiritual progress are also cultivated through bodily disciplines learned from gurus. However, the corporeal materialities on which the efficacy of *sahajiya* practices depends belong to the domain of affect in being associated with the most intimate, interior, and ineffable perceptions (Taussig 1998). Orgasmic states, evisceration, absorption, and breathing are essential experiences, not ordinarily or even easily reflected upon. Also, though I wondered what it is about bodies that makes them worth experiencing as places, my question did not make sense to my interlocutors simply because it is a matter of most intimate experience, not easily brought to language. A *sahajiya* guru finally explained that the body has a natural space-like quality since breath (and along with it *sahajiyas'* body-fluids) "passes *through* it." As it touches the body's inner walls, breath feels the affective body-as-place. In all these aspects of relative ineffability, these experiences elude language and thought—and therefore the persistent senses of subjective consciousness and sovereignty. Finally, *sahajiyas* say that their practices impact both the visceral sensations of the physical body and inner perceptive capacities.

In theorizing *sahajiyas'* experiences of the body-as-place, I extend Csordas's concept of embodiment and Casey's idea of place. Csordas (1993, 1994) locates embodiment in the realm of external intersubjectivity.[6] Similarly, in theorizing the primacy of relationship between body and place, Casey limits their intermeshed co-constitution to the dialogue of their boundaries, that is, their external relationship. While he thinks of how bodies inhabit places, I am also thinking of ways in which the body itself is cultivated and experienced as a place, that is, *sahajiyas'* interiorized experiences of emplacement, not only through but also *in* their bodies.

Persson (2007, 51) similarly questions Casey's attempts to locate the "depths" and "horizons" of places necessarily outside the body. In rethinking dimensions of embodiment and the body's relation with space, Morley (2001, 77) also insists on dissolving the boundaries between the exterior and interior. Invoking Merleau-Ponty's concept of the body as "occupied" flesh, he foregrounds the body's own intrinsic spatiality. Similarly, Sarukkai (2002), while theorizing the perceptive features of yogic breathing as passing through the body's interiors, proposes the notion of "inner body." This is similar to Hatley's (2007, 358) use of the term "inner landscape" in his discussion of Bengal's Islamic yogic practices, or Simmer-Brown's (2001, 173) imagining of the yogic subtle body as the microcosm of sacred landscapes, and yogic movements within as "the pilgrimage of inner integration." All these authors have informed my conviction that senses of place may indeed be as much internal as external to bodies.

Thus, in thinking about the *sahajiya* body, I propose the idea of body-as-place and embodiment as affective processes of interiority. My analysis falls midway between and adds to what Csordas calls an anthropology of the body, which studies the body's materiality, and the phenomenologically driven concept of "embodiment," which studies the body's perceptive relations with the (place) world (1993, 135).

Cataldi (1993) extends Merleau-Ponty's idea of "depth" to argue that the skin's perceptual gravity and emotional depth or profundity are often felt together. I borrow from her to demonstrate how *sahajiyas'* experiences of being deeply sensitive to body-interiors make their corporeal perceptions intensely affective as well as emotional. Thus, *sahajiyas* conceptualize all their affective sensations in terms of their intense love for the Vrindavan deities.

SAHAJIYA-VAISHNAVISM AND FIELDWORK METHODS

Sahajiya-Vaishnavism is not an easily discernible category in terms of either its historical origin or its contemporary forms.[7] *Sahajiya* body-practices, including sexual and ingestion rituals, breath control, and cultivation of femininity, are common among pan-Asian tantric religiosities.[8] Thus, both scholars and other Vaishnavas who deride tantric sexual practices lump *sahajiyas* together with so-called esoteric tantra-influenced groups, especially *bauls,* Bengal's famous poet-singers, who have practices similar to *sahajiyas.*

However, my *sahajiya* interlocutors strictly define themselves as Vaishnavas, and the discourses through which they communicate their religiosity are clearly mainstream ones. Thus, although scholars have often characterized *sahajiyas* and other tantric groups as subversive of the mainstream, I inferred *sahajiyas'* sectarian claim to Vaishnavism.

Although a significant complaint of other Vaishnavas against *sahajiyas, bauls,* and other similar groups is regarding the alleged monism they propound in situating Radha-Krishna in their own bodies, Navadvip's *sahajiyas* embody a rather complex monist-dualist philosophy, and assert major differences from the monistic *bauls.*

In the *sahajiya* neighborhoods I found a couple of self-professed *baul* households. They wore orange, unlike renouncer *sahajiyas,* who wear white. One evening I was drinking tea in a *sahajiya* widow's hut with other neighborhood women. A *baul* man came and joined us. The atmosphere was cordial as everyone discussed similar practices their gurus had taught them. After a while, the *baul* man left to cook dinner. Immediately, a woman remarked, "These *bauls* reside in our neighborhoods and claim to practice similar rituals as us. Yet they sing in public to earn money. With attention paid to material acquisitions, can one be a Vaishnava?" *Sahajiyas'* assertions of their clear differences from *bauls* constitute an important way in which they consolidate their identity as Vaishnavas rather than being like "other tantric groups," a claim which makes them equal competitors in Navadvip's ritual field of Vaishnava religiosity.

However, the main difference between Navadvip's *sahajiyas* and other tantra-influenced groups lies in *sahajiyas'* subtle balance between monistic religion, or what Hayes (1999, 80) calls the philosophy of "self apotheosis," and dualistic religion. While mainstream dualistic Vaishnavas maintain their faith in celestial Vrindavan, *bauls* and monistic tantric groups emphasize the unreality of all truths other than the body (Openshaw 2010, 164), thus repudiating idolism and after-life beliefs. Negotiating between these extremes, *sahajiyas* glorify their corporeal beings as veiled-Vrindavan, but they also maintain faith in the celestial realm (see also Hayes 1995, 333). While they say that corporeal experiences are sufficient to apprehend divinity, like other Vaishnavas they also worship Radha-Krishna in celestial Vrindavan. Thus, in one *sahajiya* household I saw that the woman performed daily *puja* rituals and offered food to her Radha-Krishna altar. A *sahajiya* guru explained, "We feel Radha-Krishna's erotic play in ourselves, but can we feel Radha's being jealous, or Krishna's teasing her, inside? No. Some *lilas* are inside us, some outside—Radha-Krishna inside us [implying body-fluids] and Radha-Krishna outside [implying deities]." Like *goswamis* and *babajis*, therefore, *sahajiyas* embody three senses of place: sacred Navadvip, where they reside; the sacred place they carry within them; and celestial Vrindavan, where deities perform their *lilas*.

Whether to include *sahajiyas* in my book on Vaishnavism was a difficult decision. First there was the atmosphere of disparagement wherein other Vaishnavas refuse to acknowledge them as Vaishnavas. Second, the messy classifications embodied by popular religious groups in Bengal make it difficult to distinguish between for instance *bauls*, tantrics, and *sahajiyas*. Third, I feared sensationalizing their sexual practices. However, insofar as *sahajiyas* define themselves as Vaishnavas, I decided that they must feature in my analysis as equal representatives of the religion.

Surprisingly, *sahajiyas* were less secretive about their practices when speaking to me than *goswamis* and *babajis* were. The most important reason for this is that unlike other Vaishnavas, they do not have reasons to maintain diplomacy. Already marginalized by others, they did not have anything to lose by discussing their practices. Also, many *sahajiyas* were surprised, happy, and proud that an urban, middle-class, educated woman was interested in their philosophy.

However, they treated me like a seeker-scholar, not a participant-sharer. Without initiation it is possible to know about but not to practice or observe their sexual rituals. Also, initially, *sahajiyas* never "told" me anything. In response to my questions they discussed religious issues of considerable complexity by reciting poems and charts composed by *sahajiya* gurus. The terms used in these texts are a part of mainstream Vaishnava vocabulary but with hidden meanings describing their rituals. Being illiterate, they memorize these texts through a vibrant oral culture. But once I became more familiar to some *sahajiya* friends, we gradually discussed their rituals. *Sahajiyas* are extremely articulate about their philosophy. It is a knowledge born from experiential certainty and attentiveness to gurus' teachings, rather than formal education. As with *goswamis*' and *babajis*' practices, I rely to a large extent on *sahajiyas*' narrativized experiences.

Although *sahajiyas* inhabit an extensive area around the Nadia–Bardhhaman border, I primarily focused on one neighborhood, where most of my friends resided. It has twenty-five to thirty huts or even more, with stretches of green fields on one side. In the middle there is a rudimentary temple where *sahajiyas* meet for occasional *kirtans,* and an enclosed space with a few spinning-machines for women who earn money from hand-loom work. There is a small area reserved for *samadhis.*[9] The silence of the area is interrupted by piercing sounds from passing trains on the adjacent railroad tracks. I had most of my conversations with *sahajiyas* in the open fields, or sometimes, during evenings, in their huts, in the light of dim oil lamps. Initially I found it easier to interact with women, since they felt more comfortable discussing sexual details. Gradually, I befriended men as well.

I got to know some *sahajiyas* especially well. Hariprasad was a middle-aged unmarried man who lived with Vishakha, a beautiful young girl. He was a knowledgeable guru and spent a lot of time traveling and initiating disciples. He often explained the philosophical bases of *sahajiya* rituals. Vishakha was mostly in Navadvip and earned a little by cooking during special festival occasions in other *sahajiyas*' homes. She was very kind and introduced me to a number of her friends. I had affectionate relationships with Radharani and Manjari, very old widows who lived in adjacent huts. They had taken renunciation with their husbands when very young, and did not have children. We only met in the evenings, since they would be away for a great part of the day, begging. Rohini, a pleasant, soft-spoken woman in her late twenties, with three children, was very busy with household work throughout the day. However, she was fond of me and always made time, mostly during afternoons, and we would sit for long hours and chat in the open fields. My women friends were more candid about the rituals, while the men

FIGURE 11. *Sahajiya* temple.

found it easier to discuss the accompanying philosophies. The exception was Gour, my most important interlocutor guru, who lived in a town close to Navadvip. A *sahajiya* friend initiated by Gour sent me to him when he thought I should get better guidance. Gour had gone to school. He was relatively well-off, having worked as a clerk and then retired. He lived with his wife, Sadhana, and their children. He had hundreds of disciples in rural Bengal. He was the most knowledgeable and patient teacher I have known. It was in reading books and memorizing poems he suggested and conversing intensely for hours in his house that I learned the most about *sahajiya*-Vaishnavism.

THE SOCIAL PLACE AND BODY-PLACE

Sahajiyas' narratives of their place in society and experiences of the body-as-place have interesting overlaps. The interiority of their body-geographies, I argue, helps *sahajiyas* negotiate their marginal social position.

Almost all *sahajiyas* residing at present in Navadvip migrated from what is now Bangladesh, during either Partition (1947) or the Bangladesh War (1971); the latter are the predominant group. *Sahajiyas'* life-history narratives offer analytical tools in comprehending the anthropology of their perceptions of space and place.

Vishnupriya told me: "I was sixteen when I came to Navadvip forty years ago. At that time these places were jungles. Gradually our people started flocking in. I took *diksha* with my husband while in Bangladesh. We had a daughter. My husband died soon after we had the child, and I came to Navadvip. My *diksha*-guru was in Navadvip then. He looked for another of his initiates and supervised our *malachandan*.[10] We then took *shiksha* and *sannyas* together. I stay with him now. He is much older than me and my daughter calls him *dadu* [grandfather]." She laughed.

I asked, "Don't you miss your home [*desh*] there?"

Vishnupriya said, "Not at all! I have found a place in Navadvip, Mahaprabhua's land! In any case, after *shiksha* we found our real *desh*, Vrindavan, right here." She indicated her heart.

Urmila told me: "I was in Bangladesh when my husband and I took *diksha* and *shiksha*. Then he left me for another woman and came to Navadvip, to do *karma* [sexual practices] with her.[11] Our guru and some of his disciples have been here since 1971. So he found a community. After a few months the woman died. Then he needed me and called me to him. But he had taken renunciation, so I did, too. After some years he died. His *samadhi* is next to hers."

I asked, "Do you have any regrets?"

Urmila said, "No. We are poor people. We have no place in society. Now I feel secure, beg for my meals and have close widow friends. But one regret remains. If I had the chance to take *sannyas* earlier, I would have known Vrindavan [her body] better."

In addition to the persistent social insecurities of poverty and low caste, Navadvip's *sahajiyas* faced uncertainty due to their migration. Navadvip, only around 200 km from Bangladesh, was an established Vaishnava devotional center. Thus, establishing a Vaishnava community in Navadvip was an important way in which the immigrant population tried to find a niche and establish social legitimacy in the physical place. A *sahajiya* communitarian cluster gradually developed and engendered a further influx of (*sahajiya*) population.

Sahajiyas' initiation, esoteric training, and renunciation became passports for their journeys to both the body-place and the physical place. Many of them also took *diksha* or *shiksha* while in refugee camps and came to Navadvip with their gurus. Radharani said, "Krishna says, 'I am roaming as guru from door to door. Search for me and you will find Vrindavan.'" Thus, social and affective itinerancy searches for the guru to look for the "permanent" place, in this case referring both to Navadvip, *gupta*-Vrindavan, and *sahajiyas'* bodies-as-Vrindavan.

Fluidity in conjugal bonds, common among *sahajiyas,* also helped negotiate the spatial flux. Also, while begging is a religious requirement for renouncer Vaishnavas, it also served economic purposes for the poor strangers in Navadvip. Similarly, Trawick (1994) demonstrates with respect to Tamil Paraiyars how low-caste status, sexual promiscuity and placelessness get rearticulated in terms of spatial orientations.

Sahajiyas found a place only in Navadvip's fringes, however. This is consistent with their marginal position vis-à-vis other Vaishnavas. Along railroad tracks and in small alleys and by-lanes, *sahajiyas* reside in huts with thatched or tin roofs.[12] Their insecure homes make them vulnerable to the annual floods. Compared to the town center, which has bustling shops, temples, ashrams, pilgrims, and loudspeakers blaring devotional songs, *sahajiyas'* rural neighborhoods, dotted with green fields and small ponds, are very quiet, and lit with oil lamps in the evenings.

Most renouncer couples subsist by begging. *Sahajiya* women leave their homes very early in the morning, travel to nearby villages by local trains, and receive alms from train passengers and daily house-rounds. Daily alms consist of meager sums of money and rice-grains. Sometimes they have lunch in Navadvip's temples/ashrams which reserve *prasad* for the poor, and otherwise cook one meal at the end of the day. Householder *sahajiyas* are comparatively better off. Many earn their living from small farming jobs. Others perform casual labor. They sell vegetables in carts, or do masonry; some women supply needlework orders to the market. Those among *sahajiyas* who become gurus also receive maintenance from initiates, with the occasional bonus for performing *kirtan* or holding theological discussions in initiates' homes. My understanding is that it is easier for *sahajiyas* (compared to other Vaishnavas) to become gurus and that this is also a reason for *sahajiya*-Vaishnavism's popularity in rural Bengal.

Householders and renouncers reside in the same neighborhoods. In addition to the communitarian necessity this also has a religious rationale. They share similar sexual practices. Householders stay close to renouncers and maintain the rhetoric of *"samsare thekeo tyagi"* (a renunciate mentality even while amidst everything). This rhetoric specifically implies that even though householders may have children, they share with renouncers the ideal of non-ejaculatory sexuality/spirituality. Contrary to popular impressions of asceticism as a denial of sexuality, both householders and renouncers celebrate simultaneous contradictory ideals of worldly detachment and the sensual desire of being immersed in the body-place through sexual heightening. *Sahajiya* practices thus offer a critique of the householder–renouncer binary.[13]

George's (1993, 235) study of minority religious communities in Sulawesi demonstrates that secret communities, by setting boundaries, can enjoy senses of social cohesion and spatial possession. However, he shows that "outside institutions" still maintain their censorious attitudes toward them. Similarly, *sahajiyas'* place in mainstream society is compromised. My *goswami* friend Krishnagopal exemplified this in remarking, "*Sahajiyas* are of the lowest class and castes. They are uneducated. No wonder they use their bodies in such dirty ways."

Another area of pervasive social criticism is with respect to *sahajiya* women. Hausner and Khandelwal (2006, 5) argue that women's renunciation is a way in which they deal with social problems. Yet it is precisely *sahajiyas'* practice of *yukta-vairagya* which mainstream Vaishnavas find objectionable.[14] The sexual after-life of their together-renunciation, and sexual relationships of women with their gurus, are considered to be the most immoral practices in the face of ideal ascetic modes.

Thus, while *sahajiya* body-practices form their distinctive religiosity, the interiority of their body-geography also offers a way of negotiating their insecure and lowly place in society. The *sahajiya's* body provides a corporeal place-world, a primal security of belonging. As Whitridge (2004) argues, the body forms a "topological field" bearing deep impressions of biographical histories; this is what Rich (1984, cited in Whitridge 2004, 239) refers to as "the geography closest in."

On the day of the Ras festival I met Hariprasad and Vishakha, who were relaxing in the open fields near the railroad tracks. I inquired why they hadn't gone to participate in the main town's celebrations. Hariprasad replied in a collected, firm manner: "They have nothing to do with us. It does not matter if we can't participate in their places. Real places are inner treasures; they are in us [pointing to the two of them]. We carry it with us." *Sahajiyas'* marginal position is ascribed to them by other Vaishnavas, a position *sahajiyas* deal with by emphasizing a superior form of inhabitation in turn: their emplacement in body-Vrindavan. Thus, it is not about *sahajiyas'* accepting a subaltern social location.

Sahajiyas' concerns, in the final instance, shift therefore from the body-in-place to the body-as-place, from a search for social and spatial security to the celebration of symbolic itinerancy, in "carrying the place in the body." As Casey (1993, 110) reminds us, knowing the place through our body constitutes the primary epistemological possibility.

He says that through their sense of "familiarity," "*bodies build places*" (116, italics in the original).

THE *SAHAJIYA* LANGUAGE

One of the most significant ways in which I made sense of *sahajiyas'* relations with their bodies was through sensitivity toward their highly complex linguistic sensibilities. When discussing their religion, *sahajiyas* speak in a language deploying conventional Vaishnava terms, yet imputing to them completely different meanings. These meanings pertain to what *sahajiyas* do in their sexual-religious lives. Thus, simply by hearing their language one can tell they are Vaishnavas, but till one understands exactly what they mean, one will never know they are *sahajiyas*. Their language helps *sahajiyas* tread the delicate line between maintaining their distinctive religiosity while subscribing to broader Vaishnava ideologies, and maintain secrecy from outsiders. Similar linguistic usage is common among other tantra-influenced groups. Scholars call this "intentional" or "twilight" language (*sandhya bhasha*).[15] It is intentional in that it helps religious actors maintain distance from noninitiate ordinary people; and it is "twilight" in that it preserves secrecy about their practices. *Sandhya* in fact literally means "twilight" and refers to the liminal phase between light and dark when forms are discernible, but specificities lost.

Sahajiyas distinguish their religious practices from other Vaishnavas on the basis that they can apprehend Vrindavan's pleasures through methods of *bartaman,* as opposed to others' *anuman*; similarly, they interpret Vaishnava discourses through direct bodily/sexual metaphors. Just as their religion is corporeal, so is their semantics fleshy. This is similar to Bellman's (1981) typology of secrecy as "discursive" or "deep talk," communicated through metaphors. *Sahajiyas'* use of metaphors to communicate the deepest aspects of their bodies and ontology can be interpreted through theories of cognitive science and phenomenological embodiment. Lakoff and Johnson (1999) argue that matters of the cognitive unconscious are best expressed through metaphors, and metaphors in turn are imaginatively informed by the embodied living of people. So a fleshy philosophy can understand cognitive and linguistic mechanisms as reflections of the body's perceptions, sensations, and relations. Thus, metaphors are essential both to *sahajiyas,* to communicate their philosophy, and to me, to understand and translate them. Flood (2006), however, gives a more discursive reading and says that the tantric body is constructed out of traditional cultural metaphors. *Sahajiya* metaphoric poetry, like their practices, can thus be seen as an interplay of the discursive and the affective.

Metaphors bridge the distance between the abstract and immediate, between sense and sensation (Low 1994, 140–3). Hayes (2005, 21–26), influenced by Lakoff and Johnson's (1999, 28–32) theorizations of our unconscious perceptual/conceptual systems as reflecting embodied spatial relations, argues with respect to the use of metaphors in expressing *sahajiya* religiosity that they represent alternative sacred worlds or "cognitive topologies." For instance, he speaks of "verticality schemas" embodying yogic acts of urethral suction or pulling up sexual fluids through the body, "container schemas" evoking the body's spatial sense as holding various body-substances, and "hydraulic metaphors" embodying fluids of the corporeal economy.

The entire Vaishnava vocabulary takes on new meanings in *sahajiyas'* cosmology. Krishna and Radha become the seminal essences of man and woman, respectively; *yugal-sadhana* (worshipping the deity-consort) becomes veneration of the sexual relationship between partners; *lila* (divine play) becomes the natural encounter between sexes; *rasa* (which literally means "juice" and which other Vaishnavas use to mean "emotion/mood") becomes sexual fluids; *seva* (service toward deities) can mean ingestion of sacred/sexual fluids or public devotional gatherings and feasts; the woman practitioner is known as *manjari,* and *manjari sadhana* becomes her sexual encounter with the guru-Krishna; and Vrindavan is the corporeal space which witnesses affective excesses of sexual abandon.

Similarly, *sahajiyas* worship Chaitanya as the androgynous godhead.[16] Manjari explained: "Mahaprabhu was Radha-Krishna in the same body. This means he united male and female sexual substances in his body. He taught us how to feel the same *rasa* [fluid/emotion] by enjoying Vrindavan-bliss with our partners." I asked her, "Do you interpret every word used by other Vaishnavas differently?" She was unhappy with the question. Immediately she made a gesture to get up, shook her hands vigorously, and said, "What I told you *is* what it is. *They* interpret things otherwise." In my conversations with *sahajiyas,* I discerned immense pride in their religious and linguistic practices.

Sahajiyas do not discuss their religion with outsiders. They criticize *bauls* for singing in public and thus making their linguistic-cosmological repertoire available to all. In addition to gurus directly explaining to disciples behind closed doors how to do rituals and what their significance is, *sahajiyas* discuss theological tenets among themselves during gatherings such as weekly meetings in some guru or senior devotee's house, festival occasions, and sermons given by gurus. During these public occasions, however, they never discuss rituals as such, but allude to them in their "twilight language."

One day I went to meet Hariprasad. His neighbor informed me that all neighborhood *sahajiyas* had gone to a Vaishnava devotional session (*seva*) in a nearby home. A woman had organized this gathering on the occasion of her sexual partner's third death anniversary. Fifty or sixty *sahajiyas* were seated in rows on jute mattresses, listening to the guru, Hariprasad, as he read portions of the *Chaitanya Charitamrita*, adding frequent explanations of passages.[17] At one point he said, "When I went to Bombay, I stood on the railway platform and stared in dismay! These are urban people who have read science. Yet they are so many. They don't know the basics of population control. Our gurus indicate rituals to us, and we need no pills!" This cryptic statement obviously indicated *sahajiyas'* practice of semen retention. Every time Hariprasad offered a *sahajiya* interlude to the reading, devotees raised their hands and ululated, while emotionally charged women cried and rolled on the ground.

I had chosen a discreet place for myself toward the back rows. Near where the sermon was taking place, a modest meal, sponsored by the host, was being prepared for all invitees. Vishakha, who was busy cooking, spotted me, came up and welcomed me, and invited me for lunch. This would not be a usual reaction to outsiders. But I was known to many *sahajiya* friends there and they did not mind my presence. *Sahajiyas'* linguistic usage is such, however, that sometimes the presence of outsiders may not make a difference. Once during a festival in Mayapur, I met a *sahajiya* woman friend. Although *sahajiyas* almost never visit Mayapur, she said her disciple had forced her to come. We sat under a tree where there were other pilgrims resting. After a while we began talking in detail about *sahajiya* ingestion practices. I expressed concern and pointed out that there were outsiders. She said, "But we are speaking a Vaishnava language. Only you and I understand what we are talking about."

Sahajiyas are aware that their sexualized interpretations of Vaishnava concepts come under attack from others. But they have their own justifications. Once during a conversation with a *sahajiya* couple, the woman started saying how misunderstood they are. "They [other Vaishnavas] think our rituals are dirty! Now, we know the essence of both Radha and Krishna [implying body-fluids], while they [*babaji* and ISKCON renouncers] can only know Krishna, since they have nothing to do with women. Ours is *rasa-sadhan* [worship involving love's juice], theirs only *shushko-sadhan* [dry worship]. We know how to retain our substance. If ascetics say they don't see women, then they will have nightfalls, and scandalous rape cases.[18] And then, who is dirty?"

The more I was able to tune my ears to *sahajiyas'* language and its meanings, the more interesting was my journey into their body-geographies. However, sexual practices are sensitive topics for discussion and initially I tried to be as little intrusive as possible.

Even when I had made good friends and Vishakha had introduced me to others, I preferred to talk only when they felt comfortable. So I would sit and write field notes in the neighborhood's temple compound. Gradually, someone or another would come and chat after returning from their day's begging, or taking a bath in the nearby pond, or finishing their cooking for the day. Initially there was much curiosity about me, since my clothes, my polished urban Bengali pronunciation, and my entire look were different from theirs. Then, as I became familiar, some women would call me over to their huts or while they worked in the spinning-compound or take me to the fields where no one would disturb us.

My frequent interactions initially surprised *sahajiyas* and later led to profound appreciation. Once, during an evening sermon at Gour's house, there was confusion about whether I should be allowed to participate. Gour said, "She is a modern, urban woman and yet interested in our theories. This is because she has good deeds from her past life. She is studying religion and wants to know the truth. And only *we* know the truth."

Some *sahajiyas* expressed a fear that if I practiced their teachings without initiation I might harm myself. Others were worried that I would learn enough to become a guru myself. I had to convince them that my inquiries were purely academic. Some women were unhappy about having their husbands join in our conversations when we discussed intimate practices; with them I engaged in one-to-one discussions.

Sahajiyas are given secret notebooks by their gurus. They contain details of rituals, the mantras which accompany them, and series of double-meaning esoteric poems written in ordinary Bengali. If someone reads them they would sound like any other spiritual poem involving conventional Vaishnava metaphors, but *sahajiyas* understand their hidden meanings, which exactly translate into words what *sahajiyas* experience in their bodies. The poems are often not of a high literary standard; their range is very wide. They may be short proverbs, couplets, and long or short poems which sometimes rhyme. Literate *sahajiyas* take them down while their gurus recite; for the illiterate majority of adepts, their literate gurus write them down. Memorizing the poems helps practitioners remember ritual details and keeps alive the rich tradition of esoteric poetry.

These notebooks were not shown to me, although my interlocutors frequently referred to them. The poems are incorporated into everyday manners of speaking; *sahajiyas* answered many of my questions by simply reciting poems from memory. I mostly recorded them, and when the poems were longer and more complex, I wrote them down while discussing the meanings with practitioners. While my guru-friend, Gour, who was in the habit of reading, kept the notebook handy, Rohini, who was illiterate, rarely revisited it. She emphasized, like many others, that even if she does not read it, she values the notebook immensely since it "has everything" (*shob ache*), that is, it preserves the details of their religious and poetic tradition.

One day Rohini brought out her notebook for me for a short time. She asked me to flip through the first few pages, then said, "Can you really understand by reading? I don't think so. Reading is not the issue. Understanding with the guru, and then memorizing, is." The contexts of repetitive references to these poems by gurus and senior adepts during sermons, and weekly or fortnightly theological discussions among them, lead to *sahajiyas'* memorization of these verses.

Apart from poems, there are a few *sahajiya* texts which analyze their life-worlds. Some of them are out of print. They circulate among the literate few, and I was fortunate to be given some of them during later days in the field. Sometimes gurus take excerpts from these books and write them in disciples' notebooks.[19]

For the most part, *sahajiya* tradition reproduces itself in rural Bengal through its vibrant oral tradition. While most poems were composed by gurus years ago and imparted through generations, some practitioners still compose poems in the present. Gour for instance is also a good singer. He composes poem-songs and sings them during *kirtan* sessions with disciples.

The initiated generally learn the poems before practicing their rituals. Thus, the poetic discourses *sahajiyas* memorize through association with their community have direct embodied relations with what they experience during sexual/religious rituals, since the poems directly describe the rituals, the meanings of which become evident to well-instructed practitioners. Lee Siegel (1983, 98) says about esoteric poems that they are "evidence which lovers have left behind, for the *rasika* . . . to decipher." As Rohini said, "Poems were written by gurus as after-thoughts on their *sadhana*. Poems contain the *sadhana*."

Sahajiyas' narration of different kinds of texts, like poems, proverbs, couplets, and so on, was their way of answering questions while leaving interpretations to my intelligence. Since I had already read intensively about *bauls'* use of "intentional language," I was immediately able to crack some puzzles. What I did not know before fieldwork, however, was how *sahajiyas* render particularly Vaishnava understandings through their language, for instance, their conceptualization of *manjari sadhana*. However, I usually told *sahajiyas* what I knew or understood. Elated to find that I was able to communicate through their half-revealed language, they narrated more poems. This is similar to Urban's (2003, 302) metaphor of a "spiritual slingshot" used to describe secrecy—stretched, then suddenly released. Sometimes *sahajiyas* explained the meanings of words I didn't understand, and sometimes like a fortunate rag-picker I realized the importance of unknown terms since their utterance would be followed by a hushed exclamation—"*Haribol*" (hail Krishna!). I came back every evening with text-puzzles and in a backwards brico-leur-journey put meaning-blocks in place. I constantly cross-checked my understandings with practitioners.[20] However, the mantras accompanying the rituals were never shared with me since I am not initiated.

Sitting outside in the sunny fields on a winter afternoon, I asked Vishakha and some of her friends which of their practices they consider the most important. In response, Vishakha simply recited a proverb: "You have to take Krishna's name in an egoless manner, without being found guilty." I thought for a while and said this must be referring to the practice of semen-retention, "guilt" meaning ejaculation—the symbol of self-gratificatory sex. All the women present were delighted and shouted "*Haribol!*" Another woman, visibly pleased with my understanding, smiled, leaned forward, and spontaneously recited another proverb into my recorder. "In Vrindavan there is no death or birth," she said, then explained that the pleasures of *deha*-Vrindavan are without "death" (ejaculation) or "birth" (reproductive sex).

Thus, my understandings of the poems' meanings and the rituals they describe were dependent on both my independent interpretations and thorough discussions with *sahajiyas*. In some cases the poems became clear only after I learned enough about *sahajiyas'* practices. However, there are poems I still do not understand, and confusions remain regarding a number of ritual possibilities.[21] These gray areas did not hinder my essential journey into *sahajiyas'* body-place, however.

Below I provide translations of a few texts from my field collection. They demonstrate how poetic discourses become reflections of corporeal performances.[22]

1. The following is a widely recited poem describing the body's natural constituent elements, ingestion of emitted bodily substances, and the devotee's ecstasy on successful ingestion.

> The five elements are the beginning, middle and end of creation . . .
> In their union is Chaitanya, in separation, death.
> . . .
> From these elements, the inner elements maintain rhythm.
> That [one] which [who] surpasses them
> Also surpasses Time.

In *sahajiyas'* ethno-anatomy (Scheper-Hughes and Lock 1987, 18), the body's elements correspond to the five elements of the natural cosmos: earth to feces; water to urine; fire to menstrual blood/semen/female orgasmic fluid; air to breath/semen that is pulled up with breath during *coitus reservatus*; and sky to head, where fluids are pulled up during ritual sex.[23] *Sahajiyas* say that to realize the natural state of their bodies they take back or ingest (rather than let out) these substances. The union of Radha-Krishna, represented in Vaishnava theology as Chaitanya and understood by *sahajiyas* as the combination of semen and menstrual blood, they say, gives the devotee the taste of spiritual bliss, manifesting their bodies-as-Vrindavan. "Surpassing" the elements refers to ritual sex, when self-seeking ejaculatory pleasures are overcome and both partners experience Vrindavan's original cosmic moment.

2. The following poem is also supposed to bring to the trained practitioner's mind the process of ingestion.

> He walked on to know *sahaja* [truth]
> . . .
> [He received instruction]
> . . .
> Learn to still your mind
> . . .
> Bring earth, water, and sixty-four truths together
> . . .
> To withstand the arrow's force

. . .

Do not go south, or you will fall into trouble
If you remember this, you will forever live in pleasure.

While in mainstream Vaishnava vocabulary the number 64 signifies
the rules of *vaidhi bhakti* (see chapter 3), *sahajiyas* refer to 64 months
of a woman's menstrual cycle (5 years and 4 months). If the ingestion
ritual is practiced uninterruptedly for 5 years and 4 months, then seminal retention becomes spontaneous, they say. The penis's natural ejaculatory "force" is avoided. When the practitioner performs ritual sex, he
or she must not allow seminal fluid to leave the body, or Vrindavan's
pleasures will be lost, since Radha-Krishna and their union are embodied in their sexual fluids in the body-Vrindavan.[24]

3. The following long poem is a typical instance of a kind of poetry
    that appears to be descriptive of Radha-Krishna's love-play but
    has a secret meaning as well. This was one of the very complex
    poems which I made sense of with Gour's help only after I knew
    some details of *sahajiyas'* sexual rituals.
    Vrindavan is on a lotus.
    . . .

    In the eternal place, the eternal substance resides.
    From Vrindavan it visits Navadvip from time to time.
    From the most secret lotus-stalk,
    The sea of love emanates.
    . . .

    Only the *rasika* [practitioner] is able to discover its secret.
    . . .

    Then the *rasika* sifts milk from water.
    Suddenly the beautiful girl manifests
    And in Vrindavan forests Krishna appears
    On Vrindavan's golden throne,
    In the midst of *svadhishthan*, there is a gush of *rasa*.
    . . .

    The lotus-stalk has three waves then, unable to control their
        intensity.

Here Vrindavan is the adept woman's lotus-vagina.[25] The other
Vrindavan manifests as the eternal place in the man's meditative point
in the head. The eternal substance, sperm, resides there and travels through the body's energy centers (Navadvip). The most secret

lotus-stalk is the clitoris, which in love bodies forth the orgasmic sea. The love-connoisseur (male practitioner) tastes this secret, sweet Vrindavan nectar. Then, through yogic practices, he pulls up her sexual fluid along with his and separates the two in his body. Until they are separated, the pleasures of union are not magnified in his head-Vrindavan. When Radha (menstrual blood/orgasmic substance) manifests herself in Vrindavan (vagina), Krishna (semen) appears there too. What follow in the *svadhishthan chakra*[26] are gushes of the man's sexual climax (*rasa*) and the woman's three waves (orgasms during ritual sex).

4. This poem emphasizes the need to cultivate a feminine sensibility at every stage of practice. Inverting the usual logic of male ejaculation and female absorption, *sahajiyas'* practices require both partners to be feminine by retaining or absorbing body-substances within themselves.
    One's companion/necessity in every *desh*
    Is [one's] feminine mood.

5. The following is a particularly evocative poem about the sexual bliss shared between the guru and the female practitioner.
    Manjari-tattva [theory] is very secret
    . . .
    [But] without knowing this, worship is impossible
    In his union with Radha, Krishna is delighted
    Seeing him happy, a *manjari* asks
    What makes you so happy today?
    The Lord says
    . . .
    When two *rasas* meet, it is called *prasad*
    In tasting this *prasad,* one attains Vrindavan
    The *manjari* says, then please make my body the *prasad*
    To fulfill her desire, the Lord embraces her

Unlike other Vaishnavas who stress that *manjaris* are Radha's virgin-handmaidens, *sahajiyas* refer to female practitioners as *manjaris,* venerate their gurus as Krishna's embodiments, and exalt direct sexual relationships between the woman devotee and guru-Krishna.

Sahajiyas' poetic discourses, however, were only important aids in my sustained discussions with them about their ritual world and cultivation of the body-as-place.

THE RITUAL JOURNEY

Sahajiya notebooks contain other very important linguistic tools: instructive tabular charts of ritual progression. While discussing their philosophy, most *sahajiyas* recited the charts by heart, as if they had become the summary of their spiritual lives, an involuntary body-memory.

I did a lot of talking myself by telling *sahajiyas* what I already knew about their *deha-tattva* (knowledge about the body). This knowledge was derived from general books on tantrism and approximate understandings from poems/proverbs/couplets in circulation. This assured them that I was sincere in my efforts and that they were not the first to give out their body-knowledge. *Sahajiyas* were willing to narrativize their spiritual/sexual experiences as long as they knew it was not about them but about their religious worldview. I then tallied understandings derived from conversations with charts narrated by my interlocutors. It is difficult without initiation to discern exact parallels between charts and stages of ritual practice, and almost impossible to be sure of ritual details. However, scholars often have not had access to these charts and so could not attempt to understand the parallels (Hayes 1999, 86). Thus, my ethnography seeks to contribute to the anthropology of Hinduism by providing approximate details of *sahajiyas'* ritual-sequences. Although the particulars or understandings of *sahajiya* rituals may be fuzzy or tentative, my analyses strive to intuit the central essence of their affective subjectivites.

The four ritual stages described in the four charts are called lands or places *(desh)*.[27] They describe the practitioner's spiritual stage, rituals to be performed, and emotions characterizing the devotee's affective mood. Although practitioners learn and recite the four charts at once, the ritual junctures they describe progress sequentially when the guru sanctions success at every stage.

Sthuler Desh *(Gross Place): Pre-initiation Stage*

TABLE I   STHULER DESH *(GROSS PLACE): PRE-INITIATION STAGE*

Place *(sthan)*	*Jombudvip*: karmic cycles of death and rebirth.
Time *(kal)*	Impermanent *kali*: mother's womb
Devotional object *(patra)*	Brahma: illusions of creation
Subservience to/dwelling house *(asraya)*	Parents' feet
Rituals performed *(alamban)*	Brahmanic rituals
Stimulation *(uddipan)*	Brahmanic scriptures
Kind of *bhakti (anga)*	Sixty-four disciplinary rules

This stage corresponds to the devotee's pre-initiation life, when without the guru's guidance one is still caught within Brahmanical scriptures and reproductive sex. The rituals he or she must practice to proceed toward the next spiritual stage/place are the sixty-four rules of *vaidhi bhakti*.

Pravarter Desh *(Place/Stage of Transformation): Initiation*

TABLE 2 PRAVARTER DESH *(PLACE/STAGE OF TRANSFORMATION): INITIATION*

Place	Navadvip: the devotee's heart, where Chaitanya is born
Time	Permanent *kali*: guru as Chaitanya introduces new emotions in the devotee
Object	Chaitanya Mahaprabhu
Subservience to	Guru's feet
Rituals	Chanting
Stimulation	Companionship of experienced *sahajiyas*
Bhakti	Nine rituals

This stage describes the devotee's *diksha*. On an auspicious day the devotee fasts from morning and wears new clothes. The guru gives him mantras in the right ear, a *tulsi* necklace, a sandalwood *tilak*, and chanting beads. *Diksha* mantras, devotees assert, are essential for the body's purification. *Sahajiyas* do not accept water from anyone who has not undergone initiation.

As for other Vaishnavas, the prime task at this stage is practicing the nine rules of *vaidhi bhakti*.

Repeating the initiation mantra every day, *sahajiyas* say, transforms the devotee's heart into Navadvip, where Chaitanya (saint/perceptive consciousness) is born.[28] Thus, *sahajiyas'* conceptualization of the body-as-place begins with initiation. Hariprasad, who received initiation at age 12, said, "The initiation-mantra is a part of our flesh. Krishna gives it when we are in the mother's womb. But we forget it. Then Krishna comes again as guru and reminds us the mantra. Thus, uttering it is remembering."

The common metaphor used by *sahajiyas* to explain the essence of initiation as spiritual birth is that of the *diksha*-guru, as father, planting the mantra-seed in the devotee's body-field. The body-field now needs nourishment from a mother-figure. This comes in the form of the *shiksha*-guru. Another common metaphor states that the *diksha*-guru provides a lamp and oil, and the *shiksha*-guru teaches how to light it and enlighten the hitherto dark, ignorant body.

After progress in the initiation stage, the *diksha*-guru tells the initiate to "go to the *shiksha* house" ("*shiksha-r ghore jao*") and "know

Vaishnava" ("*boishnob jano*"). *Sahajiyas* use these phrases to indicate that their supreme Vaishnava knowledge and practices begin only after esoteric training. As a *sahajiya* woman said, "After *diksha*, our onerous search begins for the *shiksha*-guru. He is responsible for our devotional bodies—the tool to know Vrindavan. He makes the road to the next *desh* easy [*sahaja*]. Then we eat only with people of the same *desh*."

If the initiated are a couple (married or otherwise), they receive esoteric mantras together, otherwise alone. The period between receiving initiation-mantras and esoteric mantras varies from less than a day to as much as ten years, depending on the devotee's spiritual progress. But *sahajiyas* say that it is important to receive esoteric mantras while young, since their bodies are then capable of producing essential substances.

Esoteric mantras are uttered in the initiate's left ear, the body's left side signifying feminine sexuality in tantric imaginings (Urban 2003, 282).

The initiate now journeys to the next land or ritual stage, experienced directly through the sense organs. These three lands correspond to the preparatory journey through the body, *gupta*-Vrindavan.

Sadhaker Desh *(Advanced Practitioner's Place): Ritual Stage*

TABLE 3   SADHAKER DESH *(ADVANCED PRACTITIONER'S PLACE): RITUAL STAGE*

Place	Vrindavan, the body-place
Time	*Dvapar*; guru-Krishna prepares the body to experience body-fluids
Object	Guru-Krishna
Subservience to	*Sakhi's* emotions: constant urge to arrange Radha-Krishna's (body-fluids') meetings
Rituals	Passionate thinking of Radha-Krishna
Stimulation	Foreplay of ritual sex
Bhakti	Five corporeal principles

Sahajiyas conceptualize the body as a cosmic reflection containing all the natural elements in its body-substances, the five *rasas*. The practices of this stage comprise realizing their spiritual potency as cosmic homologues and internalizing rather than evacuating them. Since the man's and woman's body-fluids are embodiments of Krishna and Radha, respectively, unifying and consuming them is conceptualized as retaining Vrindavan's pleasures within the body.

Sahajiyas say that ritual ingestions lead to overall health and physical beauty. One day, sitting inside their tiny hut, Hariprasad, Vishkaha, and I were discussing details of *sahajiya* ingestion practices. Vishakha said that I must know them as more than practice details, as they might seem filthy if not understood in the proper philosophical context. Herself very beautiful and with glowing skin, she explained, "Everything survives best when in its original place. This constitutes nature's well-being. When we put excreta back into our bodies, we are more healthy and beautiful. The five mantra-purified substances together taste like cosmic nectar." Hariprasad and Vishakha treated our conversation as mature philosophical talk, and did not have any disgust or shame while discussing.

Ritual specifications vary from guru to guru. But there are basic ingestion patterns. For instance, menses, known as *lal* (red), *rup* (beauty), or *phul* (flower), embody the essence of passionate femininity. Its ingestion, *laler kaj* ("work of red"), is believed to confer similar properties to the adept. Some say that on the third day of menses, blood is collected on a white cloth and its concentrate is consumed along with camphor, coconut water, and milk.[29] Others say this happens on the first night. Still others say that on all three days it is offered to the guru, used to wash his feet, and then consumed by the couple. In other narratives the guru and disciple-couple rub it in along with body-oil on the first and third days and consume it on the second.

Similarly, urine, claimed to have both spiritual and antiseptic value, is used every day for drinking early in the morning (*joler kaj* or 'work of water') and applying with turmeric on the body. Some say they do it only on three alternate days weekly. Some *sahajiyas* say they drink their own urine, while others exchange with partners.

Apart from this, all five fluids (feces, urine, semen, blood, and female orgasmic fluid) are applied on the body together and ingested along with Ganga-water, *tulsi* leaves, milk, and honey. Fluids have to be taken in the right measurements, known as *rati* (love). *Seva*, in *sahajiya* cosmology, refers to ingestion, and serving Radha-Krishna translates as consumption of seminal essences. Practitioners claim that these fluids are very powerful and that unless one knows the right methods and mantras of ingestion, one will harm oneself. Sometimes devotees perform ingestion rituals before the guru, so he can assess their spiritual progress.

Ingestion practices (re)locate passion-substances in the corporeal place. Complex interplays of control and subservience, externality and internality, inform consumption rituals. They also impart qualities of femininity and empathy, indispensable for successful ritual sex.

Ingestion of excreta, *sahajiyas* say, requires tremendous mental strength. Its successful execution is a test of practitioners' mettle of discipline. Hariprasad said, "These elements make us essentially. Our sense of ourselves rests on them. To perform these rituals, we have to leave aside *lajja* [shyness], *ghrina* [disgust], and *bhoy* [fear]. That gives a sense of immense power over our mind. Yet when I see body-substances before me, I realize my sameness with all others and therefore the ego's futility. *Rasas* are products of my passions but the passions are general. It does not belong to me but to Vrindavan."

Thus, these practices engender ego-effacement and generalized empathy. Openshaw (2010, 201) argues similarly that *baul* ingestion practices dissolve the boundaries between self and non-self and therefore are expressions of love (2002, 247).

The moment of externality of body-essences from the body-self offers the practitioner an objectivity and informed distance or abstinence from his or her elemental constitution. Their essential sameness and primal connectedness with all others establishes one's basic subservience to the empathic potentials of body-Vrindavan's fluids. Applying fluids to the body surface, the sensuous interface between the inside and outside, performs the intermesh of the singular and the general.

As in *goswamis'* and *babajis'* practices, discipline (*vidhi*) transforms into passion (*raga*) through these rituals. The term *raga* carries additional significance in *sahajiya* cosmology. It also means the passion-color red (*lal*), and *lal* in turn means menstrual blood. *Sahajiyas'* practices, though entirely different from other Vaishnavas, thus also embody principles of *raganuga bhakti*: a passionate devotion of subservience.

Hariprasad continued, "But the point is not to stop at the sense of sameness. We then consume it. If maleness is in penetration, femininity is in absorption.[30] We bring fluids back into the inside. We then want to live in this Vrindavan forever." Thus realizing one's sameness with others engenders empathy and humility, which are then internalized by consuming body-substances. Internality and humility/subservience are best characterized through social ideals of self-abnegating womanhood, and phenomenologically as absorption, being a feminine attribute. Thus, whether the practitioner is male or female, they should embody egolessness and femininity, cherished qualities of the lovers of Krishna.

Active and passive affective dimensions are co-constitutive in ritual ingestion (Morley 2001, 78). Sarukkai (2002, 465) argues that eating is a dimension of the inside and excretion of the outside, and in their simultaneous indispensability there is the primal relatedness and reversibility of self and other/world, immanence and transcendence, such that "we eat the world and the world eats us."

The phenomenology of *sahajiya* body-place thus falls between what Persson (2007, 47), following Leder, calls "ecstatic" and "dys-appearance" models of embodiment: the senses of moving outside the body, and of making the body itself the "thematic" object. When body-substances are let out and then consumed, the sense of *having* a body is established via the distance from its substances, followed by their reintegration. The body belongs to practitioners as much as is estranged from them, embodying a somatic empathy Csordas (2004, 170) calls "intimate alterity." While Radha-Krishna and their passionate love-play are within the body-Vrindavan, they are simultaneously also outside and shared by all.

These practices also help us understand how *sahajiya* philosophy borrows from classical Sanskrit rasaesthetics. Similar to the basic tenets of *rasa* theory, when dormant psychological dispositions in *sahajiyas* receive external stimuli in the form of devotional practices learned from gurus, the best possible sentiments and sensations (*rasa*) engross the *sahajiya rasika*. She or he has to be in the position of an objective, impersonal, empathic spectator to be able to realize and relish such *rasa* (Bose 1934, 20–21).

When the guru is convinced of the devotee's physical and psychological discipline, and his or her progress in embodying feminine empathy through ingestion rituals, he or she is taught how to cultivate the new perfect *siddha deha* and practice ritual sex. Devotees' feminine passion and egoless Krishna-love are then characterized as the *manjari's* emotion.

Manjari sadhana is a most concealed aspect of a practitioner's life. The devotee-couple approaches the guru when they want renunciation and to sense Vrindavan pleasures directly. Then, five other *sahajiyas*, as witnesses (*shakkhi*) of the same spiritual *desh*, grant the guru permission, and he performs ritual sex with the female adept. The guru is considered to be the best embodiment of spiritual and sexual expertise. Thus, the woman experiences perfect bliss for the first time, while her partner learns the expert methods from the guru. If the guru wishes, he pulls up his ejaculatory semen. Or he gives the mixture of his fluid and the woman's to the devotee-couple to taste and internalize. Sharing body-fluids becomes a metaphor for sharing pleasures of *sahajiyas'* body-Vrindavans (Hanssen 2006, 99). Chakrabarti (2001, 137–78) says that the female devotee, consumed by the guru, now becomes the guru-god's tasted *prasad* and is enjoyed by her partner as his blessing.

Not all devotees experience these pleasures; it is considered the greatest spiritual privilege. Radharani, lucky in this regard, bashfully said, "Guru helped me transform from bud to flower. My body-flower was then ready for offering to Krishna. He purified the body-vessel with which I could get glimpses of Radha's pleasures in Vrindavan. I went to my guru just after puberty. The bee came when the honey was ready." Like Vishakha, Radharani insisted that I understand these practices in a philosophical light, or else there is the possibility of misunderstanding.

The guru accepts food from the initiate-couple only after this transformation to the next spiritual place/land. This marks their acceptance into *sahajiya* renunciate tradition. Radharani explained, "Renunciation means giving up everything to god. Once both partners give their all to guru (she gives her body and her partner gives her), we are fit to be renouncers. As *manjaris,* we do not belong to each other. We are Vrindavan's residents."

There are contradictory appraisals of the guru's role during *manjari sadhana.* Some imagine him as Krishna, sharing his love with the Vrindavan maidens. Others view him as Radha, or her *sakhi,* or *manjari,* sharing pleasures of her body-Vrindavan with the new *manjari.* White (2000, 14), in his discussion of tantric sex, says that guru–disciple sexual intimacy is the embodiment of transfer of feminine energy. Still others imagine him as Chaitanya, teaching passionate ways of subservient love.

The couple is now ready to accept *yukta-vairagya.* This is also known as *gopi-sannyas,* or renunciation as lovers of Krishna, since both partners now embody an ego-effaced passionate feminine mood (Openshaw 2007, 320). *Sahajiya* renunciation implies not sexual abstinence but an anti-ejaculatory pleasurable sexuality such that the couple can no longer have children. The renunciate rhetoric of "giving up everything" binds *sahajiyas'* social and carnal lives. They give up material attachments to households and procreation, and beg for sustenance.

I was once invited to a married couple's renunciation ceremony. A large number of *sahajiyas* had gathered for the occasion. Led by the *sannyas* guru, they were singing *kirtans.*[31] After some time the couple arrived, in new white clothes. While white symbolizes purity, Chakrabarti (2001, 154) argues that *sahajiya* renouncers wear white also as symbolic of semen. The woman's marks of marital life—her vermillion, bangles, and so on—were taken off. The couple's heads were shaved, and they were given begging bags (*jholas*), bowls (*kamandul*), and large sticks (*danda*): typical renunciation markers.

The guru uttered the renunciation-mantra in their ears.[32] A piece of loincloth was tied across their eyes. Hanssen (2006, 108) says that tying the loincloth around the head marks the cranial abode from where the seminal seed is said to descend. Then two senior renouncers took them on a begging round to seven houses.

When they returned, the guru helped them throw three handfuls of collected rice grains behind their heads, symbolizing their obligation to pray first for the guru's food, then for other Vaishnavas', and finally for their own. Then they picked the grains from the ground and put them back in the begging-bags. *Sahajiyas* informed me that forty-five days later a feast would be arranged to celebrate the couple's new life, and those rice grains would be used then. This entire episode is also known as receiving *bhek* (renouncer's clothes) or *desh-parivartan* (transformation to a new place).[33]

Renunciation is not essential for a subsequent life of ritual sex, although it is conducive. For single practitioners, the guru assigns a partner from among his disciples, and they choose whether they want to live together, get married, or take renunciation. Married couples practice ritual sex when they no longer want children.[34]

Siddhir Desh *(Perfect Place): Final Stage/Destination*

TABLE 4 SIDDHIR DESH *(PERFECT PLACE): FINAL STAGE/DESTINATION*

Place	Eternal Vrindavan: the man's head and woman's vagina, where Radha-Krishna (sexual fluids) meet
Time	Lonely honey-night (midnight and after), when the couple perform passionate rituals
Object	Radha, who embodies highest passions
Subservience to	*Manjari*: implying both devotees' moods and the guru-*manjari*, whose instructions are followed
Rituals	Sexual love
Stimulation	Krishna's flute-sound
Bhakti	Passion

The principal practice of this stage is *pitridhan raksha,* or protection of seminal patrimony (Bottero 1991; Salomon 1995, 197). The guru now teaches the couple secrets of fluid-retention.

Sahajiyas assert that seminal retention is essential for the body's protection, that is its vibrancy, hormonal balance, and pleasure, and thus men and women pull up their fluids through appropriate breathing exercises (*domer kaj*) and mantras right at the moment of anticipated orgasm. This, they say, ensures prolonged sexual heightening and serves to preserve the deities' (fluids) love in Vrindavan within themselves. The metaphor used to express this is that the lamp (sexual pleasure) must be lit all night, without any oil depletion (ejaculation). At this stage both partners embody the impetus of "being a woman," in terms of both their retentive sexuality and a feminine mood toward love.[35]

In the neighborhood in which I primarily did my fieldwork, there was a 108-year-old man who, though partially deaf, was still able-bodied. His wife told me that in their youth he was very good at *domer kaj* (withholding breath), and this was a well-known fact among other *sahajiyas,* who revered him as an almost iconic figure. Important reasons for the significance of these rituals in the collective psyche include their association with longevity and spiritual brilliance.

My *sahajiya*-friends were willing to discuss things up to this point, after which they insisted that I learn more from a renowned guru. A local mason gave me Gour's address. Gour was the *diksha-* and *shiksha-guru* of many *sahajiyas* in Navadvip. He lived with his wife, Sadhana, in a town close to Navadvip. Sadhana was initially not comfortable with my discussing intimate sexual details with her husband. Gour's personal room, which had a lot of books and where he read and meditated, was separated from the rest of his house by a dining space. He preferred to talk to me in this personal room, so his children or wife would not disturb us. Eventually, however, I explained my academic purpose to Sadhana, and we all found it more relaxed to have her join the conversations. For a sustained period Gour tested my seriousness of purpose. He gave me poems to memorize, books to read, and a series of esoteric questions to ponder. However, the lessons progressed quickly when I told him I had practiced yoga after college and discussed my own breathing experiences. Convinced that I would be able to feel *sahajiya* discourses, he gradually paved a rough path for my journey into the interiors of the *sahajiya* body-place. We had long and intense discussions, sometimes extending to over eight hours. But we enjoyed every minute of it.

The basis of *sahajiyas'* cultivation of the body-place rests on an imagined homology between the lotus-like body and Radha-Krishna's meeting place in celestial Vrindavan, also structured as a lotus. The body-interior is divided into six circular energy-centers called *chakras* (or *mandalas,* or *padmas*). Cellular configurations are pictured as lotuses, since like lotus-petals they expand when stimulated (with sensory heightening), and contract into darkness when left in an uncultivated state.

These lotus-structures are psychic formations configured out of 72,000 nerves which ordinarily remain coiled as a dormant, snake-like energy reservoir, called *kulakundalini,* at the base of the spinal cord. In tantric understandings generally, this essential energy reservoir is imagined as passionate feminine vitality. When touched through breathing exercises, the nerves relax, elongate, and form the vertical arrangement of circular energy-centers along the spinal chord. Each *chakra* measures as long as a stretched palm. They are the *muladhar* (between anus and genitals), *svadhishthan* (energy-circuit around genitals), *manipur* (between genitals and navel), *anahata* (between navel and chest/heart), *vishuddha* (between chest and throat), and *agya* (up to the middle of the eyebrows).[36]

Apart from these, Gour mentioned another couple of *chakras* which are outside breathing ambits and absolutely essential for their practices. They are the vagina and the *shahasrar* (from the eyebrows to the top of the head, formed of a hundred lotus-petals). He said, "These are true *gupta*-Vrindavans, where Radha-Krishna meet. These are secret places where not even breath reaches, accessible only to diligent practitioners."

The point of yogic *sadhana* is to use concentrated breathing and mantras to stimulate the *kulakundalini,* reverse breath-air up the spinal cord through urethral pressure along the different *chakras,* stimulating them on the way, and send it to the *shahasrar.* As Irigaray (2002, cited in Kearns 2005, 112) notes from her own experiences, attentiveness paid to yogic breathing makes it more capable of direction.

In *sahajiyas'* ethno-anatomical understandings, three main nerves (the *ila, pingala*, and *shushumna*) run up the spinal cord. Three times a day, the practitioner practices *pranayama* (controlled breathing), exciting the nerves and pulling purified breath up the *shushumna,* the main central nerve. Through sustained practice in breathing and mantra, one masters the art of fluid-retention.

Between inhalation (*purag*) and exhalation (*rechak*) there is an almost imperceptible pause (*kumbhak*). The purpose is to increase this breath-retention time. I understood these key breathing techniques by practicing myself. Sitting with a straight spine, it is important to withhold the breath as long as possible, still the mind, and keep external distractions away.

Sahajiyas emphasize that rather than being a slave to involuntary breathing, one should know how to control it. This serves to calm the mind, without which subsequent emotions become lust-prone and self-directed.[37] Withholding breath is also said to thicken the sperm, and the more concentrated it is, the easier it becomes to retain it.

During *pranayam,* breath-air circulates in the body, creating intense undulations through the energy-centers. The four spiritual lands/places described in the charts are then said to be simultaneously present within the affective body, reflecting the adept's progressive vertical/spiritual development. The breath's journey is thus conceptualized as the practitioner's stagiest travel through body-Vrindavan.

Rousing the spiral nerve-complex in the body's base, which corresponds to uncultivated lands (*sthuler desh*), the breath rises up to the navel. The navel, the exact center of the body-mass, is imagined as like the central point of Krishna's chariot wheels. Just as air passing through the wheel-center is responsible for the chariot's perfect balance and mobility, so air travelling through the body-center stimulates its balance and journeys to the chest. Breath-air is purified in the area between the chest and neck-base. The heart-region is known as *anahata padma,* literally "the (yet) unheard lotus." The point is to arouse the purified air, which then reverberates to mantra-sounds given by the guru. Thus, this area corresponds to the transformative land/initiation stage (*pravarter desh*).[38] The more purified breath there is in the heart-space, the greater is the clarity of perception (McDaniel 1995, 43). Gour breathed slowly and indicated the upward journey of breath with his hands, saying, "Our bodies have nine openings/ doors: anus, genitals, mouth, two nostrils, and pairs of eyes and ears. When practicing controlled breathing we shut all of them. The Vrindavan *kunja* [bower] where Radha-Krishna perform their *lilas* also has nine doors, which remain shut all night. Our hearts are then transformed into Vrindavan, where through breath-retention we feel Radha-Krishna's love." From the heart air travels to the middle of the eyebrows, where practitioners claim to be able to see the deities if breathing techniques are perfect. This corresponds to the ritual place (*sadhaker desh*).

During ritual sex, Gour explained, seminal fluids also travel the introjected subtle breath-path, finally reaching the cranial center where fluids embodying deities meet and the body manifests Vrindavan.

The *sahajiya* (ideal-typical) corporeal space is imagined such that sexual fluids reside in the middle of the head, the lust-free spiritual place, Vrindavan (*siddhir desh*), and journey through the body in accordance with the waxing and waning of the moon (see also Doniger 1997, 176). This is emblematic of the constant flow of love from Vrindavan (McDaniel 1995, 50). Gour always had his notebook handy when discussing these intricate issues, so that he would not omit any details. The vagina-lotus is imagined as containing nine parts with three divisions each. Every day a single drop of the woman's sexual fluid travels from her head and fills a portion. Thus, it takes 27 days for her vagina to be brimming with sexual potency, and on the 28th day, at the full moon, her period starts. Similarly, the man's fluid journeys through his body and on the 28th day meets Radha in *gupta*-Vrindavan (vagina/head).

Alter (1994, 52, borrowing from O'Flaherty 1980, 179–90), calls such imaginative pleasurable processes "internal ejaculation."

Some *sahajiyas* said that on menstrual days the couple does not have sex since their bodies are then already experiencing the bliss of manifest Vrindavan. A couplet summarizes this: "The ocean does not have water, yet the lotus is afloat; Radha does not have Krishna, yet she smiles," meaning that the vagina is afloat on menstrual blood; semen (Krishna) does not meet blood (Radha), but the woman is still overflowing with her feminine sensibility. Some among them said that they do however unite Radha-Krishna through ingestion on these days.

The couple practices ritual sex on other days of the month. Before intercourse the man and woman calm each other's sexual excitement, while also maintaining pleasures, by rubbing each other with body-oil (*tel seva*). The man utters mantras while touching her feet, knees, vagina, navel, breasts, neck, mouth, tongue, nose, and eyes. This sanctifies every part of the body-vessel which will manifest Vrindavan. Both partners utter mantras all through the act and instead of ejaculating, reverse their fluids' flow before the anticipated climax.

Just as I can never be sure of the exact connotations of *sahajiya* terms without initiation, it is not possible to be confident about ritual possibilities. My interlocutors themselves also took very different views of these practices. However, the multiplicity of possibilities does not alter their basic theological premises of absorption/retention of divine principles and the experience of their body-as-place.

Some said that both partners pull back their fluids and experience heightened pleasure as they take them back to where they belong.[39] In this case, the deities' union is conceived in terms of the act (*kriya*) of man (Krishna)–woman (Radha) union, rather than the fluids' meeting. If the man excels in the breathing practices, the woman can experience three orgasms, the third of which when released gives the couple the taste of blissful Vrindavan. Sadhana said, "Our disciples are attracted to this path not only because of its spirituality but also because it is a sure basis of marital success. We never need condoms, contraceptives or abortions. So our bodies maintain the purity essential for worship." Thus, intrinsic to spiritual (and partnership) success is the rhetoric of pleasure, a significant source of continued membership in *sahajiya*-Vaishnavism.

But others say that the woman does not pull back fluids. Rather, the man knows techniques of pulling hers up with his own, such that the fluids/deities then meet in his head, the *gupta*-Vrindavan (see also Hayes 2000, 312). Thus, some *sahajiyas* say that Krishna meets Radha (female sexual fluid) in Vrindavan (the head) every day and her fullest embodied form when she is manifest completely in the woman's vagina/Vrindavan during her menstrual state. Thus, they claim to have ritual sex on menstrual days as well.

Still others argue that the man can pull up only his own fluid, not the woman's; and that when partners are unable to control their lust and have orgasms, they mix the fluids and consume them in equal measure, to take the sacred substances back into their bodies.

Some scholars have argued that tantric ritual sex is biased toward male spirituality, as he alone is able to make the fluids/deities unite.[40] However, I did not find this opinion among Navadvip's *sahajiyas,* who foreground the rhetoric of pleasure (*ananda*) more generally as the basis of their respective spiritual successes. Not only do both partners derive the utmost pleasure during ritual sex, irrespective of who is responsible for reverting the fluids, but this pleasure is also based on ideals of feminine empathy cultivated equally by both practitioners.

Other stereotypical ideas in the anthropology of tantrism are that practitioners embody perfect monism in considering themselves as deities, and heightened agentive self-control in the final act of redirecting fluids.[41] However, I argue that tantric practices are conceptualized differently depending on the particular ethnographic context. Navadvip's *sahajiyas,* in their claim to be true Vaishnavas, interpret their sexual experiences in a language similar to that of *goswamis* and *babajis.* While they consider their body-fluids to be embodiments of deities, they equally stress that Vaishnava divinities are also outside them. There is therefore a Vrindavan within them and a celestial Vrindavan outside. They don't imagine their sexual pleasures as the pleasures *of* deities, therefore, but rather as giving them a sense of what the deities experience. Rather than control, they say that in the final stage of ritual sex they embody subservience toward Radha-Krishna. While Narayanan (1999) argues that *bhakti* can engender *shakti* (power), *sahajiyas* embody a shift in the reverse direction, from self-power to submissiveness.

In the final, androgynous stage, the man and woman, as Hayes (1995, 337) puts it, share their feminine absorbent bodies, minds, and emotions. The experience of their own sexual-affective states as *manjaris* then is only a performance of the "originary memory" of Radha-Krishna's love, a "passivity in activity" (Husserl 1973, 108, cited in Casey 1992, 273). *Sahajiyas'* own pleasures are deemed to be glimpses of the deities' sexual experience. Here the status of both partners is equal as ras-aesthetic witnesses of objective divine affect. *Sahajiya* sexual/spiritual relations thus offer them the possibility of perfect empathy, in feeling together what Radha-Krishna feel. As in *goswamis'* and *babajis'* practices, the practitioner appreciates his or her own emotions as "impersonal" (McDaniel 1995, 46–47) and belonging to deities in Vrindavan. This further establishes *sahajiyas'* place in the broader rasaesthetic context of Bengal-Vaishnavism. At the height of affective excess, the (internal) orgasmic state, when sexual fluids as Radha-Krishna meet in the vagina/head and drown the body, the sense of the observing ego-in-control disappears. The body as the container of Vrindavan, that is, veiled-Vrindavan, then manifests the body-as-place.

Gour reflected sensitively on this state and said, "After prolonged sexual activity one feels relaxed. That is when we remember Radha-Krishna. What is in us is not ours. It is Vrindavan's *prem* that deities are enjoying in us. My *ahamkar* is then lost in subservience [*anugatya*]. It is beautiful! At this moment, we do not think 'I am Krishna' but 'I am Krishna's.' I have had Radha-Krishna's glimpse in me. Now I want to witness their beauty when I die and go to Vrindavan."

This interplay between senses of the sacred place as both within and outside the body is also apprehended during breathing practices. Practiced breathing makes the head, the topmost energy-center, feel light and spacious. The sense of the universe outside sharpens, and simultaneously the sense of bounded selfhood softens. In general, yoga is associated by scholars with cultivating a sense of emptiness. Persson (2007, 49) uses Bachelard's notion of "intimate immensity" and argues that emptiness is considered a positive experiential state in Indian spiritualities. In analyzing Satyananda yogic practices and breathing experiences, therefore, she problematizes Casey's emphasis on place and argues in favor of a productive dialogue between senses of space and place. She cites a number of phenomenological dyads as contrasting interplays of placeness and spaceness, for instance grounding/expansion, foundation/subtlety, interiority/exteriority, autonomy/unity, and control/surrender (44–46).

I agree with Persson that yogic experiences involve a subtle play of senses of space and place, and I find both Casey and Bachelard useful for my analysis. Since *sahajiyas* are not unproblematically monistic like other yogis, they conceptualize yogic space in terms of the embodied sensuous place, Vrindavan.[42] They imagine the cosmos not as an abstract empty space but as the beautiful abode where Radha-Krishna perform their *lilas*. Thus, Casey's idea of embodied place holds relevance in my case. However, Bachelard's (1994) conceptualization of interiorized place-experiences is also useful since *sahajiyas* experience the sacred place within their bodies. Thus, I extend Casey's (1993) concept of "implacement" from the body-in-place to body-as-place. But unlike Bachelard's insistence on interiorized experiences as being governed by abstract consciousness, *sahajiyas'* experiences of the body-as-place are extremely embodied.

Sahajiyas' cultivation of the body-place is also the occasion of fine-tuned sensory excess. Their breathing practices enhance inner senses. Sadhana said, "When the body's nine doors are shut and breath travels inside, when Vrindavan is manifest in the body, then external senses surrender to breath and breath develops inner senses." The interiorized body-space foregrounds theoretical insights into the anthropology of internal rather than external senses. Morley (2001, 76) suggests similarly that spiritual breathing helps in the proprioceptive act of turning toward the interior corporeal mass, translating between external and internal perception.

The affective metaphors used to describe body-Vrindavan in the final ritual stage (known as the Perfect Place in the *sahajiya* chart) are also those generally used in describing nocturnal celestial Vrindavan. Poems cite dark romantic clouds, the deep night, and the blue Yamuna as reminiscent of Krishna's skin color. Metaphors of dark nights, Cataldi (1993, 48–50) says, following Merleau-Ponty, apprehend the hidden tactility of the body's depths and interiors. Similarly, the rippling Yamuna in *sahajiya* cosmology also refers to the woman's sexual fluids. Songs describe solitary forest-bowers as deep spaces in full-moon nights where the deity-consort meet for their secret trysts. In the body-place imaginary the forest-bowers become the vagina where fluids meet during feminine sexual peaks.

Sonic and olfactory allusions by *sahajiyas* also suggest inner senses of intimacy. Practitioners state for instance that they hear the sharp buzz of crickets or smell sweet *kanara* flowers when practicing yogic breathing or performing ritual sex. Both crickets and *kanara* flowers also feature in the imagining of celestial Vrindavan forests. However, the greatest stimulant at this stage is the sound of Krishna's flute (see **table 4**). It serves as both an aphrodisiac and a post-coital soother. As Krishna inhales, he draws devotees' feminine hearts irresistibly toward him, and as he exhales, their body-pores become like flute-openings which touch Krishna's lips, and his warm breath dances up the devotees' spiral nerves echoing inner sounds. The entire body-flute resounds with the maddening melody.[43] Irigaray's (2002, 85, cited in Kearns 2005, 110) phenomenological analysis of interiorized breathing as cultivating femininity is appropriate here in making sense of the body's feminine breath-dance.

Other auditory references are to the monotonous sounds of Radha's anklets and to buzzing honey-bees coming from the middle of the heart.[44] Krishna is then compared to the bee, restless to taste the devotee's love-honeyed heart. Words are always inadequate windows to affective experiences. Being sensitive to the *sahajiya* skin required a fine balance among talking, listening, feeling, and imagining. As Nast (1998) says, the anthropologist's body-as-place must site others' affects within oneself. So when I heard about these sounds, I told Sadhana how when I practiced yoga, in a posture called *bhramar-asana* (honey-bee posture), I had to shut my eyes and ears and make the nagging sound of bees with my mouth closed. Her eyes lit up, and she said softly, "Yes, exactly—when we hear these sounds we get current-like sensations [goose bumps]. Our skin is then like *kadamphul*." The tactile metaphor of this sweetly scented marigold-like flower, whose petals are identical and blossom together, is the visual counterpart of the clarity of the insistent, repetitive, granular sounds of the love-struck buzzing bee. Thus, when the sacred place manifests, that is, when seminal fluids as embodiments of Radha-Krishna meet in body-Vrindavan, the hidden interiors of the *sahajiya* body-place delight in the vision of deities, the smell of wildflowers, passionate sounds, and the lover's touch.

OTHER SENSES OF PLACE

Sahajiyas cultivate various techniques of sexual exaltation, since they consider carnal pleasures the most significant means of realizing Vrindavan. Transformation of the body-space to Vrindavan translates as the preservation of body-fluids. Thus, *sahajiyas* experience their bodies-as-places. I have argued that *sahajiyas*' experiences of emplacement in the internal corporeal space are both discursively constructed and affectively sensed at the most immediate visceral levels.

However, my fieldwork involved the broadest possible journey among different kinds of Vaishnavisms. Travelling from Navadvip to Mayapur, across the river, was like travelling to another kind of *bhakti,* and a completely different sense of place. Mayapur's socio-religious landscape is dominated by ISKCON, which is composed of devotees from all over the world. Navadvip's Vaishnavas view ISKCON as a modern money-making institution which in its zeal for internationalization has made of their religion something superficial and bereft of philosophical rigor. ISKCON devotees, in turn, are highly critical of Navadvip's Vaishnavas and their esoteric practices. Just like Navadvip's Vaishnavas, ISKCON devotees embody Vaishnava principles of ego-effaced love and service toward the deity-couple in Vrindavan; but they interpret the tenets very differently. Rather than interiorized spaces of imagination or the body, ISKCON venerates the physical place, Mayapur, as *gupta*-Vrindavan, and devotees perform services toward deities by being productive bene-factors of monumental temples, performing developmental work in Mayapur, offering religious services to villagers, and preaching Krishna Consciousness to the entire world. It is to ISKCON's radically different idea of being a Vaishnava and experiencing and serving the sacred place that we now turn.

CHAPTER 5

Serving *Gupta*-Vrindavan: Devotional Service in the Physical Place and the Workings of the "International Society"

INTRODUCTION: SERVING THE PLACE

Fieldwork in Mayapur was completely different from fieldwork in Navadvip. The people, the place, the kind of devotion—everything was starkly dissimilar.

In a series, along the main road which cuts across the small village of Mayapur, with stretches of agricultural fields on the other side, are large, sanitized temples and guest-houses built by Gaudiya Math. Like Navadvip's *sahajiyas,* Mayapur's villagers are poor and primarily live by farming. In sharp contrast to Mayapur's rural background, however, the main attraction for pilgrims and my primary fieldwork site is 500 acres of enclosed land and a walled compound with the most modern, up-to-date facilities, unprecedented in any Indian village, within which approximately 500 Indian and foreign ISKCON devotees reside and worship. ISKCON devotees are mostly foreigners and professional, affluent, English-speaking middle-class or rich Indians, who offer financial patronage to ISKCON through unstinting donations and publicize the institution to their families and friends. Mayapur has one of the largest concentrations of foreign devotees in India.

The International Society for Krishna Consciousness (ISKCON) was founded in New York in 1966 by A. C. Bhaktivedanta, known among devotees as Prabhupad (god's servant), an English-educated man from Calcutta who became initiated into Vaishnavism and in his later life preached Vaishnavism in the West to fulfill his guru's wish of spreading "Krishna Consciousness" internationally. Over the decades ISKCON has established over 400 centers internationally, including temples, schools, and vegetarian restaurants. ISKCON's headquarters in Mayapur, instituted in 1971–72, is central for devotees since ISKCON devotees believe that Mayapur is Chaitanya's birthplace, that it has the highest standards of ritual worship, and that the regular lives led by Mayapur's devotees are exemplary for others.

ISKCON's establishment is the most influential presence in the village, since the massive pilgrimage ISKCON generates contributes toward many villagers' livelihoods—with buses bringing pilgrims from Calcutta and districts in West Bengal, boatmen ferrying pilgrims from Navadvip to Mayapur, rickshaw-pullers taking them around, and shopkeepers selling deities' idols, pictures, household *puja* goods, and *kirtan* CDs right outside ISKCON's enclosure.

ISKCON's separate enclave is distinctly different from the rest of Mayapur and from Navadvip's temples. In contrast to Navadvip's bustling town culture and general layout of devotional sites which are not centralized under any single administrative authority, ISKCON is highly organized. In the midst of an interior Bengali village it has made available to its resident devotees and pilgrims every modern facility, from pizzas and cybercafés to air conditioners, computers, and money-exchange bureaus. However, the predominant feeling one gets while walking through ISKCON's spanking-clean enclosure is one of a modern yet spiritually maintained atmosphere.

After entering the main gate one sees a small hut which has been preserved since this was where Prabhupad lived in 1972–76, before other buildings were constructed. Here devotees sing Radha-Krishna's names in rotation twenty-four hours a day. There are two massive, grand, well-maintained marble structures in the enclave: the Chandrodaya Temple, dedicated to Radha, Krishna, and Chaitanya, and Prabhupad's shrine.

The larger-than-life-size, majestically dressed idols in these temples are offered grand *pujas* with plenty of food, amidst the loud sounds of conch shells and ecstatic *kirtans* by hundreds of devotees, four to six times a day. The most significant construction taking place, however, is of the Temple of the Vedic Planetarium. Funded primarily by an ISKCON devotee, Alfred Ford (currently one of the principal stakeholders of the Ford company), its total budget is close to USD 70 million. The 35-story temple is planned to be completely covered in gold and the

FIGURE 12. Prabhupad's *samadhi* temple.

highest temple in the world. Inside, in a planetarium, devotees will be shown cosmic images as depicted in the *Bhagavata Purana*.

Apart from this, spread over ISKCON's grounds are the *goshala* (cow-shed) occupying five acres of land, where devotees' children bathe and feed cows, Krishna's favorite animal; buildings assigned as residential ashrams for celibate devotees (*brahmacharis*); a large residential area with sophisticated accommodations for married devotees; two *gurukuls* (residential schools giving children spiritual training) and two other schools for devotees' children; guest houses with modern facilities; large restaurants serving both Indian and Western food; and around six three- or four-story administrative buildings. There are also well-kept parks with benches, where pilgrims and tourists relax.

ISKCON is run like a commercial office. Devotees have designated hierarchized posts such as general manager, CEO, treasurer, or ordinary worker, and serve the institution's maintenance from large numbers of offices, known as departments, spread across the administrative buildings. The big offices are expensively equipped, with marble floors, air conditioners, and computers. Since these offices conduct spiritual work, their atmosphere is equally spiritually maintained, with recorded chants of deities' names playing in the background, the smell of incense, and large, beautiful paintings of Radha-Krishna in the celestial Vrindavan forests.

Navadvip's Vaishnavas almost never visit Mayapur, but ISKCON remains an important reference point for them. They repeatedly told me that ISKCON is improperly obsessed with spending money on opulent, grandiose structures, and that ISKCON's idea of devotion as effective management and embellishment of physical sites is superficial and not true devotional experience. Implicit in this claim is the understanding common to Navadvip's Vaishnavas that religion is true when cultivated at inner devotional levels of the body or mind, rather than being limited to the veneration of external physical spaces.

I did my fieldwork in Mayapur after my fieldwork in Navadvip. So a problem was that I had partly internalized other Vaishnavas' opinions of ISKCON, and in my initial observations I could not fathom what ISKCON's lavish expenditure on temples, its official hierarchized structure, and its devotees' modern lifestyles could have to do with Vaishnavism— till I realized that excellent organization, well-planned space and services, and a lifestyle which makes devotees productive are essential constituents of ISKCON devotees' very different understanding of Vaishnavism.

Like other Vaishnavas, ISKCON devotees seek to realize their spiritual selves in Radha-Krishna's abode through their daily religious practices. Their major difference from other Vaishnavas is that rather than interior-ized spaces of the mind-heart or body, they identify and venerate only the physical geography of Mayapur as *gupta* (veiled) Vrindavan. They argue that every physical space is a potential veiled-Vrindavan and has the capacity to manifest Vrindavan if offered appropriate devotional ser-vices. Devotees embody an intimate, sacred relationship with Mayapur by offering *seva,* which they translate as "devotional service," toward every element constituting its physical landscape, that is, the temples, the temple-deities, Mayapur's organization, and the welfare of Mayapur's people, and indeed as many people in the world as possible. Devotees agree that just as some day, after lives of spiritual perfection, they will serve the deity-couple and their devotees in cosmic Vrindavan, similarly, since Mayapur is indistinguishable from Vrindavan, their loving services there are spiritually as worthy as their services in celestial Vrindavan.

So, all the conditioned devotional senses remain engrossed in an affective rapture in ISKCON's spiritually organized atmosphere: with the sight and feel of large, clean temples, the sounds of ecstatic *kirtans,* and the smells and tastes of incense and *prasadam.* Devotees' "topo-philic" response to Mayapur's physical landscape, however, is simulta-neously directed to its being a symbol of eternal Vrindavan's transcen-dental import (Tuan 1974, 93, 150–53).

Thus, in this chapter I analyze another face of Vaishnavism and another specific dimension of the experience of place: one in which devotees conceptualize their entire life's mission as serving the physical sacred place where the deity-couple reside in grand temples, and realizing their essential selves as Radha-Krishna's servants. This commitment to devotional service involves a variety of activities, like financing, building, and embellishing temples; arranging the best possible administration and management for Mayapur; and serving the people who reside in Mayapur. ISKCON devotees unequivocally assert that rendering temple-deities the best possible *seva*—for instance, grand food, clothes, *pujas,* and most importantly love—is the best way to be a Vaishnava, rather than being improperly and prematurely concerned with divine sexuality, as practiced by other Vaishnavas.

There is a wide range of literature on ISKCON's history, philosophy, and spread to different countries, and the devotional services organized in its international centres.[1] What has however not been analyzed enough is the critical philosophy behind ISKCON's veneration of physical sacred spaces, and the related issue of the development of its different international centers. ISKCON's view of devotion, I argue, is intrinsically connected with its distinctive philosophy of place.

Unlike typical instances of South Asian populations moving westward in search of better life prospects, ISKCON has diasporic Indians who were initiated into Vaishnavism when abroad and chose to serve ISKCON there, or in Mayapur, or some other Indian place. Also, rather than Westerners only seeking "spiritual homes" in India (Khandelwal 2007), ISKCON has a combination of Westerners who serve ISKCON in the West, who have settled in India, especially Mayapur, and who switch between countries every year. ISKCON devotees' mobility therefore does not have any predetermined pattern and is characterized by flux. While Khandelwal (2007) argues for a complete acculturation of "Foreign Swamis" in the Hindu culture in India, ISKCON devotees also do not necessarily dissociate themselves from any place. Their sense of the sacred place is essentially mobile since they say that every physical site where they offer devotional services transforms into Vrindavan.

While studies of diasporas and international migratory flows focus on ways in which people either carry their senses of place and religion from the emigration site[2] or find new senses of place in the immigration site,[3] ISKCON devotees embody a distinct sense of place: of discovering Vrindavan anywhere on the global stage where there is an ISKCON temple and where devotees come together to render devotional service.

Valpey (2006, 150) argues similarly that for ISKCON the entire world is potentially Vrindavan. This philosophy guarantees immense mobility choice for ISKCON devotees, since exactly where they are located becomes immaterial, if every physical site where they offer devotional services transforms into Vrindavan, as they say. This does not simply imply a post-national scenario of migratory "ethnoscapes" (Appadurai 1996) but follows a spiritual reasoning not bound by logics of nationality. Thus, I agree with Kokot, Tololyan, and Alfonso (2004, 4) that "diaspora" and "locality," movement and fixity, may be interconnected at experiential levels. Casey (2001, 685) argues similarly that cosmopolitan mobility does not devalue the importance of experiencing a sense of place. Although the entire world is potentially experienced as Vrindavan by ISKCON devotees, Mayapur holds special importance for them, however, since it is Chaitanya's birthplace.

Like other Vaishnavas, ISKCON devotees argue that the experience of Vrindavan is effective only when the devotee cultivates ego-effacement; however, by this they mean working as a *goshthanandi,* one who derives pleasure from working collectively in an institution, rather than a *bhajananandi,* one who derives pleasure from solitary spiritual practices. ISKCON's philosophy is therefore different from other modern religious movements popular among affluent Indian classes, as discussed by Warrier (2005, 15) for instance, which foster "private" and "inward-looking" faith.

One afternoon as I was eating lunch at Govinda's, a restaurant in the ISKCON compound, I befriended a young boy of about 12 years. He had come with his parents, devotees from London, for a short stay in Mayapur. I asked, "Do you like Mayapur?" He replied confidently, "It's very nice! It's *gupta*-Vrindavan—everything is so beautiful, no one is hungry, and everyone is serving Krishna." All devotees understand "Krishna Consciousness" as willing devotional service such that the place they reside in is rendered physically attractive and organized, and the people, contented. Thus, they say, *seva* transforms any physical place into Krishna's *dham* (sacred place). The other activity all devotees identify as most significant is preaching this message of Krishna Consciousness to people. They say that spiritual love must not be confined to pleasures of the interiorized self, for instance in solitary meditation and practice (as embodied by other Vaishnavas), but should reach out to others. Reaching out to others in the contemporary world implies making religion attractive, by which they mean redefining religion to suit peoples' tastes.

FIGURE 13. Pilgrims being served *prasadam* in ISKCON's compound.

Thus, ISKCON's ideas of place and devotion are completely different from other Vaishnavas'. They realize Vrindavan by modernizing
Mayapur, building grand temples, beautifying gardens, making wide
roads for pilgrims, and serving Mayapur's villagers, Krishna's devotees,
by giving them access to life's basic facilities of food, health, and education. When temple-deities and devotees are served, the physical place
becomes Vrindavan.

My main concerns therefore are to document the everyday nature
of devotional services: toward Mayapur's effective management, elaborate temple rituals, the basic welfare of villagers, and massive preaching
ventures. Devotees of the "International Society" identify these services
as chief components of Krishna Consciousness, which transform any
physical location into Vrindavan. In order to employ members of the
global society in these common spiritual purposes, devotees downplay
all possible divisive binaries such as modern/non-modern, householder/
renouncer, and East/West. Although ISKCON's activities may seem similar to mundane work, devotees conceptualize these services as intrinsically spiritual and emotional, since they are directed with love toward
Radha-Krishna's pleasures.

Mohan,[4] a Hungarian devotee who was teaching at the boys' *gurukul* when I was doing fieldwork, said, "Our daily lives in Mayapur are
such that *everything* we do is spiritual service." Devotees rise before

four A.M., attend the grand morning *arati* in Chandrodaya Temple at four-thirty, chant deities' names (keeping count on basil seeds) for two hours sitting in the temple, and listen to senior devotees explain verses from the *Bhagavatam*, then get ready and go off for their respective devotional services. For the entire day, every single person is extremely busy serving somewhere; how busy one is is an indicator of how much one loves serving Mayapur. Idleness, devotees told me, is the mark of devotional laxity. There are devotees cooking in the temple kitchens, serving *prasadam* to pilgrims, selling books written by Prabhupada, distributing pamphlets explaining ISKCON's preaching programs, serving in the respective offices, assembling villagers and feeding them *prasadam* in villages close to Mayapur, and chanting to music on Mayapur streets. At six P.M. devotees assemble again in the temple for *arati*, listen to *Gita* explanations for an hour, and retire by nine.

ISKCON's focus on devotional service as forming the crux of emotional personhood comes close to Heidegger's idea of the work-world. He argues that one's intimate engagement with the work at hand helps the individual grasp the sense of dwelling and meaningful relation with place (Casey 2001, 684; Gibbs 2008, 2010). Kovacs (1986) also says that work is intrinsically related to transcendence. However, many devotees corrected me when I referred to their activities as "work." They are unwilling to call what they do "work"; it is simply *seva* toward gupta-Vrindavan. Material work and productivity become *seva* when practiced as embodiment of love for deities.

Routine execution of devotional services requires planned regimens of discipline and productivity. Devotees' notions of discipline are related to their understandings of emotion. Unlike other Vaishnavas, who assert that their spiritual journey is from *vaidhi bhakti* to *raganuga bhakti,* ISKCON devotees spend entire lives perfecting disciplined devotion, since they say it is easily understood and practiced by neophytes, especially foreign devotees. ISKCON's approach to devotion approximates Csordas's (2009, 4) opinion about exoteric religions: their simplicity and portability indicate possibilities of globalizing religion. ISKCON devotees follow the five essential principles of *vaidhi bhakti*: chanting, remembering Krishna's *lilas* by hearing verses from the *Bhagavata Purana* (these first two are discussed in chapter 6), worshipping temple-altar deities, serving them in association with other devotees, and residing in and serving spiritual places, in this case, Mayapur.[5] Devotees additionally argue that passionate devotional excesses are detrimental to planned, industrious efforts and organizational *seva*.

So, while Navadvip's Vaishnavas associate ISKCON's splendor, huge monetary investments, and popularity among foreigners with a shallow, materialistic, and immature appreciation of religion, the emotional exuberance embodied by these other Vaishnavas is characterized by ISKCON devotees as a way of gaining cheap popularity among disciples and as a justification for sexual licentiousness (Swami 1998).[6] A few ISKCON devotees, however, are dissatisfied in focusing exclusively on *vaidhi* and not being able to develop passionate relationships with deities, and have left ISKCON for *goswami* or *babaji* gurus in Navadvip or Vrindavan (see also Brooks 1989, 169).

However, ISKCON devotees conceptualize discipline itself as intensely emotional. One of my Bengali devotee friends had the service of helping the specialized cooks make the deities' elaborate meals. Every day at around seven A.M. she would go to the deity-kitchen of Chandrodaya Temple to cut vegetables, prepare spices, and so on. I asked her, "Isn't doing the same thing every day boring?" She smiled and said, "Prabhupad said every service must be instilled with humility and love—these are for Krishna's pleasure! Without love, would we be disciplined?"

Devotees' performances of emotions are strictly discursively constituted. ISKCON has a hierarchized structure, and devotees say or do as gurus teach them. Before saying anything, devotees add "as Prabhupad said," or "as scriptures say." ISKCON also has a thriving reading culture. Every devotee must thoroughly read books written by Prabhupad before gurus agree to initiate them. These Bengali and English books, and Sanskrit Vaishnava texts like the *Gita* and *Bhagavatam*, have been translated into many international languages. These books explain Vaishnava philosophy in simplified terms for all foreign devotees to comprehend. Thus, instances of individualized opinions are rare, and if devotees behave in any unwarranted manner, they are reported to higher authorities. Both disciplined devotion and deference to gurus are marks of humility, devotees argue, rather than cultivation of individual passionate states, which are intellectually precocious and presumptuous.

The devotees' emotive approach to their service impacts their affective body language and behavior. They are always smiling and greeting each other vibrantly, saying, "*Hare Krishna*" (hail Radha-Krishna) even while engaged intensely in their devotional services. All devotees look forward to and despite their busyness attend the daily temple-*aratis,* when with raised hands and joyous faces they chant the deities' names to music, and dance and jump in complete ecstasy. When devotees meet outsiders they are unfailingly friendly, humble, and polite, since their gurus teach them to treat every person as a potential Krishna-devotee, and everything they say as a potential preaching message.

Thus, fieldwork with ISKCON devotees was easy in many ways. They were always welcoming, though at times expecting that I would finally take initiation from their gurus. I spoke to most of them, including Indians, in English, and there was an ease in our conversations since we related to each other's social backgrounds. Since they are educated, some highly so, they immediately understood my project and said exactly what they wanted to be written about ISKCON, as that in itself is a kind of preaching. This was not a problem, since their descriptions of devotional services and self-representations as excellent organizers, public preachers, and servants of the institution constitute a significant part of my study. However, devotees are tremendously busy through the day. Thus, appointments had to be made for most interviews unless devotees invited me for lunches, snacks, or women's meetings. I befriended many more devotees in ISKCON than among *goswamis*, *babajis* or *sahajiyas*, but these relationships were often semiformal and less intense. Also, since devotees have very synchronized opinions, our conversations were repetitive, and devotees' narratives almost never contradicted each other. In comparison with my fieldwork in Navadvip, where I had to mostly rely on devotees' narrativized experiences, my fieldwork in Mayapur entailed a lot more observations of the different kinds of devotional services devotees engage in throughout the day, and understanding through conversations with them what meanings they attach to these services in *gupta*-Vrindavan.

GLOBAL SPACE, PLACE, AND SERVICE

ISKCON's philosophy and practice of devotional service question a number of binaries, such as West/East and modern/non-modern, to ensure the widest possible international participation in Radha-Krishna's services.

On a hot summer day, Tulsi had given me an appointment and we chatted in her air-conditioned office, from which she then managed an NGO carrying out developmental work in Mayapur and adjoining villages. She was a young devotee from Atlanta, who had settled with her husband in Mayapur. At one point I asked provocatively, "Why do so many foreigners leave first-world comforts and settle in this small village? On hot days like this, don't you wish you hadn't come?" She retorted softly but firmly, "Mayapur means much more than heat and dirt. Everything here is Krishna-conscious, everyone is a devotee, every work devotional service. This is our Vrindavan!" Tulsi's response was similar to those of many other devotees who reside in and visit Mayapur from all over the world.

ISKCON devotees, participants of the global-devotional space, argue that any physical location is a potential *gupta*-Vrindavan and manifests their spiritual selves as Radha-Krishna's servants, if offered devotional services. Devotional service is anything done with discipline and love toward deities. It involves no conceptual complexity—devotees stress that there should be no religious expression that cannot be preached to all.

Shyam was a middle-aged Indian devotee who along with his wife had organized a tourism bureau which preached massively about Mayapur throughout India in the previous decade and even began direct online transmissions of daily temple *aratis* and discourses by gurus for the benefit of international devotees. He said, "I do my devotional service with love. And the magic is that it is also a form of preaching, because more love means better services, means Mayapur's better organization and attraction for others across the world." Devotees in fact say that proper devotional service is in itself an effective form of preaching, and vice versa.

All devotees, including Indians, assert that they are not Hindus but Vaishnavas, since religions are divisive and not reflective of universal Krishna Consciousness. Devika, a Japanese devotee married to a Bengali, wore the *sari* since it is compulsory for all women devotees, although foreigners wear it slightly differently from Indians. Men wear *dhotis* and *kurtas*. All devotees wear *tilaks* on their foreheads and carry sling-attached cloth bags containing *jap-malas* on their shoulders. ISKCON's dress code acts as an equalizer for devotees of different nationalities. One day, seeing Devika in a red *sari* with vermillion on her forehead, by mistake I asked, "Is this because your husband is Hindu?" She exclaimed, "No! We are only Vaishnavas. Vaishnavism means *every* person's eternal relationship with Krishna and loving service toward him."

De-emphasizing nationality and religion in defining Vaishnavism ensures large-scale international participation. Also, foreigners are not asked to leave their modern way of life but simply to realize their servitude to Krishna and dedicate their lives to ISKCON. Thus, Berg and Kniss (2008, 92) argue that Indians' accepting Westerners as gurus because they sense an essential sameness with them as god's servants is unprecedented.

So, although similar to Hindu organizations which focus on *seva* as religiosity, for instance the Rashtriya Swayamsevak Sangh (RSS) or Ramakrishna Mission (RKM), ISKCON's philosophy does not entail discourses of Hindu nationalism. I agree with Waghorne (2004, cited in Hancock and Srinivas 2008, 622) that new global religiosities are ushering in states of cosmopolitan, mobile spatial forms, which do not embody fundamentalist Hindu idioms.

Also, Brajesh, a British devotee and one of Mayapur's earliest residents for over three decades, said, "We believe in practical devotion, not naive sentiment. True devotees know how to keep pace with the times." For devotees, "keeping pace with the times" and "practicality" imply a mode of sociality which blurs the boundaries of traditional/modern, East/West and renouncer/householder, in addition to nations and religions, to reach out to the maximum number of people.

Various kinds of devotees reside in and visit Mayapur. There are foreign devotees who come for a substantial period annually, participate in the devotional life, and return to their home countries; foreign devotees who reside permanently and serve in various departments; Indian permanent-resident devotees; neophyte men who come for spiritual training and are later sent to serve in other ISKCON temples; *sannyasis* who come for few months between their preaching rounds throughout the world; and pilgrim-tourists who lead regular lives in Indian cities and come for spiritual vacations. ISKCON also has life-members in Indian cities, who may not be initiates but pay a handsome sum of money to gain membership and facilities like a few annual days of free stay in ISKCON's guest houses.

There were approximately 500 resident ISKCON devotees during my fieldwork, among whom around 300 were *brahmacharis* and the rest householders. Very few single women, either unmarried or widowed, live in Mayapur, since ISKCON is careful to avoid scandals. Thus, apart from familial contexts, men and women have separate socializing situations. *Brahmacharis* live in exclusive buildings according to their particular service; for instance there are buildings for those serving in preaching activities, publishing, deity-kitchens, and so on. Their basic needs are provided by ISKCON. Householders are given a small sum for maintenance, and rent flats in an assigned complex. Those who are affluent or draw enough income from professions in the West buy housing in the complex, ranging from small flats to large, well-furnished houses. Devotees stress, however, that one must not spend on consumerism, which is thoroughly unproductive, although they may invest in modern accommodations, equipment, offices, and so on, if they are useful or productive for their devotional services.

Analysis of the life-history narratives of both foreign and Indian devotees offers distinctive insights into their devotional ethics and their negotiations between the global space and experiences of a sense of spiritual place. The narratives also help rethink binaries of West/East and modern/non-modern, when conceptualizing ISKCON's philosophy of service.

Venu, who was ISKCON's CEO during my fieldwork, said during a formal interview that the term "International Society" points to universal Krishna Consciousness rather than interaction among nationalities. Himself a Bengali, then about 35 and having lived in Mayapur for 27 years, he was trained in *gurukul,* and married to an American devotee. He spoke in a distinctly American accent, presumably due to continuous interaction with foreign children in *gurukul* since childhood. Venu added that the only important distinction is between the material and spiritual, not modern/traditional or West/East. ISKCON's working/serving atmosphere, with its emphasis on productive principles, up-to-date infrastructure, huge monetary investments, and discipline, is deemed spiritual by devotees because it is dedicated to serving Mayapur. Devotees' implicit suggestion therefore is not to conflate categories of the modern with the material, materialism being associated with selfish ego-gratification which does not care to serve deities. In other words, the modern becomes spiritual if used for devotional service; otherwise it remains material. Many devotees said that their services follow the principles of *yukta-vairagya*—"together-spirituality," or the capacity to include modern facilities in Krishna's service.[7] Venu said, "If a materialistic person found a hundred-dollar bill in the street, he would keep it for himself. An ascetic would walk past it—but a Krishna-devotee would pick it up and use it in the deities' service."

This imagining of the Krishna-devotee as one who makes prudent use of money for spiritual purposes is the ideal for ISKCON devotees. This logic fits both "world-affirming" and "world-renouncing" philosophies. Thus, unlike the Jains described by Laidlaw (1995), for whom renunciation in the true sense is an "impossible ideal," ISKCON does not view householders and renouncers, or even riches and renunciation, as starkly different. Both householder and renouncer devotees are assigned devotional services, which are considered equally important for the institution's maintenance, and devotees must be equally productive in preaching, although renouncers are expected to be preachers full-time, that is, available to preach anywhere in the world as and when necessary. Warrier (2003, 2005, 11–15) argues that although most scholarship on modern religious movements suggests that people join them because they feel disillusioned with modern living, her informants choose particular modes of religiosities *because* they are modern. ISKCON shifts the terms of this debate by insisting that the only important binary is that between materialism and spirituality.

Devotees serve in their specialized capacities from nicely decorated, often air-conditioned offices. Senior devotees' and *sannyasis'* offices have pompous decor comparable to corporate offices. Gauging my surprise at seeing his big room, late-model computer, and the number of helpers attending him, Madhava, a married devotee who then managed ISKCON's treasury, said, "Don't go by the room's look. I sit here with no material attachment to comforts. But without basic facilities, I won't be productive, and without that, no loving service to Krishna will be possible. You ask how we negotiate spirituality with modernity. But the word *modern* has no significance in spiritual life. Like Prabhupad said, I am dovetailing modern things in Krishna's service." Madhava's diasporic biography testified to this critical balance. Educated in Patna, he moved to the United States and then to the Gulf, and served for 13 years as a fashion company's CEO, but eventually decided to settle in Mayapur. He said, "Doha's material opulence could not quench my thirst for a spiritual life."

Similarly, I have seen householder devotees using modern facilities including microwaves, expensive furniture, and fancy children's toys. However, a delicate balance is achieved since televisions, considered a consumerist belonging which cannot make devotees productive in any sense, are not allowed in devotees' homes. Birthday parties (distinctly modern, Western phenomena) are held for children, but the children play only with Krishna-conscious games like puzzles, quizzes, and coloring books describing Krishna's or Chaitanya's life.

Shyamgopika, a Greek devotee who was doing her spiritual service by teaching in the international school for devotees' children, lived alone in a small flat, since her husband was away serving in London's Soho Temple most of the year. She exemplified a practical balance between traditional and modern ways of life. She wore the *sari*, put on vermillion, and took a dip in the Ganga every evening, but also used foreign household goods. Like other foreigner devotees, she prepared trendy Western food items but consumed them only after offerings to Radha-Krishna's and Chaitanya's pictures at home. She said proudly, "My daughter studies in London and loves her life there, but, true to ISKCON's philosophy, is never swayed by materialism."

As to what attracted them to ISKCON, and further, to settle in Mayapur, there are striking similarities in Indian and foreign devotees' accounts.

ISKCON puts primary emphasis on devotees' preaching Vaishnavism to others by distributing and explaining Prabhupad's books. Thus, they recruit mostly educated people. Generally people acquaint themselves with ISKCON by reading Prabhupad's books and interacting with devotees. Many devotees told me that they had begun their spiritual careers by distributing books in public places like roads, airports, and parks.

Nearly all devotees said that association with ISKCON addressed their "search for meaning in life" and "search for true love (in God)" and helped get rid of material life's boredom. Indulekha, a young devotee from Delhi, raised in Dubai, and married to Bihari, a South Indian devotee, studied medicine at elite, cosmopolitan Manipal University. She said with satisfaction, "I lost interest in TV, parties, movies, and boys, very early on in college. These material things stopped giving me inner happiness, and then by Krishna's mercy I read Prabhupad's books."

Many devotees say that ISKCON helps them understand spiritual texts "as they are," or scientifically.[8] A devotee said, "We don't give individual interpretations to texts. Prabhupad explained them as they are, and we follow him. But *babajis* and *sahajiyas* imagine what texts mean." Devotees' insistence on "scientific" religion, one which is objective, generalized, and predefined by Prabhupad, is thus linked to the understanding that proper devotion is disciplined rather than individualistic and passion-driven.

ISKCON's various preaching media, such as the posters they put up during festivals, and their books, also highlight the idea that theirs is a scientific religion. The term has the connotation that since it is objective, it has palpable effects and uses in everyday life. This claim helps ISKCON address younger generations of devotees. Nandakumar, a Bengali devotee, a veterinarian by profession, balanced his life by working in a hospital and serving Mayapur's *goshala* cows. He said, "Earlier I used to think science and religion are different. But Prabhupad said that a practical devotional approach is necessary for contemporary times. Now when I serve the cows, I think both about science and how happy Krishna is."

Other devotees told me that their parents had shed their initial skepticism about their children taking up a full-time religious life when they found that they were learning practical, scientific procedures to spiritual truth rather than abstract philosophy (often associated with Hinduism), and therefore using their professional training productively in their spiritual lives. In fact, most devotees prefer devotional services which employ their specialized skills. Achyuta gave up his lucrative job as an electrical engineer in Melbourne in 1979 to dedicate his life to serving Mayapur. His professional skills had been aptly utilized, and during my fieldwork he was in charge of building the new Temple of Vedic Planetarium.

It is difficult for devotees to sustain relationships with non-devotees, because of ISKCON's strict emphasis on "four regulative principles," which devotees also call principles of "spiritual freedom" (from material life). These are no eating of meat (or fish or eggs), no illicit sex (including sex for non-reproductive purposes), no gambling (including gambles in thought—this refers to ISKCON's "scientific" approach to religion, that is, accepting Prabhupad's books "as they are," or as non-debatable truths), and no intoxication. Along with these, devotees chant for a minimum of two hours daily. To ensure fidelity to these principles, devotees marry among themselves. Thus, cross-national marriages are common. Gurus and ISKCON matrimonial bureaus play significant roles in arranging marriages.

The "regulative principles" attract diverse groups of people, like many of my Indian friends who came from conservative Hindu vegetarian families, and Westerners who "were tired" of their shallow, materialistic lives. Weiss and Mendoza (1990, 181) similarly argue that acculturation into ISKCON brings greater senses of well-being to devotees. My American friend, Anangamanjari, then about 60 and a permanent resident of Mayapur, remembered how her life changed in the 1970s, when she was experimenting with Zen macrobiotic diets and Indian gurus, until she met ISKCON devotees in New York's Central Park. Her practice of "regulative principles," eating *prasadam,* and loud musical chanting with other devotees, leading to "inexplicable happiness and goose bumps," helped her abandon earlier "highs" she associated for instance with drugs. Like other devotees, she called ISKCON a "spiritual hospital" which cures materialism. Anangamanjari's experiences were common to other Westerners during the 1970s and '80s. Pamphlets about chanting called *Stay High Forever!* and *'Finding Ecstasy* were distributed in New York streets, and a book called *Chant and Be Happy* (Prabhupad 1987) described chanting as being "sweeter than acid, cheaper than pot, and nonbustible by fuzz" (53). Anangamanjari added, "Regulative principles are scientific—they regulate health and morality."

Thus, foreign and elite Indian devotees embody ISKCON's international spirit by being quintessential global citizens. Their educated backgrounds and philosophy of devotional service justify their mobility. Since any physical location may be transformed into Vrindavan by offering it devotional services, devotees' travels and life-philosophies problematize East/West binaries. This also ensures that devotees of optimum international exposure and professional specialization serve in Mayapur. Devotees also question binaries between householder/renouncer, modern/non-modern, and so on, and argue that anyone and everything has the capacity to be spiritual, if stripped of materialism and dedicated to the deities' service.

ISKCON'S SOCIALIZATION

Every ISKCON devotee living in Mayapur must be involved in some devotional service. Devotees do not waste time in "material" activities, and every person has a strict schedule which purports to serve Radha-Krishna through daily activities. However, devotional service begins only after the devotee has been adequately socialized into ISKCON's spiritual ideologies.

Devotees' lives are governed by ISKCON's philosophical focus on *vaidhi bhakti*, since discipline and rules aid in routine *seva* and productivity. An evening program had been arranged one day by some of ISKCON's women devotees, in one of their flats, to celebrate the initiation anniversary of the head *pujari* (priest), Brajesh. The host, a Westerner, baked a cake on the occasion. Before cutting the cake all the women discussed spiritual matters, as is usual during devotees' gatherings. That evening's topic was chanting. They were discussing what Prabhupad said about chanting, how they should try to chant for more than two hours daily, and so on. One of them, new to ISKCON, began saying that she "chants in relationship," that is, feels passionate love for Krishna when chanting. All the devotees glanced at each other, and their faces showed thorough disapproval. The host explained: "Discussing these things publicly shows cheap advertising of spirituality. Only *babajis* do that. Prabhupad said we must only chant to pray to Radha-Krishna that they engage us in humble service." But other Vaishnavas view ISKCON's sole focus on rule-bound *vaidhi bhakti* and avoidance of *raganuga bhakti* as spiritual incapacity.

ISKCON centers all over the world are run on the basis of rules laid down by the General Body Commission, which is comprised of senior devotees (mostly *sannyasis*). To keep discipline uniform internationally, devotees are grouped according to traditional Indian *varnashram* (life-cycle) models. Thus, there are rules for children receiving initial socialization, *brahmacharis* (18–25 years old) who lead disciplined lives within ISKCON without interaction with the outside world, *grhastyas* (householders), and *sannyasis,* who either never married, or married and after fifty years of age have taken permission from their wives and dedicated their lives full-time to ISKCON's preaching missions.

Devotees embody principles of ego-effaced devotional service through their different life-stages. They say their main responsibility is to serve Mayapur through concerted group activities. Socialization into ISKCON's philosophy begins in the *gurukul,* the residential training school where male children are prepared for further life-stages.[9]

The *gurukul* was built around 1975. Within ISKCON's enclosure but away from the everyday bustle, the school is surrounded by forest, and one can even hear jackals after sundown, echoing in the rural interiors. There are stony alleys all around the school built on traditional models, and the classrooms and residential buildings are made of bamboo, with clay walls. However, the benches and gardens inside are very modern, and the school's look is an interesting combination.

One of the *gurukul* teachers, Mohan, also studied there. He said, "This is not just a school. It is called Bhaktivedanta Academy. An academy gives children culture—the complete *vaidhi bhakti* training for services they will later give to Mayapur."

Mohan explained that rigorous discipline, self-sufficiency, non-materialist socialization, and modern values of time management and practical learning which will prove useful in devotional service—these are the *gurukul's* central concerns. The children, mostly foreign and from 5 to an average of 18, start their days before dawn and go to sleep right after sunset. They have very basic facilities. They bathe in cold water, even during winter; their rooms do not have electric fans. Their belongings constitute of one locker per person, a few clothes, a straw mat to sit on, a blanket, and a mosquito net. They do all the cooking and cleaning on their own. Cooking is performed on clay stoves lit with cow dung; the vegetables are often grown in the Mayapur fields, in an attempt at complete self-sufficiency. The smallest children cannot cook, so they make juices, wash vegetables, and so on. The point is to engage every child in some activity or other. Sitting on a *gurukul* bench in the cool forest breeze, I asked Mohan, who had his laptop open before him, "ISKCON gets so many donations, and devotees live in comfort. Why aren't children given more comfort?" Almost as if he was expecting the question, he said, "If they grow without material comforts, only then they will know that modern facilities are for Krishna's service, not ours."

Highly trained teachers provide classical education in Sanskrit, Vedic mathematics, Vaishnava scriptures, mantras, deity-worship techniques, and so on, such that by the time the children graduate they have all necessary ritual knowledge. Venu, who was in the *gurukul* for 14 years, clarified that the *gurukul* also ensures very contemporary training. It focuses on practical specialization, so that devotees can serve ISKCON according to their personal interests. Thus, since his interests were in administration and music, he spent extra hours learning the sacred drum (*mrdangam*), rather than doing levels of math he would not need later. Venu was a suave speaker, very polite and helpful. So he was an effective administrator. Also, sometimes when his work as CEO was slightly reduced, he would play *mrdangam* during evening musical sessions before the temple-deities. The *gurukul* also has compulsory courses on public relations, media handling, public speaking, and administrative skills, each of which is necessary for successful devotional services and preaching.

There is a separate non-residential *gurukul* for girls. Girls are trained more in cooking, dressing deities, painting, and so on, rather than temple-rituals, mantras, or methods of fire-sacrifice.

Almost all *gurukul* graduates spend their lives serving Mayapur. They take up leading roles as priests or temple presidents, or significant administrative positions. However, devotees who want to give their children a more conventional education can send them either to the International School within ISKCON grounds or to the Bhaktivedanta National School just outside. An Indian devotee teaching at the International School said, "We aim to provide children with a balance of up-to-date international education, while being grounded in Mayapur's spiritual culture by giving classes on Vaishnava scriptures, moral education, and deity-worship."

Devotees' children have the necessary training to serve Mayapur's departments as soon as they leave school. In the *gurukul,* children receive two initiations which other devotees receive later.

Outsiders who want to join as *brahmacharis* enroll themselves in the New Bhakta Training Center, an office in one of the administrative buildings. While most aspiring devotees are educated, sometimes

less-educated people from Bengal's towns and villages come for training, since a *brahmachari's* life is provided for in ISKCON. But since
every devotee will need to do *seva* and preach, an initial training is necessary. For three months they are educated in Vaishnava scriptures, etiquette, preaching techniques, and basic services like cleaning the temple
before devotees arrive for the early-morning *arati*. They spend a year
practicing what is called the ABCD—association of devotees, reading
Prabhupad's books, chanting, and vegetarian diet—and finally receive
their first initiation, *harinam-diksha* (vows to follow four regulations).
Married devotees go through the same process and are recommended
by temple authorities for initiation. First initiations are grand affairs:
500 people may be initiated at a time, when they take their vows before
the guru and receive new Vaishnava names.

A few years after *harinam-diksha,* some want the second initiation,
brahman-diksha. This initiation is not compulsory. It gives the devotee
the right to touch and cook for temple-deities. During this initiation all
devotees are given brahmanic sacred threads. This is a controversial
issue among Vaishnavas (Dasa 1982, 599–602). While ISKCON views
the distribution of sacred threads to all initiates as a democratic gesture
which avoids caste hierarchies, *babajis* assert that a Vaishnava must
condemn caste altogether by denouncing even its external markers such
as sacred threads. A Vaishnava, according to them, should be known
only as a Krishna devotee and not through any other social identity.[10]

Third initiations are rare and given to *sannyasis.* As we sat in his massive room, with its sophisticated wood flooring, comfortable sofa set,
and expensive paintings of Radha-Krishna, eating fresh fruit-*prasadam*
served by his assistant-*brahmachari,* Swami, a Bengali, middle-aged,
veteran *sannyasi,* offered an analysis of ISKCON's view of renunciation. "*Sannyasis* are not mentally attached to any given residence. They
always travel around, preaching. Although our lifestyle looks corporate—flying to different cities, lecturing in seminars, and living in posh
arrangements—we do it with a different mentality: to preach Krishna
Consciousness."[11]

Both householders and renouncers may be gurus, since the main use
for gurus is preaching to as many people as possible. Swami, for instance,
had been initiating for 30 years and had 30,000 international disciples.
Ananta, head of the General Body Commission's guru-selection committee, emphasized that who can be a guru is a practical decision. There
are international jurisdictions within which devotees preach. A devotee's capacity to be a guru is judged according to his popularity within

the allotted jurisdiction. Burr (1984, 122) argues that the leadership qualities being emphasized in choosing gurus reveal ISKCON's "this-worldly materialism." I argue, however, that she conflates pragmatism with materialism. Devotees clearly espouse a version of non-materialist but practical spirituality.

ISKCON *sannyasis* wear saffron robes. Navadvip's Vaishnavas heavily criticize this practice, which they associate with arrogance, since only Chaitanya wore saffron, while his associates and disciples wore white. I never saw any *goswami, babaji,* or *sahajiya* wearing saffron. An ISKCON devotee said, "We are international preachers. Most foreigners associate saffron with spiritually elevated personalities. Everything we do is to attract more people toward Krishna Consciousness."

Householders' main service consists in socializing their children into ISKCON's values (Judah 1974, 85). I heard many women say during women's gatherings that they preach to children, since they don't have time to preach outside. Thus, from a very young age, children are culturally well-integrated into ISKCON's ideology of devotional service. I have seen children in traditional Indian dresses work intently at cleaning the temple, making flower garlands for deities, and so on. For games, they enact stories from Krishna's or Chaitanya's life, or play toy *kirtan*-drums. Even small children touched my feet when their parents introduced them to me, and I remember how a five-year-old girl uttered Vaishnava mantras before her family began a meal with me. During a festival in Mayapur, I met a couple of *gurukul* boys of about seven. I asked playfully what they wanted to become when older. One of them said, with a serious, convinced face, "I will remain a *brahmachari* and serve Mayapur."

SERVICE AS DEVOTION, DEVOTION AS SERVICE

ISKCON devotees translate *bhakti* not as "devotion" simply, but as "devotional service," since for them active collective service is more important than solitary worship. They differentiate devotional service from both work and social service. Serving deities and their devotees in the sacred place, Mayapur, with love and humility, is their significant embodiment of devotion.

Service as devotion has gained importance since the nineteenth century among many Hindu religious movements.[12] This was when the foundations of Gaudiya Math and ISKCON devotionalism were laid. However, ISKCON, in drawing a distinction between social and spiritual service, differs from RKM, RSS, and other religious organizations which foreground service as their devotional expression. Social service, as exemplified by RKM and RSS, views people themselves as expressions of divinity and service toward them as serving God (or nation).[13] But ISKCON devotees argue that service toward people is nothing more than serving Krishna's devotees. Dualism between deities and devotees is conducive to a subservient subjectivity, contrary to RKM's monistic philosophy. Venu said, "The sense of doing social service brings pride to the servant, which is different from a Vaishnava's mentality."

Socio-religious service has been interpreted as a form of (Hindu) nationalism in many cases.[14] But ISKCON, with its emphasis on devotional service as giving pleasure to Radha-Krishna and making a good Vaishnava, understands the *social* in *social service* as clearly spiritual.

ISKCON's definition of devotional service includes any activity directed with love toward Mayapur. Thus, not only is service devotion, but devotion itself is also service. A gardener, a preacher, a publisher, an administrator, a cleaner, an author, a cook, a temple priest, and someone who simply chants all day are equally respected "servants." During my fieldwork, Vinodini, a middle-aged woman, was engaged in a number of important services. She was researching the *Bhagavatam's* 12th part; she had 40 lectures assigned to be delivered internationally; her third book was in press; and she was preparing a *Gita* edition with pictures for every chapter. Malati, an American devotee, was close to 70 and semi-paralyzed. Unable to perform any other service, she devoted all her time to painting deities' portraits, which were proudly displayed by other devotees in strategic locations within ISKCON's compound. Both Vinodini and Malati were highly esteemed devotees. Thus, ISKCON's understanding of productivity is not limited to how much work one literally does but emphasizes the mentality one cultivates to serve with love, every element constituting the functioning and publicity of Vaishnavism and Mayapur to the world.

Service, devotees emphasize, is different from work, since it is not confined to a 9-to-5 occupation but is a permanent state of mind and body. When work becomes devotionalized, productivity increases, Malati told me, for "then there is no limit to how much we want to do." In their discussions with me, married devotees were reluctant to use words like "salary" or "earnings," and referred to the small sums of money they receive from temple authorities as "maintenance." One of them said, "When I minimize my receipts, I maximize the amount available for deities' services."

There are more than thirty-five departments under which services are organized in Mayapur. Two factors determine which service one performs: ISKCON's need and the devotee's expertise. The point is "to build a knowledgeable, well-trained workforce with identifiable skills of use" (Knott 2000, 160). There are three main categories of services: for Mayapur's temple-deities, for Mayapur's maintenance, and for Mayapur's devotees.

The Pujari (priest) Department is devoted to serving the idols of Radha, Krishna, and Radha's eight main *sakhis* in one compartment and Chaitanya and his five associates in another, in the Chandrodaya Temple.[15] The life-size idols of Radha-Krishna and the *sakhis* are six feet tall, and Chaitanya and his associates, seven feet, each most beautifully carved and dressed. The department conducts services for regular worship, including making deities ready with bright-colored, sequined, gem-attached, magnificent clothing and offering four elaborate *aratis* accompanied by a wide variety of food. Almost fifty items are offered on huge plates during meals, and this number approaches a thousand during Krishna's, Radha's, or Chaitanya's birthday. The same spectacle is maintained in serving Prabhupad's idol in his shrine-temple. Brajesh, one of the head priests performing the *aratis,* said, "I am addicted to my service. I conduct it in a humble mood. I don't think that *I* am doing it, but that I'm assisting Prabhupad in serving Krishna."

In the building next to Chandrodaya Temple, during my fieldwork, thirty devotees served for twelve hours daily, preparing clothes for deities. They already had seventy such sets, and three sets are prepared every year. Each dress is very expensive. Many devotees cite the idols' magnificent size, their grand dress, and the splendor of the food-offerings as causes of their first bouts of devotion; and preaching to people by maintaining high standards of worship in Mayapur constitutes an important service.[16] Every day, hundreds of pilgrims and resident devotees flock to the temple and sit for hours gazing at the gorgeous deities.

Brajesh, along with other senior devotees, since 2007, was also involved in the service of training devotees in skills of temple-worship, in the Mayapur Academy. In addition to details of how to bathe, dress, cook for, offer food to, and perform rituals toward deities, the Academy teaches them Vaishnava etiquette, most significantly, humility while serving.

The second set of services is rendered toward the *dham's* maintenance and the welfare of the devotees residing in ISKCON's enclosure. Departments supervising these functions have separate offices, for instance Treasury, which manages accounting; Foreign Currency and

International Devotee Care, departments which take care of foreigners' needs; Housing, which distributes 120 flats at its disposal for rent or sale; Community Sevaks(servants), which manages domestic issues like marriages and divorces; and the general manager oversees legal affairs, including devotees' conduct as prescribed by the General Body Commission.

The Tourism Department was established in 2007. It advertises Mayapur internationally. Many *brahmacharis* serve the department as tour guides for pilgrims. Some travel to Calcutta, Bombay, and other cities to participate in tourism fairs, where they sell brochures, posters, and magazines explaining the spiritual importance of *gupta*-Vrindavan. I have seen how urban Indian and foreigner devotees are greeted by English-speaking *brahmacharis,* offered the best rooms in ISKCON guest-houses, given temple-*prasadam* thrice a day, and taken around places associated with Chaitanya's pastimes, when they visit Mayapur. When pilgrims leave, *brahmacharis* maintain relationships with them. Shyam, the department's head, said, "If they're not already devotees, we ensure that their experiences in Mayapur will give them the appropriate mentality."

ISKCON's most important source of preaching and income is the Bhaktivedanta Book Trust (BBT), one of the largest religious presses in the world. BBT Mayapur primarily publishes Bengali editions of Prabhupad's books.[17] A common saying among devotees is that just as the army cannot go without bullets, ISKCON cannot go without books. *Brahmacharis* serve for more than twelve hours daily, producing thousands of books every month. Almost a hundred devotees travel all over eastern India distributing books for nine months. While most of the books are sold, some are distributed for free in schools and prisons. During my fieldwork a South American group came to assist in the book-distribution service. One of them was especially lauded as he distributed 8,000 books in a month.

The third set of services is toward people and pilgrims of Mayapur in particular, and people of the world in general, especially by preaching to them. Prabhupad's biographies state that he was once very upset to see poor women and children fighting with dogs for leftover food in Mayapur. He decided that within ten miles' radius of any ISKCON temple, none would go hungry. When I asked devotees about ISKCON's philosophy, many of them narrated this story. To fulfill Prabhupad's mission, an NGO, SMVS (Sri Mayapur Vikas Sangha—development committee), was established in 1998. Funded by foreign bodies, it carries out developmental work in fifty Nadia villages. It has a food-for-life program and feeds *prasadam* to four million villagers annually. It has established a small poly-clinic and distributes water-filters and medicines to villagers at very low rates or free of cost. It also focuses on women's and child-labor education and has set up eight schools. Additionally, it provides micro-credit to villagers setting up small businesses.

Tulsi, a fieldworker for SMVS, corrected me when I called this range of services "charity." She said, "People who live in Mayapur or Vrindavan must have good *karma* from past lives. They are Krishna's devotees, and we are pleasing Krishna by serving them. This is devotional service, not social work." Tulsi was American, and her parents were also ISKCON devotees in the West. She came to Mayapur after completing college, and got married to Venu, a Bengali, and both of them actively dedicated themselves to serving Mayapur. She said, "I don't think anything is more pleasurable than serving Krishna's devotees in *gupta*-Vrindavan. I want to do everything to see them smile."

Other departments carry out similar devotional services. The Harinam Department, which organizes collective chanting on Mayapur streets every evening, also distributes free *prasadam* in villages. After the *prasadam* is distributed, villagers are asked to chant with music along with devotees. Radhananth, a middle-aged Polish devotee, was living in the housing area in ISKCON's compound during my fieldwork. He had recently developed some problems with other devotees but he continued his food distribution service without financial help from ISKCON. He said he had a wonderful rapport with villagers, and he carried big pots on boats across the river to village interiors, to cook for and feed villagers *prasadam*. This was not simply about feeding the hungry, he asserted, but more significantly, an important way to spiritualize peoples' consciousness (see also Anderson 2007, 127). Radhanath said, "When cooking, I pray, 'O Radha-Krishna, let me serve you the best food today, and please bless those who taste your *prasadam*.' I face financial difficulties these days. But I will continue this service till my last breath. There is so much pleasure in serving others."

There are three large kitchens within ISKCON's complex which serve different classes of pilgrims: affluent Indians and foreigners, life-members, and ordinary pilgrims. They charge different rates, and have different kinds of food, but they ensure that all get their sumptuous *prasadam*-meals when in Mayapur. ISKCON also has an international chain of restaurants, which provide *prasadam* and preach vegetarianism. It has a large counterpart in Mayapur, which even serves Western food items like pizzas and pastries, and caters to affluent pilgrims. I have tasted *prasadam* several times in all these places, and each can compete with the other in excellence. Serving good *prasadam* is an effective preaching technique, and all the pilgrims I know love ISKCON's *prasadam,* and many come back for it. Once during a lunch invitation in Indulekha's small flat, she offered the cooked items to her personal altar-deities, as all devotees do before meals, served me, smiled, and said, "When Krishna tastes something, it becomes nectar. Now when you taste the nectar, you will feel Vrindavan's happiness and automatically become a devotee! You will return again to Mayapur."

ISKCON's aim in preaching is to introduce Krishna Consciousness to diverse groups of people: children, youth, young couples, senior citizens, corporate officers. Every devotee ought to be a preacher in her own right. Preaching can take place anywhere—in homes, roads, temples, schools, prisons, offices—and the preacher may choose to chant Radha-Krishna's names to attractive music in strategic places, or distribute books to passers-by, and devotees whose specialized services lie in preaching offer discourses on Vaishnavism in cities and villages.

A five-story building right outside ISKCON's compound accommodates seventy-five *brahmacharis* engaged in full-time preaching. It is called the Namhatta Building, *namhatta* literally meaning "selling deities' names" in the spiritual market. The essence of *namhatta*—preaching the message of Krishna Consciousness, and missionizing and revitalizing the tradition of Gaudiya Vaishnavism through disseminating mechanisms—began in the nineteenth and early twentieth centuries and is attributed by ISKCON devotees to Kedarnath Datta (Swami 2009, 8, 10). However, ISKCON's new form of *namhatta* began around 1979 to help householders practice Krishna Consciousness from their homes (Cole 2007, 52). The emphasis for householders is on chanting, practicing the four regulations, consuming *prasadam,* reading Prabhupad's books, associating with devotees, and following practical devotion, that is, continuing professional work while dedicating it to the deities' service. With literacy increasing in villages, preachers have recently introduced this system in rural Bengal and established 2,500 small groups in districts. During the winter months, preachers set up camps in cities and villages, where they conduct religious sermons and serve *prasadam.* I have seen thousands congregate during these programs. Bengali *brahmacharis* are especially employed in preaching activities since they can communicate with villagers.

Since 1996, the *namhatta* program has developed further and a *bhakti-vriksha* preaching method has been adopted. *Bhakti* (devotional service) now caters to specialized *vriksha* (branches) of devotees. Knott

(2000) and Rochford (1982) note that ISKCON's preaching ventures adapt to different socio-historical contexts.

Most books, pamphlets, and posters distributed by the tourism and preaching departments are in English, since they mainly cater to affluent, educated Indians and foreigners. The books are of high publishing standards, with glossy paper and colorful, attractive pictures. Some devotees focus on preaching to children by designing 3D animation projects, coloring books, and cartoon films on Krishna Consciousness. Preachers focusing on services to youth have designed short courses, on completing which candidates become possible future initiates. Candidates are given the option of attending discourses by senior devotees in temples, or completing courses online. The courses are taught in contemporary, professional idioms. The course-books clearly mention that they are not esoteric texts but easy, quick, practical expositions of religion, which are compatible with present-day lives. There are journals called the Spiritual Scientist Series, for instance, and various books explain how Krishna Consciousness helps in personality development, mind control, stress management, overcoming loneliness, achieving successful relationships, and so on. Books addressing corporate executives similarly address themes like positive thinking, proactive leadership, and how to deal with recession. Apart from this there are books for novices, like *Perfect Questions, Perfect Answers*; handbooks for householders; basic philosophical books on Vaishnavism; and journals on congregational preaching for all sections of society.

During a house program in Calcutta arranged by a devotee working as a corporate manager, a *brahmachari* came to preach from Mayapur. The program had been arranged on the occasion of Radha's birthday. After *arati* having been offered to Radha-Krishna's idols, *kirtan* by devotees, and the *brahmachari's* well-articulated discourse on the need for Vaishnava spirituality in contemporary times, a college student, deeply moved, went to touch his feet. He stopped her and said, "I am only God's servant. . . . If you liked the program, come to Mayapur, associate with devotees, be a devotee and a preacher, and serve Krishna." All the devotees shouted, "Haribol!"

CONCLUSION AND OTHER SENSES OF PLACE

ISKCON devotees embody a distinctive relationship with Vrindavan through their notion and practice of devotional service—disciplined, pragmatic services rendered collectively toward every element constituting the physical sacred space of Mayapur, and through preaching missions organized for people across the world. ISKCON's philosophy of place is therefore distinctly different from that of the other Vaishnavas.

Goswamis, babajis, and *sahajiyas* all articulate three parallel senses of sacrality and place: Navadvip, *gupta*-Vrindavan, where they reside physically; cosmic Vrindavan, where Radha-Krishna reside; and interiorized affective spaces of the mind-heart or body, where they cultivate senses of pleasure they will ultimately derive from being in celestial Vrindavan.

ISKCON devotees espouse a more complex soteriology, which I argue is due to their principal emphasis on physical spaces as sacred. They do not approve of preaching about esoteric forms of religiosity or interiorized experiences of place. Also, very few devotees told me that they *want* to go to Radha-Krishna's celestial abode after death, although that is conceived of as the ultimate destination. They had interesting responses about this paradox.

Shyam said, "A true devotee does not *want* anything. It does not matter whether I go to eternal Vrindavan after death, or come back life after life to Mayapur. Mayapur is Lord Chaitanya's birthplace and he was Radha-Krishna in the same body. Mayapur and Vrindavan are the same. What is important is that I serve the deities wherever I am. If we think too much about our after-death destinations, we will lose focus on our present life's services."

Swami said, "What are we doing in Mayapur? Serving deities and devotees. What will we do in Vrindavan? Serve deities and devotees. Service always needs organization, whether here or there. Then, what is the difference? Why want something when you have it?"

ISKCON devotees, I argue, have a complicated sense of place. Since they are Vaishnavas, they believe they will ultimately travel to celestial Vrindavan after lives of spiritual perfection. But their focus on disciplined services toward the physical place engenders a strong sense of the here and now, of presentness, thus making the issue of their after-life imaginings ambiguous.

However, the similarity among all Vaishnavas is regarding the intrinsic proliferative possibilities in senses of place. Thus, while the sacred place is fixed in physical geography, it also travels in every instance. *Goswamis* and *babajis* carry Vrindavan in their imagination, and a *sahajiya* carries it in her body. Similarly, ISKCON devotees agree that, as Anangamanjari put it, "Wherever we preach is Krishna's *dham.*

Wherever we offer devotional services together is Vrindavan." Thus, while Mayapur is venerated by devotees all over the world, every international site where ISKCON has a temple, and where devotees render devotional service, is also *gupta*-Vrindavan. Similarly, a devotee writes that Prabhupad, who spent a great part of his old age in Vrindavan, left Vrindavan and set out on his preaching mission to the West, when he was 70, while ordinary people wish to retire in Vrindavan at that age. She says that this was possible because a "truly Krishna Conscious" person "carries Vrindavan with him" (Dasi 2006, 96).

Srinivas (2008, 13) argues similarly that complex spatial experiences are common to many new religious expressions. She quotes Roberts and Roberts (2003, 239), who say, in their study of Mourides, a Sufi movement based on a saint whose mausoleum is in Touba, that "any notion of Mouride travel is complicated by the idea that despite being somewhere else in the world—Amsterdam or Jidda, say—Mourides are still at home because in some sense 'Touba' has travelled too."

This experience of place as travelling with and manifesting wherever a practitioner experiences his devotion is also central to *kirtan* musical practices. All Vaishnavas claim that Vrindavan is apparent to them wherever they chant the deities' names or sing their glories. It is to the description of these musical practices, and analyses of how they manifest Vrindavan distinctively to different Vaishnavas, that we now turn.

CHAPTER 6

Listening to Vrindavan: Chanting and Musical Experience as Embodying a Devotional Soundscape

INTRODUCTION: HEARING THE PLACE

After the intense summer and monsoon, from October all the way through February villagers all over rural Bengal attend devotional musical sessions (*kirtans*) organized by Vaishnavas. *Kirtan* singers are invited to temples, devotees' homes, and village street corners, to do *kirtan* continuously for 24, 72, or 96 hours, or a week or a fortnight. These collective occasions are of two types: *nam-kirtan,* when musician groups sing Radha-Krishna's names in different melodies following the repeated chanting cycle of sixteen names (*mahamantra/sholo nam*), Hare Krishna Hare Krishna Krishna Krishna Hare Hare, Hare Rama Hare Rama Rama Rama Hare Hare; and *lila-kirtan,* when musician groups describe the deities' divine activities and love-play in celestial Vrindavan by singing songs composed by medieval Vaishnava practitioners who were also poets, and who are highly revered by Bengal-Vaishnavas.

One of the evocative memories from my fieldwork is of a typical week-long *nam-kirtan* session organized in Navadvip's Radharani temple in November 2009. Situated in a bustling area of the town, the temple was built in memory of Radharani, disciple of a *babaji* and a famous woman *kirtan* singer of Navadvip. *Kirtans* are organized on large scales by temple authorities and attract large numbers of devotees.

Parts of this chapter appear as an essay in an edited volume (Sarbadhikary 2015).

Groups were appointed to do *nam-kirtan* for three hours each, in rotation, for seven days and nights. All over the temple's broad courtyard mattresses had been laid where hundreds of men and women of all ages sat huddled together encircling and listening intently to the musicians who stood in the center singing the deities' names. The particular *kirtan* group I describe here was a male one, although women groups are also common. *Kirtan*-singers in Bengal are mostly from humble backgrounds, although since *kirtan* is immensely popular in rural Bengal, professional singers are able to ensure more or less comfortable lives. The singers wore *tilaks* and basil-seed necklaces like Vaishnavas, and an old woman went around putting sandalwood-paste *tilaks* on all the devotee-listeners' foreheads, sandalwood being considered Krishna's favorite. The main singer sang the sixteen names in different melodies and a couple of other singers followed. The tunes were mostly sad, and while singing, the singers and some members of the audience wept. The singers sang in a very high register, generating a sense of urgency among devotees, and they listened intently. Gradually, the rhythm played by two chief musicians on the main *kirtan* instruments, *khol* (barrel-drum) and *kartal* (cymbals), escalated. As the music became faster and the rhythm reached its crescendo, all the musicians, their instruments hanging from slings on their bodies, began jumping up and down with their hands stretched upwards as a mark of submission to the Vrindavan deities, just as Chaitanya is described in his biographies doing *kirtan* with other devotees. The singer then shouted the line: "Where there is *namsankirtan* [collective naming], there is Vrindavan," and listeners ran to hug each other, irrespective of familiarity and gender, and others cried bitterly and rolled on the ground. Like them, I felt the most ecstatic exhaustion at this stage, after the sheer repetition of divine names continuously, and while they sobbed, I enjoyed the auditory pleasures. The musicians continued singing and sobbing before the hanging mikes such that the sounds of their collective ecstasy reached others in Navadvip, who came and joined in increasing numbers throughout the week.

The interacting triad of place, affect, and sanctity acquire yet other very distinctive dimensions in Vaishnavas' experiences of music. Irrespective of their differences, all Vaishnavas agree that every site of utterance of deities' names or *lilas* is *gupta* (veiled) Vrindavan, which manifests the transcendental place to devotees through cultivated, attentive listening. Vaishnavas philosophically borrow from the predominant Hindu understanding that the name and named are indistinguishable, or that uttering the name makes the named apparent. Thus, in the Vaishnava context, every musical speech-act is considered a performative utterance which makes Radha-Krishna and their location in the sacred place apparent. Holdrege (2009, 4) describes this as a "multileveled ontology": the deities' presence in eternal Vrindavan, and their simultaneous "descent" to the utterance site.

To explain this to me, all devotees cited a couplet where Krishna assures us, "I am neither in any distant abode, nor in yogis' hearts. I am manifest in any site where my devotees sing [my name or doings]." Another couplet sung during *kirtans* says, "Wherever there is *kirtan,* there is Vrindavan, and the endless flow of pleasure." Another similar Bengali proverb says, "Vrindavan's love-wealth [*prem-dhan*] is deities' names."

Music is therefore one of the key means by which the critical act of Vaishnavite place-making occurs. Stage by stage, through every chapter, this book explores complex ways of apprehending, producing, and relating to Vrindavan, and simultaneous ways of cultivating religious subjectivities which are represented and understood as mystically translocating oneself to Vrindavan. All Bengal-Vaishnavas consider the practice of *kirtan* to be a most significant means of emplacing oneself in or experiencing Vrindavan, although they sense this interface of music and place in a range of different ways. These different ways of experiencing music and place have overlaps with the dimensions of place-experience discussed in previous chapters, including how chanting and music can make ISKCON devotees productive in their devotional services, and the close intertwining of the way the body's sexual responses can be cultivated and perceived in relation to the way the rhythmic sounding of voice and instrumental sound can be tuned by both performers and audiences among other Vaishnavas. In fact, to a large extent, I analyze sound issues as dimensions of Vaishnava life where the sexual-arousal and spiritual-ecstasy sides of achieving Vrindavan attain particularly rich and empowering levels of significance for devotees. Thus, chanting and music involve a lot more than the auditory sense; they involve the entire body, its sensory experiences and affective responses. So, when devotees say that Vrindavan "manifests" (*prakat hoy*) before them during *kirtan,* they mean that a sense of place is strongly engendered by their musical experiences which they conceptualize as most real, since it impacts their entire devotional bodies and sensibilities. This sense of reality of the place is achieved in different ways: through singers' describing in detail every element of Vrindavan's natural scenic beauty and the deities' erotic passions, and explaining the sense of presentness engendered therein by singing the line, "Wherever there is kirtan there is

Vrindavan"; or through the rhythmic structures of music which impact the body's immediate sexual/orgasmic sensations, sensations which give devotees the sense of ultimate bliss that Radha-Krishna experience in Vrindavan. So this chapter rounds off the discussions of place, affect, and devotion, and adds new dimensions to the arguments of preceding chapters.

My most intense ethnographic absorption in the devotional world of Bengal-Vaishnavism was through the ecstatic chanting and musical acousteme that characterizes its central aesthetic. I realized that *kirtan* is absolutely essential to the lives of all Vaishnavas living in Navadvip and Mayapur, although they conceptualize and experience it in different ways. I learned about *kirtan's* nuances both through my own listening experiences and through discussions with *goswamis, babajis,* and ISKCON devotees, all of whom chant regularly, and with professional musicians, who are often but not always Vaishnava practitioners.

When the chant of sixteen names is sung in groups it is known as *nam-kirtan,* and when muttered and iterated to oneself either aloud (*upanghsu*) or as silent meditation, hearing the sounds in the mind's ear (*manas-jap*), it is known as *japa.* Narrative forms of *kirtan* consist of remembering deities' *lilas* through reading out loud from Vaishnava texts like the *Bhagavatam* and *Gita* by practitioners (*path*), and singing of their love-acts by trained singers (*lila-kirtan*) to devotee-congregations. These different kinds of *kirtan* dominate devotees' regular lives in Navadvip and Mayapur.

Chanting is the most important element of *vaidhi bhakti,* and thus it is mandatory for Vaishnavas to chant the sixteen names (the Hare Krishna cycle) daily. All Vaishnavas possess *jap-malas,* or basil-seed necklaces with 108 beads, to keep count of the chanting when doing *japa* individually. The sixteen names are chanted for each bead, and one round of the necklace, or 1,728 names, constitutes one chanting round. ISKCON is the strictest about chanting, instructing its devotees to chant a minimum of sixteen rounds, which normally takes two hours. Other Vaishnavas are relatively flexible and chant as many rounds as possible, and increase the number of rounds or times they chant, with increasing attraction for the divine names. Thus, my *babaji* friend, Shyamchand, chanted continuously for five hours first thing in the morning. He told me, "Uttering deities' names is addictive, since names and the named are same; naming them is feeling them. I began chanting as discipline, but got captivated in passions, for the auditory space between the tongue, throat, ears, and heart sounds Vrindavan's love when naming."

Devotees agree that the syllables of the divine names have innate ritual efficacy. They say that beginning to chant is the way to awaken one's spiritual self in tune with universal auditory vibrations. Just as a sleeping person awakes with sound, transcendental sound, they say, awakens their selves in Vrindavan. This is therefore a claim about the utterance of deities' names themselves being the source of the utmost efficacious power which manifests Vrindavan for devotees. Many devotees explained this to me by saying that unlike the utterance of ordinary words, for instance "water," which obviously does not make water present before the person, just uttering Radha-Krishna's names makes their entire locational entourage, that is, Vrindavan, manifest.

ISKCON devotees argue that since chant-sounds have intrinsic sacrality, one need not and must not employ one's individual imagination in thinking of possible meanings of chanting; and that chanting has "scientific" effects which automatically make them productive in their devotional services toward Mayapur.

The mainstream opinion among Vaishnavas is that the different names in the chant are vocatives referring to Vishnu's forms. But some Vaishnavas provided meanings and interpretations which introduce Radha-Krishna's love-play in the chant. So for example they said that Hare (one who steals the heart) is Krishna's call to Radha, and Krishna (all-attractor) and Rama (pleasure-giver) are uttered in reciprocation by her. The auditory universe is thus imagined as a perpetual chant constituted by cries of separation and union between Radha-Krishna in Vrindavan, and they say that the divine sounds of deities' names which their mouths produce resonate in ways that synchronize with these cosmic forces. Thus, they seek eventual subservience to the names such that the ideal state is to habitually chant all the time, either consciously, or unconsciously under the breath.

Apart from individual devotees' daily *japa* regimens, Nadia's sacred soundscape becomes sensually imposing during different time-periods, especially dusk, when all the temples echo with the sounds of heavy drum-cymbal and ecstatic collective *nam-kirtan*. Devotees congregate after their day's work and along with temple residents repeat the sung sequences of the *mahamantra* amid loud conch-shell sounds; they sway their bodies, clap, and jump to escalating rhythms, while priests do evening-*aratis*. Then, following readings from the *Bhagavatam* or *Gita* by *goswamis, babajis,* and ISKCON devotees, there are the last temple-*aratis*. When strolling through Navadvip's alleys in the evening, one can also sometimes hear people practicing *lila-kirtan* songs or the *khol.*

ISKCON devotees focus only on chanting, individually or collectively. They do not listen to *lila-kirtan,* the songs with intricate descriptions of the deity-couple's passionate activities, which they consider inappropriate and cheap entertainment for the uneducated masses. However, the vast majority of Bengali villagers and people from small towns and urban outskirts derive the utmost delight from attending *lila-kirtan* sessions (Sil 2009, 89–91). In rural Bengal no Vaishnava festival is celebrated without appropriate *lilas* sung by trained singers. *Lila-kirtan's* popularity has been further facilitated since singers now record their songs, and their CDs and cassettes are widely circulated. In Navadvip's busy pilgrimage areas, the monthly sale of over 2,000 CDs in shops is not uncommon.

This most popular musical form describes in detail Vrindavan's beautiful scenery and seasons, and Radha-Krishna's various activities, love-moods, secret trysts, and erotic acts, normally in three-hour sessions. Thus, devotees say that like *nam-kirtan, lila-kirtan* also makes celestial Vrindavan apparent in the musical site.

Lila-kirtan traditions have been an integral part of Bengali culture ever since the spread of Chaitanyaite Vaishnavism, especially since the late sixteenth century, when Vaishnava poets composed sophisticated poetry describing Chaitanya's and Radha-Krishna's *lilas* on a large scale. *Kirtan*-singers say that over 12,000 poems were composed by Vaishnava poets over three or four centuries, of which around 6,000 have been published and 1,000 are sung.[1] *Kirtan* gurus teach these songs, and particular guru-lineages specialize in singing particular *lilas.*

Some of Navadvip's musicians have been involved in *lila-kirtan's* rich performative tradition over two or more generations. While *nam-kirtan* mostly involves simple tunes which ordinary devotee-listeners can repeat after professional singers, *lila-kirtan* is a most sophisticated art form, with complex rhythmic structures and tunes, and erudite lyrics. Thus, only expert singers who have apt training from *kirtan* gurus can perform *lila-kirtan.* While most of my performer friends were not highly educated, their rigorous musical training ensured that they understood *kirtan's* lyrics and their intricate philosophical underpinnings.

Musicians spend a lifetime cultivating musical skills and are therefore rarely devotional gurus. Most of my musician friends identified themselves as Vaishnava devotees but were not devotional gurus like *goswamis* or *babajis.* However, those who are especially good singers or drummers become *kirtan* gurus later in their lives.

However, many devotional gurus like *goswamis, babajis,* and some *sahajiyas* specialize in *path* (reading and explaining from sacred texts), which, like *nam-kirtan,* does not require as much expertise as *lila-kirtan. Kirtan* singing and *path* in contemporary Bengal are also lucrative career options. Audiences pay respect by giving voluntary sums of money to singers and readers. While many musicians are from relatively depressed backgrounds, these days those who are locally renowned are paid well for performing and for recording CDs. Trained musicians, and many *goswami* and *babaji* gurus who are good *pathaks* (readers), go on extensive tours, especially all over eastern India, Vrindavan, and Bangladesh.

What the different *kirtan* forms have in common is their capacity to manifest the sacred place, Vrindavan, to participant singers and listeners. My main concerns are to document different kinds of relationships between experiences of sacred sound or music and place-experience on one hand, and music and intense visceral pleasures on the other. I show that experiences of repetitive chanting, rhythm, and music serve different functions: from making ISKCON devotees productive in their devotional services, to helping other practitioners cultivate powerful passionate and erotic sacred sensibilities in relation to Vrindavan deities. These sexually constituted apprehensions of the divine range from being able to witness erotic *lilas* in the *manas* during individual *japa,* to feeling Vrindavan's pleasures on the skin through collective repetitive chanting, ecstatic rhythms, and participation in detailed narrative descriptions of deities' erotic *lilas,* to musicians cultivating what Hirschkind (2006, 78) calls the "entire body as an auditory instrument," which experiences deep-grained musical arousal in attentive appreciation of the materiality of drum and cymbal sounds. Thus, I analyze affective experiences of music and sacred sound, especially how they apprehend the "aural eros" (Peraino 2003, 440) of the transcendental place.

Chanting and musical practices are also common among other Indian Vaishnavas, and indeed, among most religions, including the Islamic *dhikr* tradition, and my descriptions of musical emotions also hope to contribute to general understandings of the body's experiences of sacred sound.[2] However, while it is widely recognized that devotional music in general and *kirtan* in particular evoke powerful affective sentiments in listeners, what has not been documented enough, and what is distinctive about the Vaishnava experience of music, is its capacity to bring to life a real sense of place. Thus, I bring together dimensions of place, affect, and music, and instead of theorizing *about* sound and music, I use my intense auditory memory of *kirtan's* lyrics and rhythms, individual and collective chanting, and intricate drum-cymbal sounds to theorize *through* music.[3]

Classen (1997, 401) argues that the fundamental principle of the anthropology of the senses is that senses are both physical and cultural. I concur with him, and show that the various Vaishnava soundscapes, both external and internal to the body, are both culturally constructed and experienced at the most intensely visceral, affective levels. Music as discursively constructed is best exemplified by *lila-kirtan*. Devotee-audiences are able to appreciate the spiritual import of this musical form because through repeated listening they learn to understand the detailed lyrics describing the deities and their activities in Vrindavan. Also, musician-performers and listeners exhibit stereotypical physical stimuli and emotional reactions to *nam-kirtan* and *lila-kirtan,* like sobbing, jumping with outstretched hands, and clapping. And devotees associate their intense auditory pleasures with emplacement in Vrindavan, as part of the central Vaishnava discourse which describes Vrindavan as the transcendental space of ultimate bliss. But I show throughout that relations between sound and place, and sound and visceral pleasures, are also affectively experienced. I argue that sound also has innate properties which help one sense the place one is in, and characteristics which apprehend erotic sensibilities. I show for instance that aural repetitions in chanting and escalating rhythmic patterns and their climax have bodily effects on listeners which have semblances to the sexual act and orgasm. Sound, rhythm, and repetition also stimulate visceral affective responses of aural ecstasy and heightened eros, such as goose bumps, perspiration, stupor, and trembling.[4] Thus, affective characteristics of sound and music, and Vaishnava discursive understandings, together constitute ways in which devotees experience music as transporting them to the sensuous place, Vrindavan.

In theorizing the relation between sound and place, I am influenced by Rodaway's (1994, 4) use of the terms "perception geography," "intimate geography," and "sensuous geography," which introduce new dimensions in thinking about "senses both as a relationship to a world and the senses as in themselves a kind of structuring of space and defining a place." I also borrow from Feld (1996, 94), who argues that to overcome the dominance of visualism in studies of place one should acknowledge the auditory and multisensory dimension of place-experiences.

Studies of sound locate an undeniable silhouette of presence that the auditory sense provides, its capacity to evoke nowness, a sense of being-in-place.[5] This is especially explained through sound's "tautologous accusative" nature: that is, it can have a common source and recipient. Our own sounds return to us, and we can hear ourselves speaking, singing, whispering, and so on (Margolis 1960, 82–7). This enveloping characteristic of audition gives us the rounded sense of being emplaced as sounding subjects (sources) and objects (recipients), and "the hearer or the listener (the sentient) is at the center of the soundscape" (Rodaway 1994, 85). In the Vaishnava context this translates as the utterer/listener's experience of being emplaced in Krishna's *dham* through concentrated utterance of his names and *lilas*.

Sound also has the ability to impact interiorized experiences. Many Vaishnavas assert that attentive listening sensitizes the inner sensory substrate toward sublime, erotic realizations. Thus I agree with Ingold (2000, 155–56, 268) that sounds may be felt by the hearer's external sense, as well as body-interiors. Phenomenological studies have generally argued that sound is the most insistent sense, invading our interiors even while we are asleep (Feld and Brenneis 2004, 468). Because of this penetrative effect, sound is also characterized as the most emotional sense (Gell 1995, 235; Rodaway 1994, 95).

My reflections on Vaishnava musical practices demanded sensitive autoethnography, or lending an intensely attuned ear to Vaishnava soundworlds. In comparison with other chapters, therefore, my reflections on music are more participatory, and my analyses in many cases bear similarities with phenomenology-inspired works on sound and music.

While anthropological discourses primarily foreground the "observed," I argue that methodological debates should have iconic resemblances with the object being studied (Gell 1995). So I speak through participant-hearing and the "metaphoric language of the ear" (Ihde 1976, 109). Lambek (1998) argues that both contemplation (*theoria*) and doing (*praxis*) involve intellectual capacities. I extend the proposition to argue that a feeling subject may be equally involved in contemplation. As Marsden (2005, 137) reminds us, "Listening to music requires . . . a subtle combination of thoughtful reflections and honed sensory capacities."

In writing about music and translating sound and the bodily reactions it generates into words, a tension arises about whether it is possible to narrativize others' experiences. This doubt is somewhat resolved through a sense-able process of sympathy, of feeling along with others (Leavitt 1996, 530). If an anthropological study of others helps understand the self, then an attentive disposition to one's own body also helps understand others' affective temperaments (Mitchell 1997, 79). Wikan's (1992, 471, cited in Svasek 2005, 16) musical metaphor of "resonance," or using one's own experiences to understand another's, is thus apt in this case.

I have been trained in Indian classical music since early childhood, and my music and rhythm training helped immensely in merging with the community acousteme. I honed my auditory sensibilities further to appreciate the specialized Vaishnava aesthetics. Early in my fieldwork I learned how to chant aloud with the *jap-mala*, and gradually even tried to chant in my mind whenever I had free time. Even though I started chanting aloud, I would get exhausted after some time and automatically start repeating the names in my mind's ear. Every time differential interpretations were offered by devotees about their chanting experiences, I comprehended them through my own repeated naming. I became almost addicted to attending collective *nam-kirtan* and *lila-kirtan* gatherings. Since *kirtan* is largely a rural listening practice, I bought large numbers of CDs from Navadvip, Mayapur, and the railway platforms of local trains connecting Bengal's towns and villages. The active culture of *kirtan* listening ensured that I was always surrounded by interested fellow purchasers eager to comment and advise as I made my selections. Many texts containing *kirtans* dating back to the seventeenth century were also helpful.

Along with conceptualizing *kirtan* through my own listening experiences, I had practitioner friends who discussed their chanting experiences, and trained musician friends who taught me nuances of *lila-kirtan* and drum-cymbal sounds. While most of these musicians live in Navadvip, I also befriended others living in other Bengali towns, who my friends recommended as most knowledgeable and skilled.

I had intimate experiences with people who sang to me and to whom I sang. Once, an elderly *goswami* reminisced that in his childhood there were *kirtan* singers who could evoke the most powerful sentiments in listeners. Hearing that I could sing, he asked me to sing a song. I sang a composition by Tagore which says, "O hear those sweet flute sounds as the smell of his flower-necklace fuses with the melody . . . The ripple-music of Yamuna fills my ears and eyes, O look how the honey-moon smiles at him." He gazed at me tearfully and gasped, "Will I ever be able to hear those sounds?"

CHANTING, DISCIPLINE, AND PRODUCTIVITY IN ISKCON

ISKCON's CEO offered this summary of ISKCON devotees' spiritual yearning: "Prabhupada taught us that our goal is to live in Mayapur and chant Hare Krishna twenty-four hours a day." One evening I went on a boat ride with ISKCON devotees around places close to Mayapur, organized by ISKCON's tourism department. It was during the monsoon season and suddenly there was a storm on the river. The water level kept rising, and the boat was almost sinking. I was taken completely by shock. But, to my surprise, a senior devotee maintained his nerves and told others calmly, "Please continue chanting, as that can be the only savior. If not, we are at least sure to reach Krishna's abode!" He then began singing Radha-Krishna's names, and others followed, and we all waited desperately for the storm to subside.

Chanting the deities' names is the central element of ISKCON devotees' lives. Also, rickshaw-pullers, shopkeepers, small children—everyone in Mayapur greets each other and strangers with a smiling "*Hare Krishna!*" It has become a surrogate term for "hello," "sorry," "thank you," and "excuse me," or just to get someone's attention. As part of their usual dress, devotees carry *jap-malas* in cloth bags, and they chant whenever they have time.

I argue that chanting constitutes ISKCON's devotional crux since it facilitates the institution's main aims: to develop devotees' discipline and productivity in rendering devotional services toward the physical place, and to preach to as many people as possible. With the dominance of chanting in ISKCON devotees' lives, people commonly refer to them as Hare Krishnas, and the institution as the *sankirtan* (collective singing) movement.

While preaching, ISKCON devotees ask people to begin practicing a single chanting round and gradually increase the number. Only after one habituates to sixteen rounds is one given the first initiation, *harinam-diksha* (initiation into chanting). Since initially there may be mental distractions while chanting, preachers also circulate books explaining the proper chanting techniques, which help focus the mind (see Dasa 2009; Rosen 2008).

ISKCON devotees assert that one must not employ intellectual means when chanting. This means they don't "think" of possible meanings of chanting as it might derail them from the independent, scientific effects of transcendental sounds, since *kirtan's* command "is embedded in the actual sound and not the referenced meaning of the text" (Slawek 1988, 84). Swami, the guru, said, "Sound is scientific. *Thinking* of sound only means imagination. Esoteric meanings and all—these things are propagated by *babajis*." This assertion, I argue, also addresses ISKCON's preaching philosophy of spreading Krishna Consciousness internationally. The chant itself is convenient, easy to memorize, and since uttering it does not require further understanding, its spirit is essentially democratic: anyone willing to simply hear himself chanting is an appropriate ISKCON devotee.

Devotees attend the first temple-*arati* at four-thirty A.M., chanting by muttering the deities' names and keeping count on their *jap-malas* along the way from their houses to the Chandrodaya Temple. After *arati,* they chant sixteen rounds for a couple of hours in the temple. Some sit facing Radha-Krishna's idols, some Chaitanya's, some Prabhupad's. Chanting while staring at the life-size idols keeps their minds focused on the divine sounds, they say. Some choose solitary corners and chant with eyes shut. Devotees said, and I myself found, that silent chanting in the mind is the most difficult since other thoughts automatically creep in. Thus, ISKCON instructs devotees to discipline their minds, chant aloud, and concentrate on the sound. While in the temple and public places, however, they chant only loud enough to hear themselves and not disturb others. The practiced discipline then makes them ready for their day's services.

Those who cannot complete sixteen rounds in the morning chant whenever they have time. Thus, it is common to overhear loud chanting from devotees' rooms, or to see devotees going on what they call *japa*-walks, and those with earphones constantly murmuring to themselves while occupied in other jobs. Swami often undertook international trips for preaching purposes. He said, "When travelling, we carry clickers which keep chanting counts for us." The clickers are a "portable, self-administered technology of moral health," "adapted to the rhythms, movements . . . characteristic of contemporary forms of work" (Hirschkind 2006, 73).

The chant's sonic phenomenology of constant repetition, habit, rhythm, or routine has the effect of making one patterned and subservient toward the work/service at hand. Subservience extends from the chanting body to the productive working/serving body, since service itself is devotion, in ISKCON's understanding.

Repeated chanting as augmenting discipline and focus is identifiable in ISKCON offices, where devotees often play electric chant-boxes in the background. Recorded chants are perfectly repetitive, with a monotonous voice (often Prabhupad's) chanting aloud the Hare Krishna mantra continuously. For a sustained period I played the chant-box as I read in the evenings, to comprehend its phenomenology.

The rhythmic interval of sound first generates a nervous energy of anticipation. In a while, through habit, the mind becomes calmer, and one begins to expect the repetition. The sounds are comforting, as one does not feel alone and thus does not require breaks from the lonely work. It keeps one firmly in place. As Attali (1985, 3) observes, in the modern world, "background noises" give people a sense of security; Helmreich (2007, 624) says they create "reassuring soundscapes." Habituated sounds, clicking like the regular beats of assembly-line production, engender the determination to finish the task at hand, since routine work is then in rhythm with repetitive sonic intervals. Chant-boxes thus work as background reminders for foreground services. Listening to chant, in other words, makes devotees productive in their devotional services. ISKCON's celebrity devotee, the former Beatle, George Harrison, said, "Chanting doesn't stop you from being creative or productive. It actually helps you concentrate. I think this would make a great sketch for television: imagine all workers on the Ford assembly line in Detroit, all of them chanting Hare Krsna Hare Krsna while bolting on the wheels" (Prabhupad 1987, 11).

The auditory cultures which bind Mayapur's devotee-community include both chanting and music. ISKCON is particular about disallowing songs which describe the deities' passionate activities. These unseemly songs, they say, detract from devotion's disciplinary focus. Thus, they produce their own CDs containing *kirtans* written by their gurus and selected ones of older Vaishnava poets. All devotees possess these CDs and know the songs by heart. Devotees who wish to learn music in the Bhaktivedanta Music School, within Mayapur's ISKCON compound, are also taught only the songs compiled in a special book by ISKCON gurus.

During the morning-*arati* in the temple at four-thirty A.M. devotees sing prescribed *kirtans* together to wake the deities from sleep. Men and women are cordoned separately. The temple lights are not put on, and the devotees sing soft melodies in the faint light of dawn. Then they begin unified musical chanting, and in the midst of ecstatic ululation and *arati,* the deities' day in Vrindavan begins. Similarly, after a three-hour session of *bhajan* (devotional songs) by trained devotees in the temple every afternoon, at four P.M. a small group goes around

Mayapur and nearby villages singing Hare Krishna on catchy tunes, accompanied by a small synthesizer-like instrument known as a casio. All along their route, ordinary people, grooved into the foot-tapping melodies, join in. The otherwise quiet village then resonates with Hare Krishna from every corner. The main singer explained, "Music is the best way to bind people. It's the best way to preach."

The *arati* at six-thirty P.M. draws the largest numbers. It is famous for devotees' ecstatic dancing, and that itself becomes as much a spectacle for pilgrims as the deities' spectacular idols. A group of singers stand behind the crowd and chant to the music using microphones. Like the names, the tunes and rhythms are simple, and everyone joins in. ISKCON devotees dance to the tunes with coordinated steps. As the rhythm escalates they jump rigorously with raised hands, sometimes even "headbanging." Ordinary people watch them with the greatest amazement and spontaneously emulate their devotional dancing patterns. Cooke's (2009, 189–210) informants summarized *kirtan's* popularity by saying that it is a participatory kind of "rock-n-roll" "mood music."

Thus, ISKCON's chanting and musical practices have the capacity to orient devotees toward the place they are in, to serve it with utmost productivity and to preach across larger religious topographies.

CHANTING AND REMEMBERING *LILAS* AMONG *GOSWAMIS* AND *BABAJIS*

Navadvip's *goswamis* and *babajis* embody effects of repetitive chanting which are distinct from ISKCON's focus on chanting as facilitating productivity and preaching. While ISKCON prefers loud chanting, which they say has sonic-spiritual effects on the body, *goswamis* and *babajis* also practice *manas-jap* (silent chanting in the heart-mind), as names and deities are then integrated into their affective breathing interiors. This is suitable for solitary spiritual practice and concentrating on remembering Radha-Krishna's passionate *lilas* in Vrindavan, and serving as handmaiden for the deities' erotic encounters in imagination.

Famous Vaishnavas are remembered as those who chanted all the time, and spoke little. The most famous example is a Sufi who practiced during Chaitanya's time, Haridas, who took up Vaishnavism and chanted 300,000 times a day. He is considered the paragon of chanting.[6] Similarly, Navadvip's Tinkori Goswami (twentieth century) is remembered as having spoken only twice a day, chanting constantly from three A.M. to midday and always engrossed in imagining Vrindavan. The ontology of not talking is therefore deeply associated with continuous chanting and *lila*-remembering. Solitary chanting in the mind-heart facilitates inner sound's rounded journey from and to the self, and the emplacing qualities of sound then manifest Vrindavan to the chanter/listener in the mind-heart. While the mouth remains silent, the mind-heart hears the inner voice chanting "Hare Krishna, Hare Rama" continuously. In the Islamic context, too, the heart's *dhikr* is considered superior to tongue's *dhikr* (Hatley 2007, 357). Lyons (2006) writes similarly about the biblical "murmur" that sounds become indistinguishable from breath due to the phenomenology of repetition. The murmur is the in-between of speech and silence, speaking and reflection, and therefore the best means of mind-body dissolution.

Silent chanting is much more difficult than loud chanting or even whispering the deities' names to oneself, since the mind is more prone to distractions when sounds are interiorized. I practiced *manas-jap* intensively to make sense of it. If done with open eyes, concentration is even more difficult, since external sights disturb the process. But on days when I can concentrate attentively on the meditative inner sounds with eyes shut, my body becomes relaxed, my breathing slows, and my senses turn inward toward the repeated names. For some time, even if only for five minutes, I become oblivious to what is happening around me in the external world. Practitioners with regular intensive spiritual practice claim to experience such states for much longer periods.

Concentrated inner hearing often affects the external body, and practitioners may go into fits. A renowned *goswami* is said to have experienced the "heat of names" so much that he felt his limbs burning (McDaniel 1995, 45).

Some devotees, unabashed, chant continuously as mouth-muttering. A *goswami's* wife explained candidly, "The tongue's service is continuous chanting, and through its increased attraction toward Krishna's name, which is Krishna himself, it tastes Krishna's lower lip, the source of greatest nectar-bliss."

This flesh-depth aspect of dedicating every breath to chanting is related to devotees' cultivation of subservience to the deity-couple. As Cataldi (1993, 105–06) argues, "the Flesh ontology generally places much more philosophical stock in 'the passivity of our activity'. . . . Being speaks through us—it is not we who speak of Being."

I learned the most about solitary chanting experiences from Giridhari. Disciple of a Vrindavan *babaji,* he had been in Vrindavan for a long time earlier. A serious, middle-aged man, Giridhari did not have children. His wife told me that he did not have much interest in worldly affairs, and for a long time in the day, would sit before his altar-deities, chanting. He would instruct her that no one should disturb him during this time. Giridhari was also a diligent practitioner of *manjari sadhana*. When conversing with him it was uncomfortable to see Giridhari speak, but not listen, for he chanted continuously while I spoke. His mouth moved, but the chant was silent. I expressed my discomfort, and he smiled and explained, "My full concentration lies with you. It is like breathing. Do I stop anything while I breathe? Rather, if I stop breathing, I won't be able to do anything. I can hear chant [*nam*] resounding from my heartbeat, non-stop."

This state of bodily subservience to the agency of names comes after practiced repetition. Repetition generates further attraction toward the habit. Names are repeated "till they become a part of the utterer's inner constitution" (Wolf 2006, 251; see also Deleuze 1994, 5). Repetition unclutters external distractions. Its vibrational groove induces meditative concentration (see also Morse 1990; Willis 1979, 96), creating the sedate trance-effect of a lullaby which facilitates dream-like imagination of Vrindavan.

Giridhari explained: "First I dominate the names—I fix them to rounds. Then divine taste bursts in the mouth and I do it no more for discipline but love. Then the names control. . . . I sing, dance, trance—without control and with love." Stewart (2005, 259), borrowing from Bourdieu, characterizes Vaishnavas' shift from discipline to passion as a journey from the "conscious" to the "operational" level of habitus.

Once, after a day-long musical chanting, the spiritual atmosphere became very charged. The singers had been passionately involved and left the listeners in a trance-like state. Giridhari was crying copiously. He looked at me and said, "When I speak the names aloud, my breath transforms to sound; when I hear them in my heart-mind sound transforms to breath. Where am I then? It's only Radha-Krishna and Vrindavan, outside and inside."

While ISKCON stresses not to "think" during chanting, *babajis* and *goswamis* realize meanings of chanting experiences. I argue therefore that not only is it possible to "think how it sounds" (Shiraishi 1999, 152), or to form external intellectual impressions of sounds, but also that philosophical cognition may be embedded *within* experiences of sonic name-repetition. Just as Vaishnava discipline begets passion, sustained repetition produces a state of calm and focus, makes the mind restful, and allows free play of the cognitive imaginative elements which the practitioner is socialized into.

Thus, the ravenous taste ingrained in naming also stimulates passionate synesthetic imagination. Practitioners say that "names contain *lilas*"—they are gateways to remembering Radha-Krishna's erotic activities in Vrindavan, which then shine in the "heart-mirror." Casey (1992, 273–81) similarly argues that the resonance of repeated names is apposite for passionate rememberings (see also Csordas 1994, 142).

Chandrika, then one of the most famous woman *kirtan* singers in Bengal, and a close friend, explained—and even I recognized when practicing music—"Early in the morning we repeat only the first note of the musical scale [she sang the low tone with a grave tonality]. My singing-guru explained that the first tone contains the vibration of all others. So, when repeating it, we can hear the rest in the mind-ear. Haven't you seen how a good background clarifies the whole painting? Similarly, with continuous chanting, *lilas* manifest clearly." Then she held her *jap-mala* in the middle of her chest and said, "Our hearts are the unstruck sound, *gupta*-Vrindavan. During the chanting-round of the necklace, I think I am crossing the Yamuna, and when I return to the big central bead and strike with the sound of Radha-Krishna's names, I return to Vrindavan. *Lilas* then shine in my *manas*."

What devotees mean when they say that "names contain *lilas*," therefore, is that continuous repetition engenders acute concentration, and through sustained chanting, one can imagine deities' activities in the mind-heart then experienced as Vrindavan. Philosophically, they explain this by saying that since the names are the same as the deities, when practitioners utter the names, they also passionately experience the yearning to witness the deities' *lilas*.

Besides solitary chanting, collective musical occasions also aid in imagining *lilas*. The best instance of "aural imagination" (Hedley 2008, 41) is embodied in Navadvip's Samajbari temple. For more than a century, resident *babajis* have been singing *kirtans* describing Radha-Krishna's erotic activities through eight daily periods, in the mood of deities' *manjaris,* serving them during their intimate moments. At present *kirtans* are sung a minimum of four times daily, describing the corresponding *lilas* then ongoing in celestial Vrindavan. *Babajis* copy the songs into their notebooks and do not publish or show them to outsiders, since they contain details of deities' activities realized by poet-practitioners during their personal spiritual imaginations. When devotee-singers sit and sing together on the temple grounds facing the altar-deities, the temple priest offers *aratis* to the idols. Their collective aim is to witness the deities' Vrindavan *lilas* in imagination, aided by the songs' detailed lyrics. With lowered eyes and a coy smile, the head priest added, "I also chant during *arati,* since chanting manifests *lilas.*"

The songs sung during late-night and early-morning sessions are the most passionate and graphically describe the deities' encounters before and after they retire in Vrindavan's forest bowers. Lay people are usually not present during these hours. The songs, written in archaic Bengali, describe for instance how Radha's handmaidens dress her to attract Krishna, how they sneak out from their homes and cross the beautiful nocturnal forests, how they decorate the bower in which the deity-consort will meet, how the deity-couple finally meet, and what they then say to each other. Then, leaving the deities alone for their erotic night, the curtains facing the idols are dropped, and the temple closes. Samajbari *babajis* have a distinctive, almost intoxicated style of singing. The four or five musician-devotees, led by a main singer, sing while looking at the idols, engaged in the lyrics to the extent that they share their emotional realizations with fellow singer-*manjaris* by smiling at each other when singing lyrics expressing Radha's handmaidens teasing her, for instance. Some have mild convulsions when singing about such intimate acts as Radha's sitting on Krishna's lap. The main singer's voice breaks from emotion at times, and they indicate their own body parts when describing the deities'.

NAM-KIRTAN AS EXPERIENCING VRINDAVAN

While Samajbari's *kirtans* are primarily shared among *babajis,* more common among Vaishnavas is *nam-kirtan*: public, participatory occasions of loud musical chanting. Sometimes *nam-kirtan* is more performative, and trained singers chant before the audience, which participates through attentive, embodied listening.

Devotees argue that singing the deities' names converts the auditory space into celestial Vrindavan. The deity-consort, they argue, delight in erotic pleasures at the site of musical utterance, pleasures which they too can experience. Thus, a Vaishnava proverb says, "In naming itself eros will be found." Hein (1982, 121) says similarly, about Radha-worshipping communities, that a "bond of erotic imagination" develops in devotional congregations.

This association between music and eros, I argue, is engendered by the auditory experience itself. Also, the rounded acoustic experience in this case emanates from and returns to the choral collective, giving them the sense of being emplaced together in the sacred place.

Before *kirtan* begins, the singing site is set up. A stage may be prepared, but more often the audience sits on the same level as the performers, around them or facing them. Deities' idols or pictures are present at the site, flowers are decorated, incense is lit. Lights are dimmed or turned off to intensify the mellow devotional mood. Cool, soothing sandalwood paste, considered Krishna's favorite, is put on devotees' foreheads (symbolizing their participation in the place-to-be Vrindavan), conch-shells are sounded, and naming begins on different melodies: "Hare Krishna Hare Krishna Krishna Krishna Hare Hare, Hare Rama Hare Rama Rama Rama Hare Hare . . ."

The aromatic atmosphere creates synesthetic associations draped in resounding echoes of *nam-kirtan*. The *khol* and *kartal* are instrumental accompaniments. The auditory space resonates synchronously with the heartbeat. Tactile sensibilities are equally operative as people hover, singing together (Kakar 1985, 444). The smearing of boundaries of the voice and skin of oneself from others, felt through the body-ear, creates an indomitable ego-effaced community spirit, where every embodied listener "carries an anticipation of others' bodies" (Downey 2002, 503). Thus, I often found myself swaying or clapping at a frequency similar to others.

The circular seating arrangement is considered to be the spherical stage for Krishna's appearance before his lover-singers. The circular seating and the ceaseless name-repetitions have a correspondence. The logic of *nam-kirtan* is that "in identifying the sung name of the god with divinity itself, *kirtan* singers, in the same moment, create that which they propitiate" (Slawek 1988, 90).

Nam-kirtan's spirit lies in its entrancing iterative fervor. While repetition presents an addictive propensity, it also creates a restless anticipation in the listener. Constraint and freedom together create tensions in the tuned body. While tedious routine generates an inescapable sense of habitual pleasure, the certitudes of security, one also feels the urge to break through it, and trample off-beat. Metaphorically, this tension is heard, mismatched and tussling, between the somber, hollow sounds of the *khol* and the cacophonous, impatient sounds of the *kartal*. This is also the sense of sexual impatience that the perpetual call between Radha and Krishna, as Vaishnavas assert, embodies in their continuous naming.

This acoustic anxiety manifests in the music's tempo constantly increasing. Continuously escalating rhythm is an immediate correlate of the erotic act. *Nam-kirtan* rhythm automatically involves a sense of passage, sensory arousal, and pleasurable climax.[7] This is when devotees with raised hands ululate together, roll on the ground, cry, and shout Radha-Krishna's names, and the main singer sings the line: "Where there is *kirtan,* there is Vrindavan." In other words, sonic arousal and its climax become synonymous with emplacement in the transcendental place.

So, while some have argued that music *replaces* sexual arousal, calling it "misattribution of effervescence" (Marshall 2002, 366), or that *bhakti's* eros finds indirect expression in music and dance, I argue that distinctions between music and sexuality are misplaced. Musical structures *generate* sexual auras. "Music does not make one think of tension—it is tension itself," says Pike (1970, 243). Participants swaying their bodies to *kirtan* melodies, quivering to sonic vibrations, and the entranced dances of some devotees, are only ripples of the disquiet spread over listeners' entire epidermal surfaces. Their collective rigorous clapping throughout the *kirtan* session articulates a euphoric climactic anticipation.

Just like erotic pleasure, musical satisfaction never lies in the climax's quick resolution, however. The end is incessantly postponed through continuously rising rhythms. I call this a process of devotional *longing,* or intentionally making the singing process long, so that the sonic pleasures may be experienced more and more. Repetition and anticipation inhabit the musical body where postponement itself becomes the telos. The end is simultaneously also craved for, since without it no musical experience is possible. On completing a rhythmic cycle, however, another *nam-kirtan* round begins, and this process goes on for a long time.

It is common to see devotees cry profusely during musical sessions or their exhausting, cathartic ends. These climactic tears approximate Wolfson's analysis of tears in Jewish mysticism. He says that "weeping of the eye symbolically displaces the seminal discharge of the phallus" (2004, 281). As part of *kirtan's* collective ecstasy devotees may also experience other involuntary external states, known in the Vaishnava discourse as *asta sattvika bhavas.*[8] These are "stupor, perspiration, horripilation, breaking of the voice, trembling, change of colour, tears, loss of consciousness" (Klostermaier 1974, 104). The associations of music and sexuality led Panksepp (1995, 203, cited in Becker 2004, 63) to call the chills felt during musical gatherings "skin orgasms." I have myself experienced goose bumps during rhythmic climaxes, when singers, in their high-pitched voices, passionately sing deities' names finally. I also found myself unwilling to talk too much immediately after attending *nam-kirtan* sessions.

Stewart (2010, 91) makes a discursive point in asserting that the bodily practices and responses of *kirtan* are "entextualised" and thereby authorized within Indian aesthetic theories. However, Becker (2004, 10, 52–56) argues that rasaesthetic manifestations of "deep listening" are both spontaneous and culturally learned. I similarly argue that sensory excesses are also felt naturally due to the music's affective effects. Thus, there is an established discourse about kinds of acoustic sensations. However, since the discourse is prevalent, the sensations also become culturally established and part of a celebrated sacred ideal.

Famous Vaishnavas are remembered by their affective responses to *kirtan*. A resident of Navadvip's Nitaibari Temple is said to have shouted and entered trance every time he heard Radha's name. Others fainted in emotional crescendo while dancing with raised hands. Some people become immobile for some time after the music is over. Participants often run to touch the feet of the devotee who experiences trance-states, as respect for these sensory gifts from Vrindavan.

LILA-KIRTAN AS EXPERIENCING VRINDAVAN

Equally popular as *nam-kirtan* is *lila-kirtan,* the rich performative tradition of describing Radha-Krishna's and Chaitanya's *lilas* to devotee audiences through songs performed by trained musicians in three-hour sessions.

Lila-kirtan consists of a series of poems (*padas*) of the highest literary standards, with sophisticated tunes often set to Indian *ragas*, composed by Vaishnava devotee-poets over three or four centuries, and imparted through generations of trained singers. The poems describe the deities' activities through the day, or Radha's/Krishna's/Chaitanya's love-moods.[9] A day in celestial Vrindavan is divided into eight periods when Radha-Krishna meet for secret trysts (Delmonico 1995, 263–67). Very often twenty-four-hour *lila-kirtans* are organized in which eight musician-groups describe deities' different activities throughout the day. *Lila-kirtans* also describe special romantic occasions in celestial Vrindavan such as Ras or Holi. The songs contain intricate details of how the deities look, how they are dressed by handmaidens for the particular occasion, how they feel when separated from each other, how their handmaidens arrange for their trysts, what they say to each other when they meet, how they make love, and so on. Thus, devotees argue that the elaborate performance and embodied listening of *lila-kirtan*, like *nam-kirtan*, manifests celestial Vrindavan in the sonorous site. Preceding every narrative account of Vrindavan *lilas*, songs describing Chaitanya's corresponding emotions in Navadvip are sung, since the saint is imagined to have embodied every element of the deity-consort's passions.

Unlike my spontaneous participations in *nam-kirtan*, which I could analyze through attentiveness to my own and audiences' reactions to music, understanding *lila-kirtan* required more specialist knowledge and intensive conversations with musicians. It was through attending numerous *lila-kirtan* sessions plus discussions with musicians that I developed insights into *lila-kirtan* music and its erotic power. I had very good relations with two *lila-kirtan* singers especially. Chandrika, a government-paid radio singer over 50, was the most dedicated and knowledgeable singer I knew. As a young girl she had been very poor, but had a keen interest in learning *lila-kirtan*. She stayed and studied with her *kirtan*-guru for 22 years in Navadvip, and served in his house, since she could not pay him anything monetarily. She also remained unmarried, since she did not want anything to distract her from her *sadhana* (musical/spiritual discipline). At the time of my fieldwork, she had been performing for over 35 years. She had a highly trained and husky voice due to intensive practice. She was a very popular singer throughout Bengal and had opened a *kirtan* learning center in Navadvip, where she was teaching sixty young boys and girls. Madhusudan was younger, 30–35, and formally educated, with a bachelor's degree in the humanities. My musician friends in Navadvip recommended that I meet Madhusudan, who lived in another town. He was then the most popular and highly paid singer in Bengal. He was a friendly person, and in addition to singing songs, explaining their meanings and philosophical import, and elucidating difficult *kirtan* rhythms, as Chandrika did, he also took me along on his various musical tours. He also asked his wife's *kirtan*-guru to teach me the basics of *lila-kirtan* and record some of the oldest and finest *kirtans* for me.

Kirtan performances include vivid explanations of the philosophically difficult verses for popular understanding (Christof 2001, 65, 72). Thus, singers also learn Vaishnava philosophy and effective oratory from their *kirtan*-gurus. There is a debate about whether singers need to be Vaishnava practitioners themselves, and most agree that they should. The poems were mostly composed by devotee-poets in the mood of the deities' *manjaris* and as reflections of their spiritual realizations in imagination of Radha-Krishna's passionate *lilas*. Thus, the songs, characteristic of medieval North Indian *bhakti* poetry, are written in the first person, ending with the poet's spiritual signature (*bhanita*) in their feminine moods as witnesses of divine *lilas*. Chandrika confessed that unless she knew how a *manjari* feels, she could never render the songs with apt expressions or communicate with listeners' emotions.

Hayes (1995, 335) argues that the use of spiritual signatures rather than personal names at the end of songs is an expression of ego-effacement, of disclaiming personal authority as poets in favor of conveying only the song's spiritual mood. Chatterji (2009, 64), borrowing Goodwin's idea of a "spectacle poem," adds that the poet's role as a "witness rather than an author" gives the art form a "collective signature." This enables singers and listeners to appreciate the songs in similar moods as witnesses of divine erotics.

Experienced singers also compose independent poetic interjections as couplets (*akhars*) explaining their own spiritual realizations of the original text (Wulff 2009). Along with poems, *akhars* are also imparted through guru-lineages.

In a *lila-kirtan* gathering the main singer stands in the middle, surrounded in a semicircular fashion by his musician accompanists. A supporting singer, two drummers, and cymbal-players are essential. To make the music contemporary, these days, synthesizers, harmoniums, and flutes are also used. All the musicians wear the Vaishnava adornments: *tilaks* and basil-seed necklaces. The main singer plays a pivotal role as his sonic-devotional mood percolates to the other musicians and to the listeners. During a *kirtan* class, Chandrika told her students, "As you learn singing, also learn *bhava*-expressions. You must not sing with ego. The moment one sings as Radha-Krishna's servant, her vocal renditions will naturally communicate with devotees' heart-ears; every time she cries, all listeners will also sob aloud."

The singer's empathic communication with listeners was especially evident during a three-hour *lila-kirtan*, about Krishna deceiving Radha and spending the night with another lover, performed by Madhusudan in a *babajis*' ashram in Calcutta during one of his musical tours. Typical of *kirtan* singers, he was singing in a very high register. High pitches automatically ensure a sense of urgency and attentive listening. Also, when sad *lilas* of separation between deities are sung, the tunes are melancholic, and rhythms, long-drawn. High-pitched tunes also naturally sound more feminine and almost like insistent weeping. The lyrics described what Radha told her handmaiden-friends about her waiting alone in Vrindavan bowers, her sense of being betrayed and dejected; how the handmaidens felt Radha's pain, and eventually fetched Krishna. Inherently musical and cultural elements, that is, the tunes, rhythm, and beautiful lyrics, together create the appropriate devotional aesthetic. The *babajis* listened with rapt attention, gazing at Madhusudan, and reacted appropriately as he sang. They nodded their heads, jerked their hands in disapproval, as if arguing with Krishna on Radha's behalf, cried on each other's shoulders, smiled at each other in feminine ways when the deities met, and eventually stood up and jumped with raised hands when Radha united with her lover. Both the experienced musicians and the listeners, in their sonic imaginations, witness the deities' *lilas* in their spiritual moods as devotee-*manjaris*, during *lila-kirtan*.

Kirtan-singers are deft managers of musical and affective excesses. The singer stops after singing a few lines and explains their meanings to the listeners. This is also intended, Madhusudan explained, to disallow listeners from getting emotionally too carried away in the tuned passions, since occasionally performances need to be paused when devotees lose consciousness or go into intense fits.

I have also seen Madhusudan crying copiously, for instance while describing Krishna's leaving Vrindavan or Chaitanya's leaving Nadia, while simultaneously indicating to the drummer with his hands the rhythm he wants next. Thus, kinesthetic and sensory habits during *lila-kirtan* are both naturally musical and "scripted" (Corrigan 2004, 16) and fall between what Bruckner (2001, 320), in the context of canonical text-performances, calls "spontaneous" and "controlled possession." My analysis therefore differs slightly from Marglin's (1990, 212) theorization of "spectator-devotees'" experience of "erotic emotions" while watching the ritual dance form in the Jagannatha temple, which she conceptualizes as "radically culturally constituted."

The body's reactions to rhythm during *lila-kirtan*, for instance, are both immediate and learned, affective and cultural. The drums play along with the music and their echoes pulsate in the collective ears and heart. Unlike *nam-kirtan*, where the rhythm is marked by gradual acceleration, in *lila-kirtan* the rhythm is characterized by an enjoyable unpredictability. However, experienced listeners can usually anticipate the rhythm changes. After repeated listening, even I could sometimes tell when the rhythm would change. When the rhythm is slow, a natural sense of sleepiness descends on the audience, which is conducive to relaxed imagination to witness Vrindavan *lilas* being described. Stewart

FIGURE 14. Madhusudan describing Krishna's flute.

(2005, 263) also demonstrates relations between Bengal-Vaishnava listening practices in general and visualization of Vrindavan *lilas*. The phenomenology of repetition is such that listening to *lilas* time and again helps devotees identify with those narratives, till *lilas* eventually "possess" them, he says (see also Lutgendorf 1991, 244). Palmer and Jankowiak (1996, 240) similarly argue that performance contexts often facilitate experiences of collective imagination. However, when the rhythm changes, the singer indicates with hand-movements, and the audience ululates. This generally corresponds to descriptions of Radha-Krishna's happy unions; and the musical groove automatically makes one want to dance. This rhythmic diversity helps sustain audience attention, avoids monotony, allows a range of emotions among listeners, and makes the entire listening experience spiritually consuming.

Mostly, the rhythm follows the singer's tunes; sometimes the singer repeats a line continuously, allowing the rhythm to lead in the meantime. Repeating the same lines evokes the lulling sense of contemplation and facilitates thinking about the deities' erotic pleasures described in those lines, while the heart-mind beats with the galloping rhythm. "So the musicality is not only an aesthetic gloss over the discursive content but rather a necessary condition for . . . ethical action" (Hirschkind 2006, 12).

Chandrika explained that the sonic site as Vrindavan has affective power over both singers and listeners. She said, "Through the songs' descriptions, the entire place becomes Vrindavan, and it feels like moving about in the beautiful place with other devotees, and relishing sights of the deities' *lilas.*" Throughout the performance singers indicate with their hands and on their bodies every element being described, as if it is present right there. For instance, if they sing about Vrindavan's fragrant flowers, they either make feminine gestures with their hands in the shape of flowers, or point toward some imaginary tree where they have blossomed. Also, they wear anklets and sound them when describing Radha or her handmaidens. Their facial expressions and hand-movements are also soft and feminine then. I also saw Madhusudan open his flower-necklace, bring it close to his lips and stretch it, when describing Krishna's flute. Thus, music and its embodied cultural expressions together help the devotee gathering experience the acoustic site as Vrindavan.

Toward the climax, after explicit lyrics about Radha-Krishna's union are sung in the devotee-poet's mood as witness of divine erotics, and the rhythm finally ascends, then as in *nam-kirtan,* the singer shouts into the microphone, saying, "Where there is *kirtan,* there is Vrindavan," "With pleasure, look at this honeyed-Vrindavan," and so on. The devotees' ecstatic collective sobbing or shouting then contribute to *kirtan* acoustics, and as among the Kaluli where "becoming a bird" becomes the metaphor for sound and weeping (Feld 1982, 17), in *lila-kirtan* it is "becoming a woman," or Krishna's lover. The highest rhythm played at this point is called *murchona* or "fainting," referring also to the final affective state that passionate listeners may ideally embody. Devotees ululate together at this point, and that sound, coupled with the restless cymbal jingles, gave me goose bumps repeatedly.

The three-hour *kirtan* performances tread different temporalities. The singer elaborates on some Radha-Krishna *lila,* its correlate in Chaitanya's life, and its metaphoric relationship to devotees' lives. For instance, early-morning *kirtans* may be sung to wake Chaitanya in Navadvip, then Radha-Krishna in Vrindavan, and devotees' hearts to spiritual arousal. Real musical time, devotees imagine, is congruent with cosmic time. Madhusudan explained, "Even if I sing a monsoon-*lila* in peak summer, the sonic atmosphere will give devotees the sense of a wet Vrindavan. All time condenses where Vrindavan *lilas* are sung. . . . *Lila* time is present time." This sense of presentness generates a real impact upon listeners, which they identify with the manifestation of celestial Vrindavan.

With the end of an intense *lila-kirtan* session, devotees rush aggressively to touch the singer's feet. Through a successful performance a singer comes to mean much more than a mere performer—she is the fullest embodiment of aspired devotional moods. Thus, unlike Chatterji's (1995, 437) description of a Bengali folk-dance form where *lilas* are imitations of the deities' activities, in *lila-kirtan* the music is considered to directly manifest the deities' passions, transforming the sonic site to Vrindavan. Mason (2009, 2–19) summarizes Vrindavan's theatrical performances similarly and argues that they blur the boundary between mimesis and ontology such that theatre *is* religion. Since there is a reciprocal relation between geography and performance, both theatre and religion can manifest the sacred place, he argues.

EMBODIED INSTRUMENTS AND AUDIBLE BODIES

The chief instruments used during *kirtan, the khol* and *kartal,* are sacred objects themselves. In some Bengal-Vaishnava temples, the *khol* is worshipped on the altar with the deities, and before every *kirtan* performance the drummer offers mantras to the *khol*.

Following a complex phenomenology of listening practices, musicians and instrumentalists state that by itself, careful audition of the materiality of *khol-kartal* sounds can manifest Vrindavan *lilas*. Stoller (1989, 108), a pioneer in the anthropology of senses, pointed out decades ago that the sounds of musical instruments had not been put under descriptive scrutiny, and the situation is not much better now. However, I analyze devotee-musicians' claims that the instrument sounds themselves become Vrindavan's sonic secrets, and manifest Radha-Krishna's intense eroticism. I document body-theological practices of integrating iterative chanting into the breathing interior of the musician's corporeal space, such that the inner sensate body then echoes with *khol-kartal* sounds, or Vrindavan's aural aesthetics.

Here I summarize views expressed by a few practicing musicians, especially Navadvip's *khol* players. Of them, my relationship with Govinda, one of the most renowned drummers in Bengal, proved to be most productive in honing my own listening acumen and musical imagination. Although he lived in Navadvip, I first met him in another town during a *lila-kirtan* program where he played the *khol* most beautifully and was much appreciated by the audience. Unlike other aspects of my research, the complex theology of instrument sounds is not widely known, and Govinda took pride in his extremely nuanced and rare domain of experience and knowledge. Sonic understanding of the *khol,* he emphasized, came down to him as oral lore through generations of trained instrumentalists. Govinda's father was the most respected *khol* player of the earlier generation, and many of Govinda's sensibilities were influenced by him. Govinda also accompanied important singers and held discussions with other instrumentalists of Navadvip and Vrindavan who he said had ratified his musical-spiritual understandings. Govinda was close to 60 during my fieldwork, and I had by far one of my most intimate friendships in the field with him. Our musical wavelengths matched very well, and apart from discussing the deep philosophies of *khol-kartal* sounds, Govinda occasionally also taught me some basics of *khol*-playing and helped me maintain a notebook about the significance of its multiple nuanced tunings.

Govinda exemplified the ideal combination of spiritual and musical discipline. He had been practicing the *khol* since he was a child. Also, since the age of 23 he had spent a great portion of his life in Vrindavan as a Vaishnava practitioner in the mood of a handmaiden-friend of the deity-couple. He used to have long hair and wear anklets then. It was while in Vrindavan that he explored the experiential connections between Vaishnava spiritual practices and the metaphysics of instrument sounds—between corporeal and musical acoustics.

I observed how *khols* are made in Navadvip's and Mayapur's instrument shops. *Khols* are crafted out of mud since its sound, musicians and *khol*-makers agree, is very sweet. The constituent element has an impact on sound's materiality (Hurcombe 2007, 536). The Sanskrit name for the *khol* is *mrdangam*, "body of mud." *Khols* all over Bengal are known as Nadia *khol*, since Nadia's soil is preferred in making them. *Khols* are asymmetrical, conical, barrel-like drums, 23–24 inches in length and 42–45 inches in diameter. Once the body is made, it is covered with cow skin (like other membranophones) considered sacred by Hindus, and thirty-two strings are pulled between top to bottom. The tension of these strings tunes the instrument. Finally, a small air hole is punched in one of the edges, as sounds are produced by air-passage in the inner hollow.

During *kirtan* performances the *khol* hangs from the drummer's neck with a strong cord, so that he may play it either sitting next to the singer or standing—to allow the audience to see him and the instrument clearly when he plays difficult rhythms, or when the rhythms are faster and he wishes to move about or even jump to the ecstatic rhythms he plays.

Navadvip is also famous for cymbal-makers. Large instrument shops all over Bengal outsource the work to Navadvip, and craftsmen make them in their homes. Cymbals are of different sizes. The smallest pairs (*mandira/manjari*) make a "tung tung" sound; the middle ones (*kartal*) make a similar sound but with more resonance; and the big ones (*jhompo*), weighing about a kilo together, make a loud "jh(n)a jh(n) a" sound. The shrill, sweet *kartal* sounds are due to constitutive properties of bell-metal. All cymbal varieties are generically referred to as *kartal*. *Kartals* are played in pairs and attached to the player's hands with cloth strings.

Khol and *kartal* make the ideal combination as *kirtan*-accompaniments, since their tunings suit any scale of singing. Apart from their musical properties, devotees attribute this to their innate sacredness. Graves (2009b, 105) says that the *khol* has an "affecting presence" in the Vaishnava world and is treated more as an embodied person than as a thing. I also agree with Graves (2009a, 4) that the sonic ontology of Bengal-Vaishnavism is situated at the junction of religious discourse and affective efficacy of instrument sounds. Panopoulos (2003, 640) says similarly that both bell-sounds and the meanings they acquire in a Greek island village make them significant "aural cultural artefacts." Thus, I concur with Ingold (2000, 1, cited in Chua and Salmond 2012, 106) that agentive primacies of human intention and artefacts are not discernible when cultural realities are studied in their entangled entirety.

Related to the idea of the sacrality of instrumental sounds is the parallel discourse about essential sounds of the spiritually perfected body. Govinda asserted that the *khol* is the perfect embodied correlate of the human body and that the ultimate spiritual purpose of advanced practitioner-musicians is to be able to hear the instrument sounds arising from one's own corporeal interiors, even when the physical instrument stops playing. *Khol-kartal* sounds which echo Vrindavan *lilas* then manifest in the body-Vrindavan, according to him.

Once, during a discussion with my singer friend Chandrika about *khol-kartal* sounds, she insisted that rather than only ask about them I should try to understand through my own concentrated listening. She then asked what I feel exactly when I listen attentively to the instruments. I said, "I cannot concentrate on them for too long, since the repetitive *khol*-sounds bang intensely in the middle of my chest and navel, and the *kartal*'s shrill sounds have a deafening impact." Happy with my attentive answer, she smiled and explained, "Precisely. The middle of the navel, the chest, and so on, correspond to the *chakras*, whose intrinsic, hidden sounds are then in tune with the *khol*-sounds outside.[10] And the *kartal*'s deafening sounds are the sounds of Radha's anklets. If you keep chanting well, your breath-chant will sound the body-*khol* one day." I could not understand exactly what she meant till later when Govinda told me about Vaishnava musicians' beliefs.

When Radha and Krishna decided to be reborn in Chaitanya's body, their indispensable belongings, Krishna's flute and Radha's anklets, wanted to come along. Since the flute and anklets sound together during Radha-Krishna's love-encounters, they wished that the flute and anklets incarnate as drums and cymbals for *kirtan*-music. Passion, in other words, was incarnate as music. Graves (2009b, 104) identifies this instrument incarnation as an "identity transposition."

During a conversation with a musician-couple in Navadvip, the man, who is a *khol* player, said, "When Krishna's lovers run to meet him, they giggle, and their anklets dance in pleasure. Those are the tinkling sounds *kartals* make. No wonder *kartals* are also known as *manjaris*. So when I hear the *kartal* my *manjari*-self rushes to see Radha-Krishna. Also, you will see that *kartals* play in the same rhythm in which *kirtan*-participants clap—as if Radharani's ornaments are clapping in rhythm in the devotee's heart-temple."

In general, sounds and erotic sensibilities are acutely embroiled in Vaishnavas' life-world. This is most evident in the hundreds of poems dedicated to Krishna's flute. The search for Krishna and Vrindavan is often articulated as a search for the sound of flute or anklet. The flute is often a metaphor for erotic irresistibility, its seductive sound claimed to be a direct, penetrative eros entering the body through the ears' interstices (see also Hayes 1995, 348). The poetics of the flute is described in some Vaishnava poems with the idea that as Krishna exhales his moist breath through the different holes there are different tunes, which, carrying his lip-nectar, fill the air of Vrindavan, attracting his various lovers.

The passionate flute-sounds are conceptualized as being in tune with the breathing body. I befriended a Muslim villager, 92, who lived in a village adjacent to Mayapur and was locally renowned as very knowledgeable about Vaishnava and Sufi aesthetics. He once said, "One of Krishna's flutes [*banshi*] has nine openings, and so does our body. If through spiritual practice we pull up breath-air and shut these nine doors, we trap breath-sound inside. . . . Krishna brought the flute with him; then as Chaitanya, he brought chanting. The two are the same. After sustained practice of chanting, it becomes indistinguishable from breathing. Thus breath is chant is flute-sound, and then the body-flute plays."[11] Others say that one of Krishna's flutes (*murali*) has five holes, with which he attracts the five senses. Madhusudan, in explaining a song during one of his *lila-kirtan* performances, said, "I will play as he wants to play me. He chooses to touch any pore in me, and my body sings along."

The flute and the *khol* are both hollow, such that air can pass without hindrance. That is the sounding principle in both cases. Practitioner-musicians imagine this as emblematic of the feminine heart's subservience to the lover, Krishna, without any obstruction or ego. The energy-centers in the hollow inside of the body-*khol* or body-flute can then echo Vrindavan's passions. Irigaray (2002, 84–100, cited in Kearns 2005, 110) similarly argues that yogic practices sensitive to breathing apprehend subterranean, feminine, subservient, and erotic aspects of the self. Similar to the flute-phenomenology, she suggests therefore that we are breathed as much as we breathe (113).

Which sounds will be heard in the practitioner's body is deeply in tune with how the *khol* and *kartal* sound in general. The timbre of instruments, as Balkwill and Thompson (1999, 50) remind us, determines the emotional moods accompanying them.

The repetitive rhythmic tones during a *kirtan* performance create an ecstatic atmosphere. Practitioners who prefer sonic meditation may choose to gradually stop listening to the *kirtan's* lyrics and concentrate fully on the instrumental sounds. When the rhythm reaches its climax, the musical-orgasmic pleasure bursts both in collective shouts and in the individual listener's inner body-space.

During one of Govinda's *lila-kirtan* tours, in a Vaishnava devotee's house in a Bengali town, the musicians rested before their scheduled performance. Govinda and one of his students (who had been learning the *khol* for more than fifteen years) brought their *khols,* and I brought my notebook, and we had the most enlightening discussion for four hours at a stretch. After Govinda showed me some basics of *khol*-playing, his student struck different portions of his *khol,* and both of them together explained:

> The right-hand part of the *khol* has a treble, sharp sound [*tang tang*], almost as sweet as the flute.[12] Its echo resonates for a long time after it is struck. There are large, round bangles around the *khol's* edges, like Radha's ornaments. When we strike the *khol*, the bangle also sounds [*chn chn*]. The *kartal*, also like Radha's different ornaments, echoes for almost thirty seconds after it is struck. As the sharp rebounds resonate, our mind-hearts travel on the echo-trail left by the instrument-sounds, to Vrindavan, and we can hear/see Radharani dancing, her ornaments sounding in rhythm with Krishna's flute. The left side has a deep, hollow, bass sound. As its repeated *dhakdhak-dhak* or *gurgurgurgur* strikes, the heartbeat also pounds, as if in the excitement of seeing Radha-Krishna together.

Rodaway similarly says that auditory experiences are synchronous with the body's biorhythms (1994, 91).

The *khol* rhythms taught by gurus are called *bols*. Govinda explained how different *bols,* as devotional embodiments, say different things to the deities. For instance, the *khol* might say, "I will only speak of Krishna," "O hear how the flute plays," or "Hail Radhe, Hail Krishna." Advanced practitioners, he explained, are able to embody these words of subservience when they concentrate on the rhythms. Similarly, in Sinhalese Buddhist rituals drum-beats sound like spoken sentences (Becker 2004, 32). Jankowsky (2006, 389) also demonstrates that among sub-Saharans the Gumbri drum communicates with listeners like a speaking voice. Similarities can be observed in sonic conceptualizations across cultures, I argue, because music, albeit cultural, has sonic elements with affective generalities.

In similitude with *khol* rhythms, *kartals* play, and people clap. *Kar-tal* literally means "keeping rhythm with the hands," which also refers to keeping count on the fingers while chanting. Just as there are 32 strings which tune the *khol*-sounds, the two *kartals* are divided into 32 portions, each of which has a tone aligned with the *khol's* sounds. Govinda said, "Why do you think there are 32 possible sounds in *khol-kartal*? Because there are 32 syllables in the Hare Krishna chant. Keep chanting, and *khol-kartal* sounds will come from inside."[13]

My conversations with Govinda, our listening to *khol* together, his continuous reflection on sound, and our introspective ruminations convinced me that the Vaishnava sound-world is as much about internal as about external sounds. For a sustained period I was unable to concentrate on any other work. I was continuously counting chant on my fingers. I listened to *khol* records even before going to bed, and at times I felt that I could hear *khol* or anklet sounds just before going to or after waking from sleep. I discussed this with Govinda, who said it was typical for anyone who paid sincere attention to "sacred sounds."

In a particular yogic posture called *bhramar asana* (honey-bee posture), one is supposed to pull in one's breath and shut the eyes, ears, mouth and nose and create the repeated reverberation of the sound "mmm" inside. Beyond a point, the timbre echoes right in the chest cavity (see also Fillippi and Dahnhardt 2001, 355). I especially enjoyed practicing this *asana* while in college. In the Vaishnava discourse, pulling in the breath signifies shutting the body's doors so that sonic-affective upsurge is introjected rather than let out (McDaniel 1995, 50–51).

Govinda drew the connection and said, "In our sonic philosophy, the sound 'mmm' apprehends the sense of dreamless sleep. When the honey-bee hums, it is the same nagging sound. Krishna, as honey-bee, comes to savor the interior space of the body-lotus, of a Vaishnava who has curbed her ego and let herself be submerged in divine sounds. This is possible through constant chanting in the *manas*. Krishna then breathes into the body and it sounds the *khol* in her body-Vrindavan. She hears the buzzing bee [*gunnngunnngunn*] in the middle of the chest." The metaphor of the bee is commonplace among Vaishnavas. Vrindavan's maidens are repeatedly compared to flowers and buds, whose hearts, when steeped in honey/love, are cherished by Krishna, the black bee.

The sensory vibration of the bee-buzz has a monotonous insistence. It also has a calm, from within which shines forth the sense of clear perception, a mirror-like reflective quality. This grain-like clarified sensation is similar to the vibrating resonances of string instruments. Indeed, in *nada-yoga* (sonic meditation) traditions, "the word nada signifies the reverberating tone of vocal sound, especially the buzzing nasal sound with which the word AUM fades away" (Beck 1993, 82).

The body's nasal "mmm" sound is replicated in a number of *khol bols* (*jhna, jhni, najhi, nako, jhini* etc.). These are also like heavy anklet-sounds. Musicians often complain of getting "lazy hands" after playing the *khol* for a long time. The sensation of the lazy hand, once again, has a sensory similitude with the nagging, grainy feeling of the "mmm," and has a nasal name itself—*jh(n)i jh(n)i*. Similarly, cricket sounds are also called *jh(n)i jh(n)i* in Bengali. Govinda said that his guru asked his students not to stop playing the *khol* despite the tired, lazy sensation in the hands, since the exhaustion is a yogic blessing.

Nasal sounds are also said to echo in the body when a practitioner, with a straight spine, pulls up the breath via the central yogic nerve known as *shushumna*.[14] When pulling up the breath the energy-centers are also pulled up. From the anus to the chest is, in the sonic-yogic imagination, the journey from silence to sounds.[15] When the sounds finally travel from the middle of the eyebrows to the head, Vrindavan is said to manifest with its passion-acoustics in the "touch-hearing geography" (Rodaway 1994, 100).

Innate properties of sounds being linked to deeply felt cultural values is a widespread phenomenon. The Songhay, for instance, imagine high-pitched violin sounds as wailing cries, and the drum's "clacks" in association with them as making ancestor-spirits present in the site of sounding (Stoller 1989, 112). Similarly, *khol-kartal* sounds make the sacred place Vrindavan's immediate presence felt by sensitive listener-devotees.

However, while I have been describing imaginings of the *khol*-in-the-body, the *khol* is also imagined to be the exact corporeal counterpart of the practitioner's body. The interior space of the *khol,* in other words, is compared to the inner body-space. Thus, there is also a body-in-the-*khol.* Both are veiled-Vrindavans, waiting to be manifest to those with sensitive hearing. Govinda explained: "Like the *khol*, we have a small opening for breath in the nose; and just as our navel maintains bodily balance, the *khol's* middle-portion is essential for sonic balance.'

The small black patch on the *khol's* right side, musicians say, is Krishna's embodiment, and the white patch on its left side, Radha's.[16] As the two are struck together, when Radha and Krishna are in erotic vibration, sounds overflow in the instrument's affective body-space. A *khol* player living in Navadvip, who was around 86 years of age during my fieldwork and who had played the *khol* for 62 years, read a couplet to me from his notebook. It said, "A little air stays inside the *khol*. It breathes/chants Radha-Krishna all the time." He explained, "Friction makes sound, and friction gives pleasure. As the *khol's* edges shiver in sound, the couple vibrates in love." Similarly, in the yogic discourse, the body, from the navel down, is the embodiment of feminine vitality, and upwards, of masculine energy. When breath connects the two, it sounds the desired love (Beck 1993, 101).

In the "intuitive imagery" of the "inner senses" (Csordas 1994, 89), the body's energy-centers are imagined as lotuses. Each of these, Govinda explained, has its own distinctive sounds, and is assigned alphabetic characters with phonetic resemblance to those sounds.[17] Which letters reside in which energy-center is a practitioner's secret. However, when the practitioner-musician pulls up the breath and as the breath traverses the different *chakras,* the petals of the lotuses are supposed to blossom, and the sounds within reverberate.[18]

The *khol* is similarly imagined as divided into corresponding *chakras,* some below the middle portion (the navel) and some above. The same alphabet combinations can be played on the *khol* as *bols*. When a sensitive listener hears the repetitive *khol* rhythms, he is able to hear the same sounds within the body, rising ecstatically from the appropriate *chakras*. When the *khol* player, with intensely shut eyes, plays the instrument hung from his shoulders and leans his ears toward it, then the entire kinesthetics of striking the *khol* and shaking the body proves that his *khol*-in-the-body and *khol*-on-the-body are entirely in sync. Sometimes the body sounds/hears the flute, sometimes anklets, ornaments, bees, drums, thunder, and so on. There are many more sounds, which no practitioner was willing to disclose.

Beck (1993, 91–97) similarly speaks about yogic traditions of subtle "mystical auditions" and an "esoteric physiology of sound," through which the practitioner rises to higher levels of sonic perception. He says that what a musician plays externally and what he hears internally, that is, the link between instrumental sounds and sonic meditation, has not been studied (110). I hope to have partially filled in an ethnographic lacuna in this respect.

Govinda, indicating both the instrument-*khol* and body-*khol,* summarized, "Now I do no other *puja.* I only worship my *khol,* for it contains the essence of Vrindavan *lilas.* I drown myself in sounds, and the rest simply follows."

Helmreich's (2007) notion of "transductive ethnography" has been useful for me in thinking about the phenomenology of instrument sounds, sensitizing my ethnographic ear to the tactile in the sonic, to the bodily interior as a reverberator of sound, and rethinking the boundaries between external and internal soundscapes. In this case, however, the intimate "immersion" has been in the deep oceanic recesses of the body's interior.

CONCLUSION

Devotees venerate every site of sacred-sonic utterance as *gupta* (veiled) Vrindavan, which manifests the transcendental place to them through cultures of attentive, embodied listening. While senses of sacred sound, music, and rhythm are discursively cultivated and conceptualized through Vaishnava discourses, they also intensely impact the body's affective, visceral orientations. I have also argued that acoustic experiences and senses of place may be cultivated at the level of the musician's inner sensate body. Thus, senses of sacred sound and place may be experienced as both external and internal to the devotee's spiritually cultivated body and self.

CHAPTER 7

Conclusion

This book has primarily tried to demonstrate that senses of (sacred) space and place may not be restricted to external physical geographies but also intensely experienced in internal states of the body, mind, and senses. Extending Edward Casey's theorizations of being-in-place or body-in-place, I have shown how different groups of Bengal-Vaishnavas also experience their body-*as*-place, mind-*as*-place, and/or internal auditory sensibilities as apprehending senses of place. While both the anthropology of place and the anthropology of emotions, affect, and senses have been skeptical of theorizing interiorized experiences since they associate dimensions of interiority with disembodied ideas of consciousness and the mind, and therefore with paradigms of an autonomous, conscious, bounded subject, I have shown through different chapters how senses of place, in every instance, including when they are experienced in internal sites of the body or mind, are thoroughly embodied. I have also argued that the varied senses of place are both cultivated through discursive practices and affectively experienced at extra-subjective, ineffable, and visceral levels of breath, absorption, imagination, and sonic sensations. These affective experiences are often pre-conscious or supra-conscious and therefore overwhelm notions of a conscious subject. Also, senses of place, by being both external and internal to individuals, render the body's and mind's boundaries porous, that is, able to open toward senses of place both inward and outward, thus once again evading ideas of a bounded subject. My book therefore brings together and seeks to contribute to the anthropology of place and anthropology of emotions/affect by foregrounding the importance of conceptualizing both embodied relations with physical geographies and interiorized experiences of place, since internal place-experiences may be not solely the prerogatives of a thinking mind but equally of embodied and affective sensations and sensibilities.

In concluding the book I now want to raise a different kind of question, the answer to which is deeply imbricated within my theorizations of place and emotions, although extending them further. Given the immense diversity of the devotional traditions and practices of the Bengal-Vaishnava groups I studied, a question I found myself asking during and after fieldwork was: What conditions of experience account for or constitute the simultaneous importance, popularity, and continuity of all these different Vaishnavisms? This question is a most general one, and all anthropologists of religion surely ask themselves versions of the same question, put most generally as: What fosters the persistence of religious traditions? This question obviously has different answers in different contexts, and I will think about this issue from the perspective of analyses I have already proposed in the book. Simply put, common to all Bengal-Vaishnava groups is a proliferative impulse which is embodied in and strengthened by their different philosophies and practices of place-experience and affective community formations. In other words, Bengal-Vaishnava practices render efficacious certain characteristics of place-experience and community ethics which are ideal for the proliferation of Vaishnava religion. Interiorized states of experiencing place and community support this proliferative tendency. Interiorized experiences, I argue therefore, are not only about solitary states, as commonly imagined, but are social practices indispensable for the continuity of Bengal-Vaishnavism. Although different Vaishnava gurus appeal to different kinds of devotees, and despite the stark differences in their religious practices, in concluding, I am more interested in their similarity: their capacity to disseminate themselves.

I have argued in the book that all Bengal-Vaishnavas have three parallel senses of place: the sacred physical landscape of Navadvip-Mayapur in which they reside, and which supports a thriving pilgrimage industry; their imagining of celestial Vrindavan as the desired after-life destination; and the varied religious practices which help them locate their senses of space in affective capacities of their imagination, body, sonic sensibilities, or physical sites where they render devotional services. A major implication that follows from this is that senses of place are essentially creative: they may be fixed in external geography but also capable of mobility. Thus, a *goswami's* or *babaji's* sense of Vrindavan travels with him in his imagination; a *sahajiya's* sense of place travels with her in her body; an ISKCON devotee experiences the pleasures of serving Vrindavan wherever she renders her devotional service; and all Bengal-Vaishnavas experience Vrindavan's spiritual/sonic bliss in the sites of their musical performances.

Therefore, while Casey (1993, 306) invokes the concept of "de-literalization" to argue that one may journey while fixed in a single place, I am also arguing that one may carry the same place with oneself while journeying. Places acquire their capacity of mobility especially when interiorized in the devotee's mind or body, that is, when the devotee experiences the mind-as-place, body-as-place, and so on. This dimension of mobility in senses of place is in turn particularly suitable for the spread of religion, through mobility's intrinsic feature of geographical expansion. Inherent in Bengal-Vaishnava senses of place, therefore, are their multiplicities, that is, their potential to reproduce themselves infinitely. Thus, any Vaishnava guru, whether a *goswami, babaji, sahajiya,* or ISKCON devotee, can offer his potential disciples and teach the existing ones techniques through which they can experience the sacred place wherever and whenever they wish. Irrespective of whether a devotee is in Navadvip, Vrindavan, Chennai, or Boston, therefore, he is guaranteed the most sensuous experience of Radha-Krishna's divine abode, and his own spiritual self emplaced there. This convenience of the mobile place-experience and its expansive spirit, I argue, ensure continued membership in the religion, or the experiential basis for every devotee to belong to an age-long devotional tradition, and the religion's geographical spread, since people potentially from all over the world are able to embody its central principle of emplacing and experiencing oneself in the deities' abode.

In conceptualizing the interiorized dimensions of place-experience I have been influenced by Gaston Bachelard (1994) in two related ways. The first, about which I have written in the introduction, follows from Bachelard's argument that one can apprehend senses of place in spaces interior to oneself, especially in one's imagination. The second is his related idea of a layered geography: a closed sense of place opening up from within itself to a larger sense of space/place. He suggests that the more one drowns in the deep intimate spaces of one's interiorized self, the greater is one's ability to apprehend "the large that extends beyond all limits" (ix, 205). He identifies in these "personal cosmoses"

(viii) the dialectic of the intimate and immense, within and without (xxxviii). The immensity of space, in other words, manifests itself as "inner immensity" (185) in the individual's "inner space" (205). Also, as Bachelard says, "Associated with the immensity within us are aspects of the sacred and depth" (186). I find Bachelard's theory of "intimate immensity" particularly useful in analyzing Vaishnavas' conceptualizations and experiences of interiorized place—but with a difference.

For Bachelard, all place-experiences remain confined to the interior spaces of the solitary subject. I argue, however, that Bengal-Vaishnavas' place-experiences, even when interiorized in the devotee's mind or body, engender the capacity for sociality, without which community formation would not be possible. This capacity for sociality, in turn, is made possible by being oriented toward two kinds of others: the deities in the celestial place, and other devotees of the community. In both cases of being oriented toward the other, the notion of the bounded, self-contained, sovereign subject is destabilized. Thus, interiorized experiences, rather than remaining only the abstract mental processes of an autonomous subject, as the anthropology of place and affect have criticized, in this case also become the basis of embodied, affective, and intersubjective relations with others. Similarly, Csordas (1994, 158; 2004) summarizes the basic kernel of religion, the characteristic feature which ensures its persistence, as the "preobjective sense of alterity," the sense of otherness which is the ground both for the self's "indeterminacy and for the possibility of an intersubjective relationship" (157). Robbins (2006, 287), similarly, in suggesting what anthropology can gain from theology, identifies theology's main functions as evoking a proper idea of otherness and writing in a "community building idiom."

All Bengal-Vaishnavas, through their different religious practices, aim to cultivate intensely emotional relationships with, get glimpses of, hear, or serve, that is, sensually emplace themselves in, Radha-Krishna's celestial abode, Vrindavan. From within their most "intimate" visceral domains, therefore, they claim to understand and experience the cosmic "immensity," the divine place of sensuous bliss. Thus, Bengal-Vaishnavism offers the unique devotional possibility of devotees' carrying the sense of their after-life destination with them. In their varied senses of place devotees are thereby always already oriented toward others: toward Radha-Krishna and an-other place, different from the one they are in, yet one they learn to understand, experience, and emplace themselves in through their present lives' practices of imagination, devotional service, sexual heightening, and/or musical ecstasies.

In popular understandings of Hinduism, it is monistic yogis who best characterize interiorized experiences in meditation. Through meditation they aim to realize the supreme almighty in themselves, and all the rest of the world as an illusion (*maya*). But Bengal-Vaishnavas are dualists and realists. They emphasize the difference of deities from themselves, and the reality of both the celestial place in which deities reside, and the immediacy of their pleasurable present-life experiences. Thus, even through interiorized spiritual experiences in their bodies and minds, they claim to apprehend an-other place, outside themselves. That is what gives them the sense of soteriological certitude, of knowing their death and their after-life, and not fearing but loving it.

However, of greater anthropological interest are the myriad social, intersubjective relationships among members of the community engendered through Vaishnavas' varied spatial practices. Like mobile place-experiences, the possibilities of different kinds of collective participation and empathic senses of community they generate, I argue, underwrite the proliferative impulse of Bengal-Vaishnavism. Also, every Vaishnava group, in its own distinctive way, offers devotees the most embodied ways of realizing their spiritual selves in relation to the deities and other devotees. Both the dimensions of pleasurable devotion and conditions of collective embodiment have tremendous popular appeal and lead to devotees' sustained involvement in the Bengal-Vaishnava traditions. Indeed, the strong emotional and affective religiosities of *bhakti* traditions in general are prime reasons for their high status among the majority of Hindu devotees. I have also shown through the different chapters that all Vaishnavas emphasize the importance of cultivating ego-effaced subservience toward the Vrindavan deities, and subservience as a general virtue also ensures commitment to the continuing fabric of religion.

The interfaces of place-experience and community building as factors contributing to the perpetuation of Bengal-Vaishnava religious traditions are effectuated in highly complex ways. Among the many ways of constructing and experiencing place discussed in the various chapters, it is relatively easier to understand how pilgrimage practices, ISKCON's devotionalism, and musical traditions facilitate community sentiments. Pilgrimage in the Navadvip-Mayapur region is a collective act, not simply because pilgrim-devotees come in groups but also because their pilgrimage experiences and also resident practitioners' ways of emotionally relating to the sacred landscape are structured according to contested routes which reflect the collective sentiments and mutual conflicts of individual Vaishnava groups. I argued in chapter 2 that Nadia's consecrated landscape embodies the differentiated community identities of all the religious practitioners who claim it. Nadia's physical landscape is therefore a congealed embodiment of collective sentiments.

The essence of *kirtan* also lies in its collective appeal, in the communal occasions of musical chanting and narrative music remembering the deities' love-acts in Vrindavan. Collective musical occasions are generally effective in creating intersubjective, participatory communion (Burrows 1980, 242–43; Edelman 2009, 44). Such "acoustemologies" (Feld 1996, 91) give a sense of deindividuation, and affective and corporeal oneness with others (Cohen 1995, 444). Thus, *kirtan* is popularly known as *sankirtan*: collective singing. Its massive popularity throughout Bengal is precisely due to the inevitable collective ecstasy it spreads among devotee-singers and listeners. I showed in chapter 6 that during these performances devotee-listeners have similar bodily reactions to the collective music and rhythms, which they identify as intensely sensuous experiences of the divine place. McDaniel (1995, 42) says similarly about Bengali devotional traditions that religious ecstasies sensitize waves of intense emotions (*bhavataranga*) across crowds. Thus, Vaishnava musical traditions also facilitate senses of empathic, participatory communion and affective connectivity among sensitive listeners.

ISKCON devotees similarly define themselves as *goshthanandi*: those who derive pleasure/happiness from serving in and toward the community. I showed in chapter 5 that ISKCON devotees promulgate a Vaishnava ethic based on collective devotional service (*seva*) toward Mayapur and its people. Thus, it has been successful in employing members of the global society in the common spiritual purpose of serving the temple and its adjoining areas in Mayapur. Indeed, ISKCON devotees venerate every physical site where they render collective services as Vrindavan. Thus, ISKCON's philosophy also productively engages ideas of place-experience and community ethics.

It is relatively more difficult to understand how the solitary interiorized practices of *goswamis*' and *babajis*' imagination, or *sahajiyas*' sexual rituals, engender notions of the community. I argue, however, that not only do both householders and renouncers live in community structures to carry out their religious practices, but more importantly, that the practices themselves facilitate community formation.[1] In other words, I argue that Bengal-Vaishnavas exemplify unique religious states wherein interiorized experiences of the mind and body are oriented toward others in the community, and therefore are essential for fostering senses of collectivity. So, while Cook (2010b) argues that Thai Buddhist meditative practice, rather than being an asocial activity, generates interiorized realizations of religion which translate into different kinds of social action and community relationships, Bengal-Vaishnava practices of interiority not only translate into social relationships in the external world but have ways of relating to others that are contained within the religious experiences themselves.

Imagination would ordinarily be understood as the epitome of a solitary, abstract, mental act. But in case of *goswamis* and *babajis,* it is a thoroughly social activity. This is significantly but not only because the techniques and content of imagination are learned, and its effects understood, through rigorous training received from gurus. The community of practice, including the guru and his other disciples, is itself also internalized in the practitioner's imagination. Thus, every practitioner follows a script of imagination which defines his role in relation to others in his guru-lineage. As I showed in chapter 3, every member of the guru-lineage has a place in his imagination such that, when his mind-as-place is manifest as Vrindavan, then the practitioner, in his imagination, along with all others, assists the guru in serving Radha-Krishna. Thus, the practitioner is bound in reciprocal relations with his guru and others in the community. This reciprocity is necessary for the continued importance of the script, imagination, service to Vrindavan, and therefore Vaishnavism. In being necessarily oriented toward others in their imagination, *goswamis'* and *babajis'* sense of place intensifies their community spirit. Their spiritual selves and therefore their religion will not be sustained unless they are in a relation of chained subservience to others holding crucial positions in their imagination. My analysis concurs with that of Mittermaier (2011, 3–5), who argues that dreams/imagination, insofar as they relate to the other/divine, are not self-consumed subjective spaces but interrelational ones capable of constructing senses of community.

Sahajiyas' interiorized senses of the body-as-place are also oriented toward others and establish community sentiments. *Sahajiyas'* cosmology, which highlights the importance of breathing routines, ingestion rituals, and sexual pleasure, relates to the body's interior affective capacities. *Sahajiyas* conceptualize each of these experiential conditions as embodying dialectics of the self and world, inside and outside. Breathing for instance is the most immediate visceral experience which connects the individual to the space outside, the self to the universe. Similarly, I showed in chapter 4 that *sahajiyas* interpret their ingestion of excreta as internalizing the sense of every human being's essential corporeal sameness. In other words, they say that since excreta constitute every person's elemental constitution, ingesting excreta is the most immediate way of internalizing the other within the self. *Sahajiyas* also exchange body fluids among themselves in an intersubjective sphere. I have discussed various occasions of such exchange: partners exchanging their urine, the man consuming the woman's menstrual blood and sexual fluid, and the woman consuming his semen. Similarly, the female adept performs ritual sex with the guru in the presence of her partner, and both the male and female practitioners then taste the guru's semen or its mixture with the woman's sexual fluid. Similar exchanges follow when partners have ritual sex. Some *sahajiyas* also mentioned a secret communal ritual known as *chakra-seva,* where a man and woman are dressed and worshipped as Krishna and Radha, respectively, and hinted thereafter at communal ingestion practices. In some cases, when the *sahajiya* woman reaches menopause, she and her partner borrow menstrual blood for ingestion from younger *sahajiya* women in their community.

On all these diverse occasions, exchanging body fluids becomes the most immediate way of establishing affective connectivity, or what Gregory (2011) calls "skinship," with others in the community. *Sahajiyas'* basic understanding is that since the elemental constitution of all beings is the same, the experience of Vrindavan's pleasures in the body is essentially shared and collective. In a similar analysis, Irigaray (1992, 59, cited in Casey 1998, 325) theorizes the woman's body-as-place, which in its capacity to take in or internalize another is always open toward the other. As in *goswamis'* and *babajis'* practices, therefore, it is *sahajiyas'* practices pertaining to the affective interiors of the body which propel communitarian ethics.

Bengal-Vaishnavas' philosophies and practices of place-experience and community formation have a similarity: they are characterized by infinite reproducibility. Vaishnavas embody a mobile sense of place, that is, the potential to apprehend and experience themselves as emplaced in Vrindavan, whenever and wherever they wish. I therefore concur with Stewart (2010, 273–316, 2011), who demonstrates through a historical analysis of Bengal-Vaishnava theology that Bengal-Vaishnavism has a "self-replicating" mechanism such that it reproduces and perpetuates notions of the cosmic place and community through continuously flexible and expanding structures.

Similarly, the basic tenet of Bengal-Vaishnava philosophy is that all human beings, in essence, are Radha-Krishna's servants. This serves as the most significant rationale for all Vaishnavas' preaching exercises. For instance, ISKCON preaches "Krishna Consciousness" on a large international scale, and all ISKCON devotees say that their main aim is to make everyone realize their eternal relationship of servitude to Krishna.

Similarly, *goswamis* and *babajis* cultivate their imagination according to a pre-given script which is marked by intrinsic creativity and proliferation. Thus, every devotee is assigned by his guru a particular position in a pictorial chart representing Vrindavan. This picture/Vrindavan is imagined as a lotus flower, and all devotees are placed in its sub-petals. However, this chart is imagined as always incomplete, with the potential to incorporate more people in its sub-petals, since all human beings are imagined to have a location in it, that is, in relation to Radha-Krishna, who occupy the central petal. This implies that there is potentially no limit to how many people can be initiated into *goswamis'* and *babajis'* kind of Vaishnavism. Thus, their practices of imagination have an essentially expansive spirit. Also, every devotee's position in the pictorial chart is permanent—that is, every devotee of the particular guru-lineage retains his importance in the script, unaffected by his physical death. Each member of the community continues to hold permanent relevance in the spiritual imaginations of other community practitioners, since they are all linked in relations of prescribed, chained subservience to the guru-lineage. There is therefore a long-standing intersubjective relationship of a very different kind among *goswamis* and *babajis*.

Sahajiyas similarly conceptualize their ingestion and sexual practices as understanding the corporeal sameness of all beings. Theirs is a notion of a transcendental community, where practitioners relate to each other and can potentially relate to as many others as possible, through universal, visceral dimensions of physical bodies: breath, body fluids, and sexual relationships. Thus, *sahajiya* religiosity has the capacity to connect with the largest possible numbers on the basis of the most elemental experiences. However, while I agree with Hirschkind (2006) that religious traditions perpetuate themselves through devotees' cultivation of bodily, visceral substrates, I have shown throughout the book that Bengal-Vaishnava experiences are both cultivated and affectively sensed.

I began this conclusion with a most general question: What conditions of experience enable the persistence of the very diverse Bengal-Vaishnava traditions? I have tried to suggest two answers emanating from my ethnography. Although these answers may sound too general, my observations pertain only to the continuity of Bengal-Vaishnavism, a religion with utmost popular appeal across a wide geographical region. I have tried to understand the central logics of Bengal-Vaishnava discursive practices, and imagine what far-reaching consequences they may have in contributing to the religion's longevity.

I argue that the main factor contributing to the religion's continuity and massive appeal, now even internationally through ISKCON, is its expansive spirit. I have identified two factors facilitating this proliferative tendency: the symbolic itinerancy in senses of place, that is, practitioners' capacity to embody mobile place-experiences, which lead to the religion's geographical spread; and a zeal toward community formation, which leads to the religion's popular appeal.

Finally, I have discussed that the anthropology of place and affect have largely been critical of studying interiorized experiences of place, arguing that notions of interiority are predisposed toward Cartesian dualism, especially with respect to the mind and consciousness, and are therefore both disembodied and self-contained or subjectivist. While I have demonstrated throughout the book that interiorized experiences of place may equally be most embodied and affective, I have argued in concluding the book that all Bengal-Vaishnavas, including those whose practices pertain to the mind's or body's interior, also embody and highlight notions of sociality or communitarian empathy. In fact, I have argued that their intersubjective community sentiments and affective sympathies derive force from their practices of interiority. Thus, the mind's or body's inside opens itself to the outside, the self to the community, and senses of place apprehend the sense of cosmic space: celestial Vrindavan.

Notes

1. INTRODUCTION

1. I use the word *idol* because it comes closest to the Bengali term *vigraha*. One must however bear in mind that the term often had a problematic disparaging use in the colonial discourse: to signify Hinduism's irrational trends.

Throughout the book I will use phrases such as "deity-consort," "divine couple," and "deity-couple" to refer to Radha-Krishna.

2. I retain the category of Bengal-Vaishnavism since my ethnography was based in West Bengal, although scholars have suggested that it is better to use the term Chaitanyaite Vaishnavism (Case 2000, 28), given the wide geographical spread of Chaitanya-influenced Vaishnavism in eastern and northern India, especially Vrindavan, and in Bangladesh.

3. For detailed analyses of Bengal-Vaishnava theology, see Chakrabarti (1996, 62), De (1986, 277, 282, 225–47), Dimock (1963, 109,115), and Stewart (1999, 83, 99–106, 431–52, 458–59).

4. Parry (1994) describes Banaras for instance as the quintessential city of death, helping souls travel to the next life-cycle.

5. Devotees articulate spatial understandings in multiple ways. This is because in Bengali the terminology for space, place, sites, etc. is diverse and dependent upon the context of use. Thus, *jayga* or *sthan* refers to any space/place/site, *dham* to a sacred physical place, and non-physical sites such as the body or mind are often referred to as *bhanda/patra* (vessels), which manifest Vrindavan if appropriately cultivated. In view of this flexible vocabulary, to minimize confusion I generally use English phrases such as *sacred place* when analyzing Bengal-Vaishnava place-experiences.

6. See Lutt (1995) and van der Veer (1987).

7. See Chakrabarty (1985, 85), Pinch (2003, 179), and Sarkar (1992).

8. Chaitanya, although married, did not have children.

9. Next in number are the descendants of Chaitanya's associate, Advaita Acharya.

10. On debates about "subaltern" agency see Banerjee (2002), Bhadra (1989), Chatterjee (1989), Openshaw (2002, 240–52), Sarkar (1989), and Urban (2001).

11. See also Adams, Hoelscher, and Till (2001), Basso (1996), Ingold (1993, 2000), Low and Lawrence-Zuniga (2003), Munn (2003), and Smith et al. (2009).

12. See Massumi (2002) for this distinction between emotion and affect.

13. See Lutz and Abu-Lughod and Lutz (1990), Appadurai (1990), Hirschkind (2006), Lutz and White (1986), and Palmer and Occhi (1999).

14. See Csordas (1993, 1994), Feld (1996), Howes (2003), and Stoller (1989).

15. See also Haberman (1988) and Lynch (1990).

16. Athanasiou, Hantzaroula, and Yannakopoulos (2008), Clough and Halley (2007), Gregg and Seigworth (2010), and Thrift (2008), among others, champion this theoretical shift.

17. This is why Navaro-Yashin (2009) argues that ethnography in its most productive moments is often trans-paradigmatic, the paradigms in my analysis of Bengal-Vaishnava experiences being the phenomenological, discursive, and affective ones.

18. Not all theorists agree with the notion of *rasa* as impersonal, however; some argue that it is of a personal nature (Haberman 2003, xlvi–vii).

19. For detailed discussions of rasaesthetics, see Chakrabarti (1996), De (1986, 166–225), Haberman (2003, esp. xxix–lxxiv), Hardy (1983, 557), and Stewart (1999, 99–106).

2. DISCOVERING *GUPTA*-VRINDAVAN

1. Gourango or Gour, "the fair-skinned one," is Chaitanya's epithet, others being Nimai, "born under a Nim tree," and most commonly Mahaprabhu, "the great god."

2. See Eck (1999), Ghosh (2005), and Morinis (1984, 14).

3. See also Bharati (1968, 54) and Das Babaji (1987, 8–9).

4. Texts produced as glorifications of Hindu pilgrimage places.

5. On the relation between "background" and "foreground," see Hirsch and O'Hanlon (1995, 14).

6. South Asianists have written extensively on discourses of modernizing Hinduism in general and Bengal-Vaishnavism in particular. See Anderson (1991, 91), Pinch (2003, 179), Sarkar (1948, 221 [cited in Chakrabarty 1985, 85], Sarkar (1992).

7. This eighteenth-century Vaishnava text is cited by proponents of both birthplaces as their prime geographical/historical reference. In chapter 12 of the book, the author, Narahari Chakrabarti, mentions that Navadvip, the nine islands, are together shaped like a lotus, within which, in a site called Mayapur, Chaitanya's house is located (Chakrabarti 1912, 710–13, esp. 713).

8. Stewart (2010, 309) similarly argues that the *Bhaktiratnakara* makes extensive use of rhetorical strategies and is thus not considered historically accurate by scholars.

9. *Nava* can mean both "nine" and "new" in Bengali.

10. Divine images being shifted due to changes in royal policies was a common South Asian phenomenon. Peabody (1991), for instance, describes how western Indian Vallabha statues used to be hidden in royal authorities' turbans under the fear of Mughal emperors; and Stewart (2010, 278) speaks about Jagannatha's image being similarly relocated in sixteenth-century Orissa.

11. An exception is the famous *babaji*-owned Samajbari temple, located in the hub of pilgrimage-routes.

12. *Taste* here is a shorthand translation of *asvadan*, refined spiritual savoring. Vaishnavas use the term *asvadan* to describe the act of enjoying any emotion or mood which brings them pleasure.

3. IMAGINING IN *GUPTA*-VRINDAVAN

1. Bengal-Vaishnavism views the relation between Radha and Krishna as an extramarital one. Love without possession increases the passionate relish, according to them.

2. *Manjari sadhana,* as the essence of emotional *bhakti* in Bengal-Vaishnavism, developed after the seventeenth century (Haberman 1988, 108–09) and further during the twentieth (113). For philosophical/ritual details of the practice, see Haberman (1988, 1992) and Wulff (1984).

3. Imagination, in other religious contexts like Christianity and Buddhism, has mostly only been understood in terms of visualization (see Caro 1995; Lewis 1995; Lyons 2006; Williams 1997).

4. This is most probably an abbreviation of the term Jiva Goswami uses to describe the devotee's perfected self: *antas-cintitabhista-tat-sevapoyagi-deha,* or an inner cognized body which is suitable for Krishna's service (Haberman 2003, liii–iv).

5. Worshipping and serving divinity in a feminine, subservient mood, and imagining the consort's sexuality without desiring it for oneself are experiences shared by devotees in other South Asian contexts as well (Marglin 1985, 1990; Narayanan 1999, 42; van der Veer 1987, 691–92, 1988, 162).

6. Stewart's (2011) observations support the arguments I make in this chapter.

7. See Collins (1997), Cook (2010b), Jordt (2006), and Willis (1979).

8. van der Veer (1989, 458) argues that in the Hindu context, body and mind are not separate entities.

9. Interestingly, the Bengali word *dharan* refers to the spatial logic of holding in a container, and *dharana,* to thinking/intuition, thus hinting at a spatial sense of the mind (McDaniel 1995, 44).

10. See chapter 1 for an analysis of the autonomy of affect.

11. For debates in Indian philosophy on the impossibility of ascertaining the ontological differences between dream-life and waking-life, see Chakrabarty (2009).

12. In Hindu culture, touching the dust on someone's feet symbolizes reverence for that person. Marglin (1990, 228) also argues that Krishna's desire for his lovers' foot-dust has sexual connotations of his desiring their sexual fluid.

13. Bengal-Vaishnavism has a stronghold in the Indian state of Manipur, and a significant number of Manipuris live and worship in Navadvip.

14. *Aratis* are performed in Samajbari temple eight times a day. Of these, two *aratis* are performed privately and witnessed only by the priest, since they commemorate the deities' most intimate erotic pastimes.

15. Her biography (Bhattacharya 1998) is sold in shops outside Samajbari. Although Bengali does not have pronouns depicting gender differentials, throughout the chapter I will refer to "he" and "she" as devotees' spiritual genders embodied during different stages of practice.

16. These convulsions were a manifestation of one of the eight signs (*asta sattvika bhavas*) well attested in Vaishnava literature as external expressions of heightened internal devotional states (Das 2014, Part 2, 1680; Haberman 2003, xxxviii, 242–71).

17. *Bindis* are round colored pastes put on women's foreheads; *alta* is a red liquid Bengali women paint around their feet.

18. **Figures 7** and **8** are not from my fieldwork collection. Borrowed from Stewart (2011), they are typical instances of the kind of *yogapitha* pictures practitioners possess.

19. I use typical Vaishnava names as pseudonyms for practitioners. I also do not mention which temples/ashrams they live in.

20. Some of these books are written in verse-forms describing deities' *lilas* from the author's perspective in the mood of Krishna's lover and Radha's hand-maiden-friend. Some describe life-events and ritual discipline of practitioners, and others, compulsory Vaishnava rituals. Some contain pictures and descriptions of the lotus-shaped spiritual places (see Babaji 2004; Das 1975; Das 2003; Das 2004–2008; Das Babaji 2001; Das Babaji undated).

21. Delmonico (1995, 245) similarly argues that in the Vaishnava context, no cognitive remembering is possible without mantras.

22. Ideally, one may embody any of five emotional moods (*bhavas*) toward the deities: ordinary peaceful subservience (*santa*), servility (*dasya*), companionship (*sakhya*), parental affection (*vatsalya*), and erotic (*madhur*). Bengal-Vaishnavism, and Rupa Goswami especially, privilege the last one, influenced by the *srngara rasa* of Sanskrit poetics (De 1986, 197; Haberman 2003, lxiv, 355–63, 381–83, 396–546; Stewart 1999, 611–31). However, the devotee's eroticism is further qualified as the *manjari's* love in real practice.

23. For similar arguments on the generative capacities of pain, see Asad (2003), Scarry (1987), and Schimmel (1997, 275).

24. As we will see, *smaran* is a technical term and part of the ritual structure of sixty-four *vaidhi bhakti* acts (Das 2014, Part 1, 897, Part 2, 1678–79; Haberman 2003, 57).

25. This is similar to what Humphrey and Laidlaw (1994, 5) identify as the "peculiar fascination of ritual," where "actors both are, and are not, the authors of their acts."

26. Most of my interlocutors narrated the sensitive experiences of *manjari sadhana* through references to paradigmatic or exemplary spiritual figures, rather than talking about their personal experiences. These exemplary figures were sometimes characters from famous Vaishnava scriptures, sometimes practitioners of older generations, and at other times distant friends.

27. Details of these *vaidhi bhakti* acts can be found in Bhatta (1911), Haberman (2003, 35–71), and Stewart (1999, 697–702). Gopal Bhatta's *Haribhakti Vilasa* is in fact an essential text of the Vaishnavas. It states 137 rules and minute details of the correct methods of worship, including rituals of the body, initiation, fasts, *pujas* for special occasions, and idol installation and worship.

28. A widely circulated anecdote says that townspeople often saw a young girl walk out of an ascetic's room late in the night. Suspicious, they went in to check. They discovered that the girl was the ascetic; during his intense imagination, the man's demeanor changed completely to his essential form as a young girl.

29. Three or four senior *babajis* alternately perform this service in the temple. Once annually, on a special Vaishnava festival, nine *babajis* wear the *sari* and perform *arati* together. However, whether or not a practitioner may adorn the physical body in a feminine form is a debated issue among Vaishnavas (Haberman 1988, 94–103).

30. For details of *ragatmika* and *raganuga bhakti,* see Haberman (2003, 77–85) and Stewart (1999, 702–05).

31. The eight periods (three hours each) are early morning, pre-noon, noon, afternoon, evening, late evening and very late night/dawn. For details, see Rupa Goswami's *Astakaliyalilasmaranamangala stotram* (cited in De 1986, 673–75).

32. Hardy (1983, 100–04) argues that engaging sensuous *bhakti* with practices of intellectual *bhakti yoga* is a way of sublimating erotic principles into disembodied ones. In *manjari sadhana*, however, we see a very productive engagement of both.

33. Unlike most other practitioners, Kunjabihari knows elementary English. He used the words *discipline, sense, concentration,* and *practice.* This phenomenology of breathing approximates the balance between "intensive concentration" and "mindful awareness" that Cook (2006, 125) describes in case of Theravada Buddhist meditation. McDaniel (1995, 40–41) mentions, too, that in Indian philosophical systems, cultivation of mental calm is associated with clarity in perception and sensation.

34. This shift from the *karan sharir* to the *manjari svarup* (essential self) corresponds to the transformation of *jiva-sakti* to *svarup-sakti* theorized by Jiva Goswami. The relation between Krishna and the devotee's feminine self as part of Krishna's own *svarup* is one of simultaneous sameness-and-difference (De 1986, 313–14).

35. Stewart (2011, 307) argues that the concept of *mandala* is used in the *yogapitha's* imagining.

36. This is why some *manjaris* are placed in the lotus's innermost sub-petals.

37. Haberman attributes such instances to "intense religious voyeurism" (1988, 189). However, I would not use the term *voyeurism* in these cases, since Navadvip's practitioners make a clear case against self-gratificatory aesthetics.

38. This approximates Scheper-Hughes and Lock's (1987, 16) idea of the "body image" as an individual's imagining of the body in relation to its perception, memory, affect, cognition, and action.

39. Some practitioners follow an even more complex route. They first imagine and serve Chaitanya and his associates in Navadvip (in the form and mood of a Brahmin boy of around 12 years), and then proceed to Vrindavan, since Navadvip is spiritually equivalent to Vrindavan.

40. Recent anthropological studies of the senses have similarly questioned the false agonism between the body's felt dimensions and mind's thinking potentials (Gell 1995; Leavitt 1996, 514; Lutz and White 1986; Mitchell 1997, 84).

41. This episode has a striking resemblance to one cited in the *Brahmavaivarta Purana* and mentioned by Jiva Goswami (Haberman 2003, 90). This shows the discursive connections in such paradigmatic recollections.

42. These emotional states are described in *Ujjvala Nilamani* by Rupa Goswami (De 1986, 214–15; Haberman 2003, lxvii).

43. See also Goswami (1982), Hawley and Wulff (1982), and Rosenstein (1998, 2000). Radha's gaining greater pleasure than Krishna is the foundation of the argument for the androgynous dual incarnation of Chaitanya: Radha-Krishna fused in one body so Krishna could apprehend the bliss that Radha enjoys by loving him (Stewart 1999, 99–106).

44. On details of the difference between *kama* and *prem*, see Stewart (1999, 454).

45. Bengal-Vaishnavas use gastronomic metaphors of *asvadan* and *rasa* to explain emotional processes.

4. BODYING *GUPTA*-VRINDAVAN

1. Once initiated, however, they are only recognized as Vaishnavas, since Vaishnavism is ostensibly an anti-caste religion. Thus, it was impolite to probe Vaishnavas about their exact caste backgrounds.

2. There are a couple of exceptions—temples in Navadvip within which some *sahajiyas* reside. For anonymity reasons I am not naming them.

3. See Dimock (1966, 35–36) and Hayes (1995, 333, 2000, 308).

4. Some scholars refer to *sahajiyas'* or tantrics' bodies as "microcosmic" entities reflecting macrocosmic truths. But White (2009, 175) argues that "microcosm" is a Western concept with no Sanskrit correspondence and that practitioners' bodies must be conceptualized as universes in themselves.

5. On *sahajiyas'* philosophy and practices, see Basu (1932), Bose (1986), Chakrabarti (1996, 143–50), Das (1988), Dasgupta (1976, 113–56), Dimock (1966), and Goswami (2008).

6. See also Coakley (1997, 4) and Ingold (2000, 170).

7. For discussions on *sahajiyas'* origins, see Klaiman (1983, 37) and O'Connell (1989). For debates on whether the *sahajiya* religion developed before or after Chaitanya, see Bose (1986, 156–59) and Dasgupta (1976, 116). For the history of the relation of Vaishnavism with *sahajiya* religion, see Dimock (1966, 25–67).

8. See Brooks (1990, 1995), Cashin (1995), Flood (2006), Schomer and McLeod (1987), Shaw (1994), Urban (2010), and White (1996, 2000).

9. Renouncer *sahajiyas* are not burned, like ordinary Hindus, but buried, since renunciation already symbolizes their death to the social world. They are seated in a yogic posture with a cloth tied around their heads and turmeric, sandalwood, *ghee,* honey, and flowers put on their bodies after bathing.

10. This refers to *sahajiyas'* marriage practice, which is completely different from orthodox Hindu marriages. They exchange garlands (*mala*) and put sandalwood paste (*chandan*) on each other's foreheads. The flexibility that such a simple ceremony offers is criticized by others as a mark of *sahajiyas'* licentiousness.

11. Unlike in ordinary Hindu discourse, where *karma* refers to the ethics of living and its relations with transmigratory cycles of life and death, *sahajiyas* use the term to refer to their spiritual practices. In the ordinary discourse there is a teleology inherent in the term such that good *karma* implies good fruits, and bad *karma,* negative results. In the *sahajiya* discourse, however, the term connotes a distinct ethicality of presentism. Thus, *karma* (sexual practices of the right kind) must aim at no "fruit" of sexual action, that is progeny, but desire present sensual pleasure for its own sake.

12. Many refugee settlements have developed along railroad tracks in Bengal (Jalais 2005, 1760).

13. Gold (1999, 70) says that tantric cults exemplify these overlaps.

14. *Yukta-vairagya* literally means being *yukta* (associated) with this-worldly affairs, while also being a *vairagi* (renunciate); or conversely, maintaining a renunciate mentality within the material world (Das 2014, Part 1, 630). In the *sahajiya* context this would mean a non-ejaculatory ethic of sexual relationships.

15. See Banerjee (2002, 12), Gold (1987, 124), and Salomon (1995, 190).

16. See Morinis (1985, 212) and Hayes (2000, 311).

17. As for other Vaishnavas, the *Chaitanya Charitamrita* is a most significant text for *sahajiyas* since it presents the philosophy of the *Bhagavata Purana* and rasaesthetics in a systematic manner (Bose 1986, 270). But *sahajiyas* interpret it in terms of their own practices. Stewart (2010, 348–62) argues that *Vivarta Vilasa,* by Akinchana Das, presents an essentialized reading of the *Chaitanya Charitamrita* through the lens of *sahajiya* theology and thus is an important text for *sahajiyas.* Few of my interlocutors referred to this text.

18. In the past there have been rumors of ISKCON devotees' being involved in rape cases.

19. *Sahajiyas'* discursive culture problematizes assertions about the non-explanatory rituals of "folk" religion. For similar debates, see Openshaw (2010, 150), Parry (1985), and Sontheimer (1991, 231).

20. Other scholars have also stressed the importance of oral explanations when studying secret religious/sexual practices (Hayes 2003, 167; Simmer-Brown 2001, xvi).

21. Bose (1932, 1934) provides an excellent collection of *sahajiya* poems and their philosophical meanings. He does not provide any ritual explanations

of the texts, however, and that is natural, since it is only possible to be tentative about those meanings.

22. I am not providing the texts' vernacular forms, in view of issues of fair use.

23. The literal equivalences of "fire" and "air" are provisional. I am not sure that there is any singular correlation.

24. Other possible tantric readings of this poem (composed by the poet Chandidas) are provided by Bose (1934, 1–2, 27–28) and Dimock (1966, 59).

25. In *sahajiya* cosmology, the tantric *chakras* (the body's energy-centers) are referred to as lotuses.

26. This refers to the genitals' energy-region. It literally means place (*adhish-than*) of the self (*sva*).

27. Bose (1986, 141) and Das (1988) also mention them. Das (1988, 79, 82, 92) says that they first appeared in a seventeenth-century *sahajiya* text, *Amritaratnabali,* by Mukundadev Goswami. I also found references to them in a few vernacular texts from my fieldwork collection.

28. Chaitanya means "perceptive consciousness." Thus *sahajiyas* imply both its literal meaning and the saint's name.

29. I believe that the other substances are added to ameliorate the odor. But *sahajiyas* never said this because they ascribe divinity to body-fluids.

30. Khandelwal (2001, 160) similarly argues that seminal retention is experienced alongside psychosexual withdrawal.

31. Apart from *diksha* and *shiksha* gurus, renouncer *sahajiyas* also have a *sannyas* guru. During this occasion, a senior renouncer-woman is appointed as a symbolic mother for their new lives and is known as *bhikkha ma* (beggar-mother).

32. Some receive new names at this stage.

33. Openshaw (2007, 323–26) describes a similar renunciation ceremony among *bauls.*

34. When women reach menopause, some men look for other partners, while others continue to live together and borrow body-substances like menstrual blood from other *sahajiyas.* Only a few *sahajiyas* said that they stopped their ingestion and sexual rituals after renunciation.

35. See also Bose (1934, 1–2, 1986, 42–44) and Dimock (1966, 158–61). *Sahajiyas* think of rule-bound sexuality as procreative (*kama*), and spiritual sexuality, or *raganuga bhakti,* as pleasure-for-itself (*prem*) (213–14).

36. This classification of *chakras* comes close to that of the Hindu tantras (Bose 1986, 125–32; Dimock 1966, 176–77).

37. These logics are similar to those of *goswamis* and *babajis* (see chapter 3).

38. Fillippi and Dahnhardt (2001, 353) show that Ananda Yoga practices depend on similar experiences of air/sonic vibrations within the empty heart-space.

39. While some said that they pull back fluids before orgasm, others seemed to suggest that they take the mixture of fluids back into the body after the fluids meet in the vagina.

40. See Khandelwal (2001, 165–66), Salomon (1995, 195), Urban (2003, 286), and White (2000, 18). Hausner and Khandelwal (2006, 27) argue against this view.

41. See Fillippi and Dahnhardt (2001, 356) and Hayes (2000, 310).

42. This is different from monist *bauls*, who associate the cranium with transcendental space (Salomon 1994, 272).

43. Gold (1999, 73–74) says similarly that in Nath cosmological understandings, *bindu* (sperm) converges with *nad* (sound).

44. Sarukkai (2002, 469) says that when the external senses are subdued through yogic postures, inner body-sounds can be heard.

5. SERVING *GUPTA*-VRINDAVAN

1. See Bryant and Ekstrand (2004), Gelberg (1983), Knott (1986), Nye (2001), Rochford (1982), and Zaidman-Dvir and Sharot (1992).

2. See Baumann (2004), Jaffrelot and Therwath (2007), Kokot, Tololyat, and Alfonso (2004, 3), and Williams (2001, 2).

3. See Inda and Rosaldo (2002, 12, cited in Srinivas 2010, 32).

4. Devotees receive Vaishnava names once initiated.

5. See De (1986, 174), Haberman (2003, 71–77), and Stewart (1999, 699–700) for discussion of these five main principles of the sixty-four *vaidhi bhakti* acts.

6. There have also been persistent international rumors of ISKCON's involvement in mysterious deaths, sex scandals, and weapons hoarding, which are also popularly narrated by Bengalis generally and in Navadvip particularly.

7. Even foreigners, through intensive reading practices, understand and use Sanskrit and Bengali terms with theological import. The significance of the concept of *yukta-vairagya* was discussed in chapter 4. See also Haberman (2003, 75).

8. The *Bhagavad Gita* for instance has an extensive commentary by Prabhupad (1986), titled *The Bhagavad Gita As It Is*.

9. See Bozeman (2000, 385–86) and Rochford (1995, 156–57, 2007, 60–61).

10. On Bengal-Vaishnava debates on caste, see Dimock (1963, 112).

11. This ideal of the corporate *sannyasi* is yet another embodiment of the philosophy of *yukta-vairagya*.

12. See Babb (1986), Juergensmeyer (1991), and Matringe (2001).

13. See Beckerlegge (2000, 2003, 2004, 2006, 2007, 2010), Kamble (2008), and Watt (2005).

14. See Dalmia and Steitencron (1995, 25), Menon (2006), and Miller (1999).

15. On details of the idols' installations, see Brahmachari (2007), Dasi and Dasi (2004), and Svami (2004).

16. For an analysis of "attending Krishna's image" as a form of *vaidhi bhakti*, see Packert (2010) and Valpey (2006).

17. English editions are published by BBT Mumbai.

6. LISTENING TO VRINDAVAN

1. Some critical anthologies are Bhadra (1902), Dimock and Levertov (1981), Majumdar (1962), Ray (1915–1931), Sanyal (1989), and Sen (1935).

2. On analyses of *kirtan* traditions, see Broo (2009), Sanyal (1989), Schultz (2002), Schweig (2005), and Thielemann (1998, 2000).

3. Attali (1985, 4) makes a similar point about theorizing through rather than about sound.

4. These physical responses are part of *asta sattvika bhavas,* mentioned in note 16 of chapter 3.

5. Sound-experience is intimately connected to place-experience. The homophonic pair "hear" and "here" points to the ear's tendency to locate the present here and now. Thus, sound studies trace "locality" in the "nature of sound" (O'Shaughnessy 1957, 483). Most studies *situate* or emplace the sources, objects, and/or directionality of sound (Pike 1970; Schryer 1992, 219). So Connor (2004, 153–72) speaks about the "umbilical continuity" or "sonic tactility" sounds have with their sources, and Pasnau insists on "putting sound back to where it *belongs*" (1999, 325, emphasis added).

6. See Stewart (1995, 564–77, 1999, 812–25, 904–09).

7. My analyses here have strong resemblances to Shannon's (2004) discussion of *dhikr* experiences.

8. For details of Vaishnava divine ecstasy during *kirtan,* and its relation with classical rasaesthetics, see Stewart (2010, 82–96). On Chaitanya's experiences of these ecstatic states, see Stewart (1999, 926–35).

9. The poems were composed in Bengali, Sanskrit, and Vrajabuli, a medieval Bengali dialect.

10. I realized later that the energy-center around the chest is known as *anahata,* literally "unstruck sound," which she meant is struck when the *khol* plays.

11. Schimmel (1997, 279) similarly demonstrates the importance of the flute-aesthetic in Sufism.

12. The strings are tighter and the surface smaller at this end. Thus, its sounds are sharper and higher-pitched.

13. Sonic imaginations similarly connect chanting and instrument sounds in Japanese theatre (Ingold 2007, 29).

14. See also Gold and Gold (1984, 120) and Williams (1997, 223).

15. In contrast, in Buddhist meditative imaginings, the gradual movement is from silence, to sounds, to silence (Cooper 2001, 182).

16. Krishna is imagined as the dark lord, and Radha as the fair maiden.

17. See also Beck (1993, 94, 104) and Davidson (1995).

18. See also Ernst (2005, 26), Gold (1999, 73), and Salomon (1995, 190).

7. CONCLUSION

1. See Burghart (1983) and Cook (2006, 2010b) for related debates on the community bases of renouncers' religious lives, and thus necessary revisions of Dumont's theories.

Glossary

ACHAR ritual
AHAMKAR ego
AISHWARYA Krishna's warrior moods
AKHRA BABAJIS' residential ashram
ANANDA happiness/pleasure
ANUMAN inference
ARATI light-offering made to deities
ASTA-KALIYA eight daily periods in celestial Vrindavan
ASTA SATTVIKA BHAVAS eight physical manifestations of internal Vaishnava devotional states
ASVADAN taste
BABAJI male renouncer Vaishnava
BARTAMAN present/immediacy
BHAKTI devotion
BHASHA language
BHAVA emotion
BHEK Vaishnava renunciation
BHOG food-offering to deities
BOL KHOL rhythm
BRAHMACHARI male celibate practitioner/monk
CHAKRA energy region in the body
DARSHAN spiritual gaze
DEHA body
DESH place of residence/land/spiritual stage
DHAM sacred place
DIKSHA initiation
GOPI Krishna's lovers

GOSHALA cow shed
GOSWAMI householder Brahmin Vaishnava
GUPTA unmanifest/hidden/secret
GURUKUL school providing spiritual training
GYAN knowledge
HOLI festival commemorating Radha-Krishna's passionate play with colors
JAPA chanting and keeping count
JAP-MALA basil-seed necklace used for counting while chanting
KAMA self-directed lust
KARTAL cymbals used in KIRTAN
KHOL sacred drum used in KIRTAN
KIRTAN Vaishnava devotional music
LILA divine play
LILA-KIRTAN performance of songs describing the deities' love-acts by trained
    singers before devotee-audiences
MADHURYA Krishna's sweet moods
MAHAMANTRA uttering Vishnu's sixteen names
MALA necklace
MANAS mind-heart
MANDIR temple
MANJARI Radha's handmaiden friend
MANTRA ritual efficacious utterance
MRDANGA Sanskrit name for the KHOL or sacred drum used in KIRTAN
NAM name
NAM-KIRTAN loud musical chanting of the deities' names in a group
PADMA lotus
PATH reading from scriptures by Vaishnava practitioners for devotee-audiences
PRACHAR preaching
PRAKAT manifest
PRANAYAM controlled breathing
PRASAD/PRASADAM food-offering tasted by deities
PREM (spiritual) love
PUJA worship
RAGA passion
RAGANUGA passionate devotion
RAS festival commemorating Krishna's autumnal dance with his lovers in
    Vrindavan
RASA thick sap/concentrated emotion/aesthetic mood
RASIKA aesthete/devotional connoisseur
SADHAK religious practitioner
SADHANA spiritual discipline
SAHAJA natural/easy/spontaneous
SAHAJIYA Vaishnava with practices similar to tantrics
SAKHI Radha's girlfriends
SAMADHI burial
SAMPRADAYA tradition
SANKIRTAN collective singing

SANNYAS renunciation
SEVA service, public feasts
SHARIR body
SHIKSHA knowledge/(esoteric) training
SHUKHHO subtle
SIDDHA perfected, essential
SMARAN remembering
STHUL gross
SVARUP essential self
TILAK sacred design made on a Vaishnava's forehead with sandalwood paste
TULSI basil-seed considered sacred by Vaishnavas
TYAGI renouncer
VAIDHI disciplined devotion
VAIRAGYA mentality of renunciation
VAISHNAVA follower of Vaishnavism
VAISHNAVISM tradition of worshipping the Hindu deity Vishnu and his incarnations
YOGAPITHA place of the deities' union
YUGAL deity-couple
YUKTA together

Bibliography

Adams, P., S. Hoelscher, and K. E. Till, eds. 2001. *Textures of Place: Exploring Humanist Geographies*. Minneapolis: University of Minnesota Press.

Ahmed, S. 2004. "Affective Economies." *Social Text* 79(22/2):117–39.

Alter, J. S. 1994. "Celibacy, Sexuality, and the Transformation of Gender into Nationalism in North India." *Journal of Asian Studies* 53(1):45–66.

Anderson, B. 1991. *Imagined Communities: Reflections on the Origin and Spread of Nationalism*. London: Verso.

Anderson, K. 2007. "Spiritual Solutions to Material Problems: ISKCON and the Modern World." In *The Hare Krishna Movement: Forty years of Chant and Change*, edited by G. Dwyer and R. J. Cole (121–33). London: I. B. Taurus.

Appadurai, A. 1986. "Theory in Anthropology: Center and Periphery." *Comparative Studies in Society and History* 28(2):356–61.

———. 1988. "Place and Voice in Anthropological Theory." *Cultural Anthropology* 3(1):16–20.

———. 1990. "Topographies of the Self: Praise and Emotion in Hindu India." In *Language and the Politics of Emotion*, edited by C. A. Lutz and L. Abu-Lughod (92–112). Cambridge: Cambridge University Press.

———. 1996. *Modernity at Large: Cultural Dimensions of Globalization*. Minneapolis: University of Minnesota Press.

Asad, T. 1983. "Notes on Body Pain and Truth in Medieval Christian Ritual." *Economy and Society* 12(3):287–327.

———. 1987. "On Ritual and Discipline in Medieval Christian Monasticism." *Economy and Society* 16(2):159–203.

———. 1993. *Genealogies of Religion: Discipline and Reasons of Power in Christianity and Islam*. Baltimore, MD: Johns Hopkins University Press.

———. 2003. "Thinking about Agency and Pain." In his *Formations of the Secular: Christianity, Islam, Modernity* (67–99). Stanford, CA: Stanford University Press.

Athanasiou, A., P. Hantzaroula, and K. Yannakopoulos. 2008. "Towards a New Epistemology: The 'Affective Turn.'" *Historein* 8:5–16.

Attali, J. 1985. *Noise: The Political Economy of Music,* translated by B. Massumi. Manchester: Manchester University Press.

Babaji, R. 2004. *Sadhak Kanthamala* [A Practitioner's Necklace]. Calcutta: Ramkrishna Sarada.

Babb, L. A. 1986. *Redemptive Encounters: Three Modern Styles in the Hindu Tradition.* Berkeley: University of California Press.

Bachelard, G. 1994. *The Poetics of Space,* translated by M. Jolas. Boston: Beacon Press.

Balkwill, L., and W. F. Thompson. 1999. "A Cross-Cultural Investigation of the Perception of Emotion in Music: Psychophysical and Cultural Cues." *Music Perception* 17(1):43–64.

Banerjee, S. 2002. *Logic in a Popular Form: Essays on Popular Religion in Bengal.* Calcutta: Seagull Books.

Basso, K. H. 1996. *Wisdom Sits in Places: Landscape and Language among the Western Apache.* Albuquerque: University of New Mexico Press.

Basu, M. M. 1932. *Sahajiya Sahitya* [The Literature of the Sahajiyas]. Calcutta: Calcutta University Press.

Bose, M. M. 1986. *The Post-Chaitanya Sahajiya Cult of Bengal.* Delhi: Gian.

Baumann, M. 2004. "A Diachronic View of Diaspora, the Significance of Religion and Hindu Trinidadians." In *Diaspora, Identity and Religion: New Directions in Theory and Research,* edited by W. Kokot, K. Tololyan, and C. Alfonso (170–88). London: Routledge.

Bayly, S. 2004. "Conceptualising from Within: Divergent Religious Modes from Asian Modernist Perspectives." In *Ritual and Memory: Toward a Comparative Anthropology of Religion,* edited by H. Whitehouse and J. Laidlaw (111–34). Oxford: Altamira Press.

Beck, G. L. 1993. *Sonic Theology.* Columbia: University of South Carolina Press.

———. 2005. "Krishna as Loving Husband of God: The Alternative Krishnology of the Radhavallabha Sampradaya." In *Alternative Krishnas: Regional and Vernacular Variations on a Hindu Deity,* edited by G. L. Beck (65–90). Albany: State University of New York Press.

Becker, J. 2004. *Deep Listeners: Music, Emotion and Trancing.* Bloomington: Indiana University Press.

Beckerlegge, G. 2000. "Swami Akhandananda's *Sevavrata* (Vow of Service) and the Earliest Expressions of Service to Humanity in the Ramakrishna Math and Mission." In *Gurus and Their Followers: New Religious Reform Movements in Colonial India,* edited by A. Copley (59–79). New Delhi: Oxford University Press.

———. 2003. "Saffron and *Seva*: The Rashtriya Swayamsevak Sangh's Appropriation of Swami Vivekananda." In *Hinduism in Public and Private:*

Reform, Hindutva, Gender and Sampraday, edited by A. Copley (31–65). New Delhi: Oxford University Press.

———. 2004. "The Rashtriya Swayamsevak Sangh's 'Tradition of Selfless Service'." In *The Politics of Cultural Mobilization in India*, edited by A. Wyatt and V. Hewitt (105–35). New Delhi: Oxford University Press.

———. 2006. *Swami Vivekananda's Legacy of Service: A Study of the Ramakrishna Math and Mission*. New Delhi: Oxford University Press.

———. 2007. "Responding to Conflict: A Test of the Limits of New-Vedantic Social Activism in the Ramakrishna Math and Mission?" *International Journal of Hindu Studies* 11(1):1–25.

———. 2010. "'An Ordinary Organization Run by Ordinary People': A Study of Leadership in Vivekananda Kendra." *Contemporary South Asia* 18(1):71–88.

Bellman, B. L. 1981. "The Paradox of Secrecy." *Human Studies* 4(1):1–24.

Bender, B., and M. Winer, eds. 2001. *Contested Landscapes: Movement, Exile and Place*. Oxford: Berg.

Bennett, P. 1990. "In Nanda Baba's House: The Devotional Experience in Pushti Marg Temples." In *Divine Passions: The Social Construction of Emotion in India*, edited by O. M. Lynch (182–211). Berkeley: University of California Press.

Berg, T. V., and F. Kniss. 2008. "ISKCON and Immigrants: The Rise, Decline and Rise Again of a New Religious Movement." *Sociological Quarterly* 49:79–104.

Beuke, C. J., M. Garry, and S. J. Sharman. 2004. "Imagination or Exposure Causes Imagination Inflation." *American Journal of Psychology* 117(2):157–68.

Bhadra, G. 1989. "The Mentality of Subalternity: Kantanama or Rajdharma." In *Subaltern Studies VI*, edited by R. Guha (54–91). Delhi: Oxford University Press.

Bhadra, J., ed. 1902. *Gaura-pada-tarangini* [Songs in Honor of Chaitanya]. Calcutta: Bangiya Sahitya Parishad.

Bharati, B. 1968. *Sri Gourharir Atyadbhutchamatkari Bhoumolila: Nabadvip Bilash* [Sri Chaitanya's Miraculous Lilas on Earth: Navadvip Episodes]. Kolkata: Tridondiswami Srimadbhaktibilash Bharati Maharaj.

Bhatia, V. 2009. *Devotional Traditions and National Culture: Recovering Gaudiya Vaishnavism in Colonial Bengal*. PhD dissertation, Columbia University.

———. 2011. "Images of Nabadwip: Place, Evidence, and Inspiration in Chaitanya's Biographical Tradition." In *Time, History and the Religious Imaginary in South Asia*, edited by A. Murphy (167–85). Abingdon: Routledge.

Bhatta, G. 1911. *Haribhakti Vilasa*. Calcutta: Kolikata Rajdhanyam.

Bhattacharya, D. 1998. *Sri Sri Lalita Sakhi Ma*. Calcutta: Sri Sri Nitai Gourango Trust.

Bose, M. M. 1932 (Part 1)/1934 (Part 2). "Ragatmika Pader Byakhya" [Explanation of Ragatmika Poems]. *Journal of the Department of Letters* 22/24.

Bottero, A. 1991. "Consumption by Semen Loss in India and Elsewhere." *Culture, Medicine and Psychiatry* 15:303–20.

Bowen, J. R. 1995. "The Forms Culture Takes: A State-of-the-Field Essay on the Anthropology of Southeast Asia." *Journal of Asian Studies* 54(4):1047–78.

———. 2002. *Religions in Practice: An Approach to the Anthropology of Religion.* Boston, MA: Allyn and Bacon.

Bozeman, J. M. 2000. "ISKCON's Extensive Reform Efforts." *Nova Religio* 3(2):383–91.

Brahmachari, S. D. 2007. *Mayapure Sri Sri Radha Madhava* [Radha Madhava in Mayapur]. Mayapur: Bhaktivedanta Book Trust.

Broo. M. 2009. "The Vrindavan Goswamis on Kirtana." *Journal of Vaisnava Studies* 17(2):57–71.

Brooks, C. R. 1989. *The Hare Krishnas in India.* Princeton, NJ: Princeton University Press.

Brooks, D. R. 1990. *The Secret of the Three Cities: An Introduction to Hindu Sakta Tantrism.* Chicago, IL: University of Chicago Press.

———. 1995. "Esoteric Knowledge and the Tradition of the Preceptors." In *Religions of India in Practice,* edited by D. S. Lopez Jr. (609–26). Princeton, NJ: Princeton University Press.

Bruckner, H. 2001. "Fluid Canons and Share Charisma: On Success and Failure of a Ritual Performance in a South Indian Oral Tradition." In *Charisma and Canon: Essays on the Religious History of the Indian Subcontinent,* edited by V. Dalmia, A. Malinar, and M. Christof (313–27). Oxford: Oxford University Press.

Bryant, E. F., and M. L. Ekstrand, eds. 2004. *The Hare Krishna Movement: The Postcharismatic Fate of a Religious Transplant.* New York: Columbia University Press.

Burghart, R. 1983. "Renunciation in the Religious Traditions of South Asia." *Man* (n. s.) 18(4):635–53.

Burr, A. 1984. *I Am Not My Body: A Study of the International Hare Krishna Sect.* New Delhi: Vikas.

Burrows, D. 1980. "On Hearing Things: Music, the World and Ourselves." *Musical Quarterly* 66(2):180–91.

Carman, T. 2008. *Merleau-Ponty.* London: Routledge.

Caro, R. V. 1995. "An Ignatian Meditation: 'Carrion Comfort'." *Studies: An Irish Quarterly Review* 84(334):152–59.

Carter, P. 1987. *The Road to Botany Bay: An Essay in Spatial History.* London: Faber and Faber.

Case, M. 2000. *Seeing Krishna: The Religious World of a Brahmin Family in Vrindaban.* New York: Oxford University Press.

Casey, E. S. 1992. "Remembering Resumed: Pursuing Buddhism and Phenomenology in Practice." In *In the Mirror of Memory: Reflections of Mindfulness and Remembrance in Indian and Tibetan Buddhism,* edited by J. Gyatso (271–98). New York: State University of New York Press.

———. 1993. *Getting Back into Place: Toward a Renewed Understanding of the Place-World.* Bloomington: Indiana University Press.

———. 1996. "How to Get from Space to Place in a Fairly Short Stretch of Time." In *Senses of Place*, edited by S. Feld and K. H. Basso (13–52). Santa Fe, NM: School of American Research Press.

———. 1998. *The Fate of Place: A Philosophical History*. Berkeley: University of California Press.

———. 2000. *Imagining: A Phenomenological Study*. Bloomington: Indiana University Press.

———. 2001. "On Habitus and Place: Responding to My Critics." *Annals of the Association of American Geographers* 91(4):716–23.

Cashin, D. 1995. *The Ocean of Love: Middle Bengali Sufi Literature and the Fakirs of Bengal*. Stockholm: Association of Oriental Studies.

Cataldi, S. L. 1993. *Emotion, Depth and Flesh: A Study of Sensitive Space: Reflections on Merleau-Ponty's Philosophy of Embodiment*. Albany: State University of New York Press.

Chakrabarti, A. 2009. "Play, Pleasure, Pain: Ownerless Emotions in Rasa-Aesthetics." In *History of Science, Philosophy and Culture in Indian Civilization*, Vol. XV, Part III, edited by D. P. Chattopadhyaya and A. Dev (189–202). New Delhi: Centre for Studies in Civilizations.

Chakrabarti, H. 1940. *Panchatattva O Gyanamrita Katha*. Navadvip: Sri Devimadhava Chakrabarti.

Chakrabarti, N. 1912. *Bhaktiratnakara*. Murshidabad: Sri Ramdev Mishra.

Chakrabarti, R. 1996. *Bonge Vaishnava Dharma: Ekti Aitihashik ebong Samajtattvik Adhyayan* [Vaishnavism in Bengal: A Historical and Sociological Exercise]. Kolkata: Ananda.

Chakrabarti, S. 2001. *Baul Fakir Katha*. Kolkata: Lokoshongoshkriti Kendra.

Chakrabarty, A. 2009. "Is This a Dream? Analytical Reflections on Objecthood and Externality." *Journal of Indian Council of Philosophical Research* 26(1):29–44.

Chakrabarty, R. 1985. *Vaisnavism in Bengal (1486–1900)*. Calcutta: Sanskrit Pustak Bhandar.

Chatterjee, P. 1989. "Caste and Subaltern Consciousness." In *Subaltern Studies VI*, edited by R. Guha (169–209). Delhi: Oxford University Press.

Chatterji, R. 1995. "Authenticity and Tradition: Reappraising a 'Folk' Form." In *Representing Hinduism: The Construction of Religious Traditions and National Identity*, edited by V. Dalmia and H. V. Steitencron (420–41). New Delhi: Sage.

———. 2009. *Writing Identities: Folklore and Performative Arts of Purulia, Bengal*. New Delhi: Aryan Books.

Christof, M. 2001. "The Legitimation of Textual Authority in the *Bhagavata Purana*." In *Charisma and Canon: Essays on the Religious History of the Indian Subcontinent*, edited by V. Dalmia, A. Malinar, and M. Christof (62–76). Oxford: Oxford University Press.

Chua, L., and A. Salmond. 2012. "Artefacts in Anthropology." In *The SAGE Handbook of Social Anthropology*, edited by R. Fardon and J. Gledhill (101–14). London: Sage.

Classen, C. 1997. "Foundations for an Anthropology of the Senses." *International Social Science Journal* 49(153):401–12.

Clough, P. T., and J. Halley. 2007. *The Affective Turn: Theorising the Social.* Durham, NC: Duke University Press.

Coakley, S., ed. 1997. *Religion and the Body.* Cambridge: Cambridge University Press.

Cohen, S. 1995. "Sounding Out the City: Music and the Sensuous Production of Place." *Transactions of the Institute of British Geographers* 20(4):434–46.

Cole, R. J. 2007. "Forty Years of Chanting: A Study of the Hare Krishna Movement from Its Foundation to the Present Day." In *The Hare Krishna Movement: Forty years of Chant and Change*, edited by G. Dwyer and R. J. Cole (26–53). London: I. B. Taurus.

Collins, S. 1997. "The Body in Theravada Buddhist Monasticism." In *Religion and the Body*, edited by S. Coakley (185–204). Cambridge: Cambridge University Press.

Connor, S. 2004. "Edison's Teeth: Touching Hearing." In *Hearing Cultures: Essays on Sound, Listening and Modernity*, edited by V. Erlmann (153–72). Oxford: Berg.

Cook, J. C. 2006. *Vipassana Meditation and the Monasticisation of Popular Buddhism in Thailand.* PhD dissertation, University of Cambridge.

———. 2010a. "Ascetic Practice and Participant Observation, or, The Gift of Doubt and Incompletion in Field Experience. In *Emotions in the Field: The Psychology and Anthropology of Fieldwork Experience*, edited by J. Davies and D. Mihavlova (239–66). Stanford, CA: Stanford University Press.

———. 2010b. *Meditation in Modern Buddhism.* Cambridge: Cambridge University Press.

Cooke, J. 2009. "Why Has Kirtan Become So Popular in the West?" *Journal of Vaisnava Studies* 17(2):185–212.

Cooper, P. C. 2001. "Clouds into Rain." *Journal of Religion and Health* 40(1):167–83.

Corrigan, J., ed. 2004. *Religion and Emotion: Approaches and Interpretations.* New York: Oxford University Press.

Cort, J. E. 1999. "The Gift of Food to a Wandering Cow: Lay-Mendicant Interaction among the Jains." In *Ascetic Culture: Renunciation and Worldly Engagement*, edited by K. Ishwaran (89–110). Leiden: Brill.

Cox, C. 1992. "Mindfulness and Memory: The Scope of Smriti from Early Buddhism to the Sarvastiivadin Abhidharma." In *In the Mirror of Memory: Reflections on Mindfulness and Remembrance in Indian and Tibetan Buddhism*, edited by J. Gyatso (67–108). New York: State University of New York Press.

Csordas, T. J. 1990. "Embodiment as a Paradigm for Anthropology." *Ethos* 18(1):5–47.

———. 1993. "Somatic Modes of Attention." *Cultural Anthropology* 8(2):135–56.

———. 1994. *The Sacred Self: A Cultural Phenomenology of Charismatic Healing.* Berkeley: University of California Press.

———. 2002. *Body/Meaning/Healing.* Hampshire, NY: Palgrave Macmillan.

———. 2004. "Asymptote of the Ineffable: Embodiment, Alterity and the Theory of Religion." *Current Anthropology* 45(2):163–85.

———. 2009. *Transnational Transcendence: Essays on Religion and Globalization*. Berkeley: University of California Press.

Currie, G. 2002. "Imagination as Motivation." *Proceedings of the Aristotelian Society* (n. s.) 102:201–16.

Dalmia, V., and H. V. Steitencron, eds. 1995. *Representing Hinduism: The Construction of Religious Traditions and National Identity*. New Delhi: Sage.

Das, B. *Krishnatattvarasamrita Gyanmanjari* [The Nectar of the Essence of Knowledge]. Calcutta: Mascot Press.

Das, H. 2003. *Sri Sri Gaudiya Vaisnava Jivan* [Biographies of Gaudiya Vaishnavas]. Navadvip: Sri Haribol Kutir.

———. 2014. *Sri Sri Gaudiya Vaishnava Abhidhan*. Kolkata: Sanskrit Book Depot.

Das, J. 2004–2008. *Sadhaner Pothe* [In the Path of Spiritual Discipline]. 4 vols. Navadvip: Puraton Bhajan Kutir.

Das, K. 1975. *Manjari Svarup-Nirupan* [Ascertaining the True Manjari Self]. Vrindavan.

Das, P. 1988. *Sahajiya Cult of Bengal and Pancha Sakha Cult of Orissa*. Calcutta: Firma KLM.

Das, R. P. 1992. "Problematic Aspects of the Sexual Rituals of the Bāuls of Bengal." *Journal of American Oriental Society* 112(3):388–432.

Dasa, B. 2009. *Japa: Nine Keys from the Siksastaka to Improve your Japa*. Vrindavana: Vrindavan Institute for Higher Education.

Dasa, S., ed. 1982. *Sri Namamrta: The Nectar of the Holy Name (from writings of A.C. Bhaktivedanta Swami Prabhupada)*. Mumbai: Bhaktivedanta Book Trust.

Das Babaji, J. Undated. *The Holy Life History of Siddha Sri Jagannath Das Babaji Maharaj*. Navadvip: Puratan Bhajan Kutir.

Das Babaji, K. 2001. *Sadhak Smaran* [Practitioners' Remembrance]. Calcutta: Sri Sri Nitai Gourango Gurudham.

Das Babaji, M. 1987. *Sri Gourango Mahaprabhu-r Sathik Janmasthan* [Sri Chaitanya's True Birthplace]. Navadvip: Prachin Mayapur Gourango Janmasthan.

Das Brahmachari, S. 2006. *Jogote Amra Kothay?* [Where Are We in This Universe?] Mayapur: Bhaktivedanta Book Trust.

Dasgupta. S. 1976. *Obscure Religious Cults as Background of Bengali Literature*. Calcutta: Calcutta University Press.

Dasi, A. G. 2006. *The Nectar of Congregational Preaching*. Sri Mayapur Dham: Bhaktivedanta Book Trust.

Dasi, B. S. D., and Dasi, R. D. 2004. *Eighteen Days: Sri Panca-tattva's Mayapur-lila*. Delhi: Thomson Press.

Davidson, R. M. 1995. "The Litany of Names of Manjusri." In *Religions of India in Practice*, edited by D. S. Lopez (104–25). Princeton, NJ: Princeton University Press.

Dawson, A., and M. Johnson. 2001. "Migration, Exile and the Landscapes of the Imagination." In *Contested Landscapes: Movement, Exile and Place*, edited by B. Bender and M. Winer (319–32). Oxford: Berg.

De, S. K. [1961] 1986. *Early History of the Vaisnava Faith and Movement in Bengal*. Calcutta: Firma KLM.

Debes, R. 2009. "Neither Here Nor There: The Cognitive Nature of Emotion." *Philosophical Studies* 146:1–27.

de Certeau, M. 1984. *The Practice of Everyday Life*. Berkeley: University of California Press.

Deleuze, G. 1994. *Difference and Repetition*, translated by P. Patton. London: Continuum.

Deleuze, G., and F. Guattari. 2004. *A Thousand Plateaus: Capitalism and Schizophrenia*. London: Continuum.

Delmonico, N. 1995. "How to Partake in the Love of Krsna." In *Religions of India in Practice*, edited by D. S. Lopez Jr. (244–68). Princeton, NJ: Princeton University Press.

Derrida, J. 1978. "Structure, Sign and Play in the Discourse of the Human Sciences." In *Writing and Difference*, translated by Alan Bass (351–70). London: Routledge and Kegan Paul.

Dimock, E. C., Jr. 1963. "Doctrine and Practice among the Vaisnavas of Bengal." *History of Religions* 3(1):106–27.

———. 1966. *The Place of the Hidden Moon: Erotic Mysticism in the Vaisnava-Sahajiya Cult of Bengal*. Delhi: Motilal Banarsidass.

Dimock, E. C., Jr., and Denise Levertov. 1981. *In Praise of Krishna: Songs from the Bengali*. Chicago, IL: University of Chicago Press.

Doniger, W. 1997. "Medical and Mythical Constructions of the Body in Hindu Texts." In *Religion and the Body*, edited by S. Coakley (167–84). Cambridge: Cambridge University Press.

Downey, G. 2002. "Listening to Capoeira: Phenomenology, Embodiment and the Materiality of Music." *Ethnomusicology* 46(3):487–509.

Dubow, J. 2001. "Rites of Passage: Travel and Materiality of Vision at the Cape Town of Good Hope." In *Contested Landscapes: Movement, Exile and Place*, edited by B. Bender and M. Winer (241–56). Oxford: Berg.

Dumont, L. 1960. "World Renunciation in Indian Religions." *Contributions to Indian Sociology* 4:33–62.

Eck, D. 1999. "The Imagined Landscape: Patterns in the Construction of Hindu Sacred Geography." In *Tradition, Pluralism and Identity: In Honour of T. N. Madan*, edited by V. Das, D. Gupta, and P. Uberoi (23–46). New Delhi: Sage.

Edelman, J. B. 2009. "Argument and Persuasion: A Brief Study of Kirtana in the *Bhagavata Purana*." *Journal of Vaisnava Studies* 17(2):37–56.

Entwistle, A. W. 1991. "The Cult of Krishna-Gopal as a Version of the Pastoral." In *Devotion Divine: Bhakti Traditions from the Regions of India: Studies in Honour of Charlotte Vaudeville*, edited by D. L. Eck and F. Mallison (73–90). Paris: Groningen/Egbert Forsten, Ecole Francaise Extreme-Orient.

Ernst, C. 2005. "Situating Sufism and Yoga." *Journal of the Royal Asiatic Society* 3(15/1):15–43.

Fabian, J. 2003. "Forgetful Remembering: A Colonial life in the Congo." *Journal of the International African Institute* 73(4):489–504.

Feld, S. 1982. *Sound and Sentiment: Birds, Weeping, Poetics and Song in Kaluli Expression*. Philadelphia: University of Pennsylvania Press.

———. 1996. "Waterfalls of Song: An Acoustemology of Place Resounding in Bosavi, Papua New Guinea." In *Senses of Place*, edited by S. Feld and K. H. Basso (91–136). Santa Fe, NM: School of American Research Press.

Feld, S., and D. Brenneis. 2004. "Doing Anthropology in Sound." *American Ethnologist* 31(4):461–74.

Fernandez, J. W. 2003. "Emergence and Convergence in Some African Sacred Spaces." In *The Anthropology of Space and Place: Locating Culture*, edited by S. M. Low and D. Lawrence-Zuniga (187–203). Malden: Blackwell.

Fillippi, G., and T. Dahnhardt. 2001. "Ananda Yoga: A Contemporary Crossing between Sufism and Hinduism." In *Charisma and Canon: Essays on the Religious History of the Indian Subcontinent*, edited by V. Dalmia, A. Malinar, and M. Christof (350–59). Oxford: Oxford University Press.

Flood, G. 2006. *The Tantric Body: The Secret Tradition of Hindu Religion*. London: I. B. Tauris.

Foucault, M. 1988. "Technologies of the Self." In *Technologies of the Self: A Seminar with Michel Foucault*, edited by L. H. Martin, H. Gutman, and P. H. Hutton (16–49). Amherst: University of Massachusetts Press.

Fuller, J. D. 2003. "Re-membering the Tradition: Bhaktivinoda Thakura's 'Sajjanatosani' and the Construction of a Middle-Class Vaisnava Sampradaya in Nineteenth-Century Bengal." In *Hinduism in Public and Private: Reform, Hindutva, Gender and Sampraday*, edited by A. Copley (173–210). New Delhi: Oxford University Press.

———. 2005. *Religion, Class and Power: Bhaktivinode Thakur and the Transformation of Religious Authority among the Gaudiya Vaishnavas in Nineteenth-Century Bengal*. PhD dissertation, University of Pennsylvania.

Funkhouser, E., and S. Spaulding. 2009. "Imagination and Other Scripts." *Philosophical Studies* 143:291–314.

Gelberg, S. J., ed. 1983. *Hare Krishna Hare Krishna: Five Distinguished Scholars on the Hare Krishna Movement in the West*. New York: Grove Press.

Gell, A. 1995. "The Language of the Forest: Landscape and Phenomenological Iconism in Umeda." In *The Anthropology of Landscape: Perspectives on Place and Space*, edited by E. Hirsch and M. O. Hanlon (232–54). Oxford: Clarendon Press.

George, K. M. 1993. "Dark Trembling: Ethnographic Notes on Secrecy and Concealment in Highland Sulawesi." *Anthropological Quarterly* 66(4):230–39.

Ghosh, P. 2005. *Temple to Love: Architecture and Devotion in Seventeenth-Century Bengal*. Bloomington: Indiana University Press.

Gibbs, P. 2008. "What is Work? A Heideggerian Insight into Work as a Site of Learning." *Journal of Education and Work* 21(5):423–34.

———. 2010. "A Heideggerian Approach to Higher Education as Workplace: A Consideration of Academic Professionalism." *Studies in Philosophy and Education* 29:275–85.

Gold, A. G. 1988. *Fruitful Journeys: The Ways of Rajasthani Pilgrims*. Berkeley: University of California Press.

Gold, A. G., and D. Gold. 1984. "Fate of a Householder Nath." *History of Religions* 24(2):113–32.

Gold, D. 1987. *The Lord as Guru: Hindi Saints in the North Indian Tradition.* New York: Oxford University Press.

———. 1999. "Nath Yogis as Established Alternatives: Householders and Ascetics Today." In *Ascetic Culture: Renunciation and Worldly Engagement,* edited by K. Ishwaran (68–88). Leiden: Brill.

Goswami, B. 2007. *Bishnupriya Prananath Nadiya Bihari* [The King of Bishnupriya's Heart: Nadia's Chaitanya]. Navadvip: Porama Press.

Goswami, N. 2008. *Manober Muldhon* [Man's Essence]. Navadvip: Sri Nitai Gour Seva Ashram.

Goswami, S. 1982. "Radha: The Play and Perfection of Rasa." In *The Divine Consort: Radha and the Goddesses of India,* edited by J. S. Hawley and D. M. Wulff (72–88). Berkeley, CA: Graduate Theological Union.

Graves, E. 2009a. *Rhythmic Theology: Khol Drumming in Caitanya Vaisnava Kirtan.* PhD dissertation, Tufts University.

———. 2009b. "Chaitanya Vaishnava Perspectives on the Bengali Khol." *Journal of Vaisnava Studies* 17(2):103–26.

Gregg, M., and G. J. Seigworth. 2010. *The Affect Theory Reader.* Durham, NC: Duke University Press.

Gregory, C. 2011. "Skinship: Touchability as a Virtue in East-Central India." *Journal of Ethnographic Theory* 1(1):179–209.

Haberman, D. L. 1988. *Acting as a Way of Salvation: A Study of Raganuga Bhakti Sadhana.* New York: Oxford University Press.

———. 1992. "Krsna-lila as Perceived in Meditation and Pilgrimage." In *Vaisnavism: Contemporary Scholars Discuss the Gaudiya Tradition,* edited by S. J. Rosen (305–26). New York: Folk Books.

———. 1994. *Journey through the Twelve Forests: An Encounter with Krishna.* New York: Oxford University Press.

———. 2003. *The Bhaktirasāmrtasindhu of Rūpa Gosvāmin.* Delhi: Indira Gandhi National Centre for the Arts and Motilal Banarsidass.

Halliburton, M. 2002. "Rethinking Anthropological Studies of the Body: Manas and Bodham in Kerala." *American Anthropologist* (n. s.) 104(4):1123–34.

Hancock, M., and S. Srinivas. 2008. "Spaces of Modernity: Religion and the Urban in Asia and Africa." *International Journal of Urban and Regional Research* 32(3):617–30.

Hanssen, K. 2006. "The True River Ganges: Tara's Begging Practices." In *Women's Renunciation in South Asia: Nuns, Yoginis, Saints and Singers,* edited by M. Khandelwal, S. L. Hausner, and A. G. Gold (69–94). New York: Palgrave Macmillan.

Hardy, F. 1983. *Viraha-Bhakti: The Early History of Krsna Devotion in South India.* Oxford: Oxford University Press.

Hastrup, K. 2007. "Performing the World: Agency, Anticipation and Creativity." In *Creativity and Cultural Improvisation,* edited by E. Hallam and T. Ingold (193–206). New York: Berg.

Hatley, S. 2007. "Mapping the Esoteric Body in the Islamic Yoga of Bengal." *History of Religions* 46(4):351–68.

Hausner, S. L., and M. Khandelwal. 2006. "Introduction: Women on Their Own." In *Women's Renunciation in South Asia: Nuns, Yoginis, Saints and Singers*, edited by M. Khandelwal, S. L. Hausner, and A. G. Gold (1–38). New York: Palgrave Macmillan.

Hawley, J. S. 1981. *At Play with Krishna: Pilgrimage Dramas from Brindavan*. Princeton, NJ: Princeton University Press.

Hawley, J. S., and D. M. Wulff, eds. 1982. *The Divine Consort: Radha and the Goddesses of India*. Berkeley, CA: Graduate Theological Union.

Hayden, R. M. 2002. "Antagonistic Tolerance: Competitive Sharing of Religious Sites in South Asia and the Balkans." *Current Anthropology* 43:205–31.

Hayes, G. 1995. "The Vaishnava Sahajiya Traditions of Medieval Bengal." In *Religions of India in Practice*, edited by D. S. Lopez Jr. (333–51). Princeton, NJ: Princeton University Press.

———. 1999. "The Churning of Controversy: Vaisnava-Sahajiya Appropriations of Gaudiya Vaisnavism." *Journal of Vaisnava Studies* 8(1):77–90.

———. 2000. "The Necklace of Immortality: A Seventeenth-Century Vaisnava Sahajiya Text." In *Tantra in Practice*, edited by D. G. White (308–25). Princeton, NJ: Princeton University Press.

———. 2003. "Metaphoric Worlds and Yoga in the Vaisnava Sahajiya Tantric Traditions of Medieval Bengal." In *Yoga: The Indian Tradition*, edited by I. Whicher and D. Carpenter (162–84). London: Routledge.

———. 2005. "Contemporary Metaphor Theory and Alternative Views of Krishna and Radha in Vaishnava Sahajiya Tantric Traditions." In *Alternative Krishnas: Regional and Vernacular Variations on a Hindu Deity*, edited by G. L. Beck (19–32). Albany: State University of New York Press.

Hedley, D. 2008. *Living Forms of the Imagination*. London: T. and T. Clark International.

Heidegger, M. 1975. "Building, Dwelling, Thinking." In his *Poetry, Language, Thought*, translated by A. Hofstader (141–60). New York: Harper and Row.

Hein, N. 1982. "Comments: Radha and Erotic Community." In *The Divine Consort: Radha and the Goddesses of India*, edited by J. S. Hawley and D. M. Wulff (116–24). Berkeley, CA: Graduate Theological Union.

Helmreich, S. 2007. "An Anthropologist Underwater: Immersive Soundscapes, Submarine Cyborgs, and Transductive Ethnography." *American Ethnologist* 34(4):621–41.

Hirsch, E., and M. O'Hanlon, eds. 1995. *The Anthropology of Landscape: Perspectives on Place and Space*. Oxford: Clarendon Press.

Hirschkind, C. 2006. *The Ethical Soundscape: Cassette Sermons and Islamic Counterpublics*. New York: Columbia University Press.

Holdrege, B. A. 2009. "From Nama-Avatara to Nama-Samkirtana: Gaudiya Perspectives on the Name." *Journal of Vaisnava Studies* 17(2):3–36.

Horstmann, M. 1995. "Towards a Universal Dharma: Kalyan and the Tracts of the Gita Press." In *Representing Hinduism: The Construction of Religious Traditions and National Identity*, edited by V. Dalmia and H. von Stietencron (294–305). New Delhi: Sage.

———. 2001. "Charisma, Transfer of Charisma and Canon in North Indian Bhakti." In *Charisma and Canon: Essays on the Religious History of the*

Indian Subcontinent, edited by V. Dalmia, A. Malinar, and M. Christof (171–82). Oxford: Oxford University Press.

Howes, D., ed. 2003. *Sensual Relations: Engaging the Senses in Culture and Social Theory*. Ann Arbor: University of Michigan Press.

Humphrey, C., and J. Laidlaw, eds. 1994. *The Archetypal Actions of Ritual: A Theory of Ritual Illustrated by the Jain Rite of Worship*. Oxford: Clarendon Press.

Hurcombe, L. 2007. "A Sense of Materials and Sensory Perception in Concepts of Materiality." *World Archaeology* 39(4):532–45.

Ihde, D. 1976. *Listening and Voice: A Phenomenology of Sound*. Athens: Ohio University Press.

Ingold, T. 1993. "The Temporality of the Landscape." *World Archaeology* 25(2):152–74.

———. 2000. *The Perception of the Environment: Essays on Livelihood, Dwelling and Skill*. London: Routledge.

———. 2007. *Lines: A Brief History*. London: Routledge.

Jaffrelot, C., and I. Therwath. 2007. "The Sangh Parivar and the Hindu Diaspora in the West: What Kind of 'Long-Distance Nationalism'?" *International Political Sociology* 1:278–95.

Jalais, A. 2005. "Dwelling on Marichjhanpi: When Tigers Became 'Citizens', Refugees 'Tiger-Food'." *Economic and Political Weekly* 40(17):1757–62.

Jankowsky, R. C. 2006. "Black Spirits, White Saints: Music, Spirit Possession, and Sub-Saharans in Tunisia." *Ethnomusicology* 50(3):373–410.

Jordt, I. 2006. "Defining a True Buddhist: Meditation and Knowledge Formation in Burma." *Ethnology* 45(3):193–207.

Judah, J. S. 1974. *Hare Krishna and the Counterculture*. New York: John Wiley and Sons.

Juergensmeyer, M. 1991. *Radhasoami Reality: The Logic of a Modern Faith*. Princeton, NJ: Princeton University Press.

Kakar, S. 1985. "Psychoanalysis and Religious Healing: Siblings or Strangers?" *Journal of the American Academy of Religion* 53(4):841–53.

Kamble, M. T. 2008. "Bengal in Karnataka's Religious Reform Movement: A Case Study of the Ramakrishna Math and Mission, 1890–1947." In *Colonialism, Modernity, and Religious Identities: Religious Reform Movements in South Asia*, edited by G. Beckerlegge (126–46). New Delhi: Oxford University Press.

Kapstein, M. 1992. "The Amnesic Monarch and the Five Mnemic Men: 'Memory' in Great Perfection (Rdzogs-chen) Thought." In *In the Mirror of Memory: Reflections on Mindfulnesss and Remembrance in Indian and Tibetan Buddhism*, edited by J. Gyatso (239–68). New York: State University of New York Press.

Kar, B. 2007. *Framing Assam: Plantation Capital, Metropolitan Knowledge and a Regime of Identities, 1790s-1930s*. PhD dissertation, Jawaharlal Nehru University, New Delhi.

Kaviraj, S. 1995. "The Reversal of Orientalism: Bhudev Mukhopadhyay and the Project of Indigenist Social Theory." In *Representing Hinduism: The*

Construction of Religious Traditions and National Identity, edited by V. Dalmia and H. V. Steintencron (253–82). New Delhi: Sage.

Kearns, C. M. 2005. "Irigaray's *Between East and West*: Breath, Pranayama, and the Phenomenology of Prayer." In *The Phenomenology of Prayer*, edited by B. E. Benson and N. Wirzba (103–18). New York: Fordham University Press.

Kennedy, M. T. 1925. *The Chaitanya Movement: A Study of Vaishnavism of Bengal*. Calcutta: Oxford University Press.

Khandelwal, M. 1997. "Ungendered Atma, Masculine Virility and Feminine Compassion: Ambiguities in Renunciant Discourses on Gender." *Contributions to Indian Sociology* 31(1):79–107.

———. 2001. "Sexual Fluids, Emotions, Morality: Notes on the Gendering of Brahmacharya." In *Celibacy, Culture, and Society: The Anthropology of Sexual Abstinence*, edited by E. J. Sobo and S. Bell (157–79). Madison: University of Wisconsin Press.

———. 2007. "Foreign Swamis at Home in India: Transmigration to the Birthplace of Spirituality." *Identities* 14:313–40.

Klaiman, M. H. 1983. "Religious Tradition and Religious Revolution: The Case of Vaishnavism in Bengal." *South Asia: Journal of South Asian Studies* 6(1):33–43.

Klostermaier, K. 1974. "The *Bhaktirasamrtasindhubindu* of Visvanatha Chakravartin." *Journal of the American Oriental Society* 94(1):96–107.

Knott, K. 1986. *My Sweet Lord: The Hare Krishna Movement*. Wellingborough: Aquarian Press.

———. 2000. "In Every Town and Village: Adaptive Strategies in the Communication of Krishna Consciousness in the UK, the First Thirty Years." *Social Compass* 47(2):153–67.

Kokot, W., K. Tololyan, and C. Alfonso, eds. 2004. *Diaspora, Identity and Religion: New Directions in Theory and Research*. London: Routledge.

Kovacs, G. 1986. "Phenomenology of Work and Self-Transcendence." *Journal of Value Inquiry* 20:195–207.

Krell, D. F. 1982. "Phenomenology of Memory from Husserl to Merleau-Ponty." *Philosophy and Phenomenological Research* 42(4):492–505.

Laidlaw, J. 1995. *Riches and Renunciation: Religion, Economy and Society among the Jains*. Oxford: Clarendon Press.

———. 2004a. "Embedded Modes of Religiosity in Indic Renouncer Religions." In *Ritual and Memory: Toward a Comparative Anthropology of Religion*, edited by H. Whitehouse and J. Laidlaw (89–110). Oxford: Altamira Press.

———. 2004b. "Introduction." In *Ritual and Memory: Toward a Comparative Anthropology of Religion*, edited by H. Whitehouse and J. Laidlaw (1–10). Oxford: Altamira Press.

———. 2005. "A Life Worth Leaving: Fasting to Death as Telos of a Jain Religious Life." *Economy and Society* 34(2):178–99.

Lakoff, G., and M. Johnson. 1999. *Philosophy in the Flesh: The Embodied Mind and its Challenge to Western Thought*. New York: Basic Books.

Lambek, M. 1998. "The Sakalava Poiesis of History: Realizing the Past through Spirit Possession in Madagascar." *American Ethnologist* 25(2):106–27.

———. 2002. *A Reader in the Anthropology of Religion.* Oxford: Blackwell.

Leavitt, J. 1996. "Meaning and Feeling in the Anthropology of Emotions." *American Ethnologist* 23(3):514–39.

Leder, D. 1990. *The Absent Body.* Chicago, IL: University of Chicago Press.

Legat, A. 2008. "Walking Stories; Leaving Footprints." In *Ways of Walking: Ethnography and Practice on Foot*, edited by T. Ingold and L. Vergunst (41–61). Hampshire: Ashgate.

Levy, R. I. 1984. "Emotion, Knowing, and Culture." In *Culture Theory: Essays on Mind, Self and Emotion*, edited by R. A. Shweder and R. A. LeVine (214–37). Cambridge: Cambridge University Press.

Lewis, T. T. 1995. "The Power of a Mantra: A Story of Five Protectors." In *Religions of India in Practice*, edited by D. S. Lopez Jr. (227–43). Princeton, NJ: Princeton University Press.

Low, K. E. Y. 2006. "Presenting the Self, the Social Body, and the Olfactory: Managing Smells in Everyday Life Experiences." *Sociological Perspectives* 49(4):607–31.

Low, S. M. 1994. "Embodied Metaphors: Nerves as Lived Experience." In *Embodiment and Experience: The Existential Ground of Culture and Self*, edited by T. J. Csordas (139–62). Cambridge: Cambridge University Press.

Low, S. M., and D. Lawrence-Zuniga. 2003. "Locating Culture." In *The Anthropology of Space and Place: Locating Culture*, edited by S.M. Low and D. Lawrence-Zuniga (1–47). Malden: Blackwell.

Luhrmann, T. M. 2006. "Subjectivity." *Anthropological Theory* 6(3):345–61.

Lund, K. 2008. "Listen to the Sound of Time: Walking with Saints in an Andalusian Village." In *Ways of Walking: Ethnography and Practice on Foot*, edited by T. Ingold and L. Vergunst (93–104). Hampshire: Ashgate.

Lutgendorf, P. 1991. *The Life of a Text: Performing the Ramcharitmanas of Tulsidas.* Berkeley: University of California Press.

Lutt, J. 1995. "From Krishnalila to Ramrajya: A Court Case and Its Consequences for the Reformation of Hinduism." In *Representing Hinduism: The Construction of Religious Traditions and National Identity*, edited by V. Dalmia and H. von Stietencron (142–53). New Delhi: Sage.

Lutz, C., and G. M. White. 1986. "The Anthropology of Emotions." *Annual Review of Anthropology* 15:405–36.

Lutz. C. A. 1988. *Unnatural Emotions: Everyday Sentiments on a Micronesian Atoll and Their Challenge to Western Theory.* Chicago: University of Chicago Press.

Lutz. C. A., and L. Abu-Lughod. 1990. "Emotion, Discourse and the Politics of Everyday Life." In *Language and the Politics of Emotion*, edited by C. A. Lutz and L. Abu-Lughod (1–23). Cambridge: Cambridge University Press.

Lynch, O. M. 1990. *Divine Passions: The Social Construction of Emotion in India.* Berkeley: University of California Press.

Lyons, J. D. 2006. "Meditation and the Inner Voice." *New Literary History* 37(3):525–40.

Mack, A. 2004. "One Landscape, Many Experiences: Differing Perspectives on the Temple Districts of Vijayanagara." *Journal of Archaeological Method and Theory* 11(1):59–81.

Majumdar, P. 1962. *Banglar Kirtan* [Kirtan of Bengal]. Kolkata: Sankar Mitra Kirtan Shikshalay.

Majumdar, S. 1992. *Mayachhonno Mayapur* [The Mystery of Mayapur]. Navadvip: Sri Sri Gourango Mahaprabhu Janmasthan Trust.

———. 1995. *Sri Chaitanya Janmasthan Bitorko, Tar Truti O Samadhan* [The Dispute over Sri Chaitanya's Birthplace, Its Deficiencies and Mitigations]. Navadvip: Sri Gourango Janmasthan Prachin Mayapur Unnayan Parishad.

Mahmood, S. 2001. "Rehearsed Spontaneity and the Conventionality of Ritual: Disciplines of 'Salat'." *American Ethnologist* 28(4), 827–53.

Malinar, A. 1995. "The Bhagavadgita in the Mahabharata TV Serial: Domestic Drama and Dharmic Solutions." In *Representing Hinduism: The Construction of Religious Traditions and National Identity*, edited by V. Dalmia and H. von Stietencron (442–67). New Delhi: Sage.

Marglin, F. A. 1985. *Wives of the God-King: The Rituals of the Devadasis of Puri*. New York: Oxford University Press.

———. 1990. "Refining the Body: Transformative Emotion in Ritual Dance." In *Divine Passions: The Social Construction of Emotion in India*, edited by O. M. Lynch (212–36). Berkeley: University of California Press.

Margolis, J. 1960. "Nothing Can Be Heard but Sound." *Analysis* 20(4):82–87.

Marsden, M. 2005. *Living Islam: Muslim Religious Experience in Pakistan's North-West Frontier*. Cambridge: Cambridge University Press.

Marshall, D. A. 2002. "Behavior, Belonging and Belief: A Theory of Ritual Practice." *Sociological Theory* 20(3):360–80.

Mason, D. V. 2009. *Theatre and Religion on Krishna's Stage: Performing in Vrindavan*. New York: Palgrave Macmillan.

Massumi, B. 2002. *The Autonomy of Affect*. http://www.brianmassumi.com/textes/Autonomy%20of%20Affect.PDF.

Matringe, D. 2001. "The Re-enactment of Guru Nanak's Charisma in an Early 20th Century Panjabi Narrative." In *Charisma and Canon: Essays on the Religious History of the Indian Subcontinent*, edited by V. Dalmia, A. Malinar and M. Christof (205–22). Oxford: Oxford University Press.

McDaniel, J. 1989. *The Madness of the Saints: Ecstatic Religion in Bengal*. Chicago: University of Chicago Press.

———. 1995. "Emotion in Bengali Religious Thought: Substance and Metaphor." In *Emotions in Asian Thought: A Dialogue in Comparative Philosophy*, edited by J. Marks and R. T. Ames (39–63). New York: State University of New York Press.

Menon, K. D. 2006. "Passionate Renouncers: Hindu Nationalist Renouncers and the Politics of Hindutva." In *Women's Renunciation in South Asia: Nuns, Yoginis, Saints and Singers*, edited by M. Khandelwal, S. L. Hausner, and A.G. Gold (141–70). New York: Palgrave Macmillan.

Miller, D. 1999. "Modernity in Hindu Monasticism: Swami Vivekananda and the Ramakrishna Movement." In *Ascetic Culture: Renunciation and Worldly Engagement*, edited by K. Ishwaran (111–26). Leiden: Brill.

Mitchell, J. P. 1997. "A Moment with Christ: The Importance of Feelings in the Analysis of Belief." *Journal of the Royal Anthropological Institute* 3(1):79–94.

Mittermaier, A. 2011. *Dreams That Matter: Egyptian Landscapes of the Imagination.* Berkeley: University of California Press.

Mondol, M. 2002. *Nabadviper Itibritto: prothom khondo* [The History of Navadvip, Part 1]. Navadvip: Sujaya Prakashani.

Morinis, A. 1985. "Sanctified Madness: The God-Intoxicated Saints of Bengal." *Social Science Medicine* 21(2):211–20.

Morinis, E. A. 1984. *Pilgrimage in the Hindu Tradition: A Case Study of West Bengal.* New Delhi: Oxford University Press.

Morley, J. 2001. "Inspiration and Expiration: Yoga Practice through Merleau-Ponty's Phenomenology of the Body." *Philosophy East and West* 51(1):73–82.

Morse, M. 1990. "An Ontology of Everyday Distraction: The Freeway, The Mall and Television." In *Logics of Television: Essays in Cultural Criticism,* edited by P. Mellencamp *(193–221).* Bloomington: Indiana University Press.

Munn, N. D. 2003. "Excluded Spaces: The Figure in the Australian Aboroginal Landscape." In *The Anthropology of Space and Place: Locating Culture,* edited by S. M. Low and D. Lawrence-Zuniga (92–109). Malden: Blackwell.

Narayanan, V. 1999. "Brimming with *Bhakti,* Embodiments of *Shakti:* Devotees, Deities, Performers, Reformers, and Other Women of Power in the Hindu Tradition." In *Feminism and World Religions,* edited by A. Sharma and K. K. Young (25–77). Albany: State University of New York Press.

Nast, H. J. 1998. "The Body as 'Place': Reflexivity and Fieldwork in Kano, Nigeria." In *Places through the Body,* edited by H. J. Nast and S. Pile (69–86). London: Routledge.

Navaro-Yashin, Y. 2009. "Affective Spaces, Melancholic Objects: Ruination and the Production of Anthropological Knowledge." *Journal of the Royal Anthropological Institute* (n. s.) 15:1–18.

Nelson, R. S., and M. Olin, eds. 2003. *Monuments and Memory, Made and Unmade.* Chicago, IL: University of Chicago Press.

Nichols, S. 2007. "Imagination and Immortality: Thinking of Me." *Synthese* 159:215–33.

Nye, M. 2001. *Multiculturalism and Minority Religions in Britain: Krishna Consciousness, Religious Freedom, and the Politics of Location.* Richmond: Curzon Press.

O'Connell, J. T. 1989. "Were Chaitanya's Vaisnavas Really *Sahajiyas*? The Case of Ramananda Raya." In *Shaping Bengali Worlds, Public and Private,* edited by T. K. Stewart (11–22). East Lansing: Asian Studies Center, Michigan State University.

Openshaw, J. 2002. *Seeking Bāuls of Bengal.* Cambridge: Cambridge University Press.

———. 2007. "Renunciation Feminised? Joint Renunciation of Female-Male Pairs In Bengali Vaishnavism." *Religion* 37(4):319–32.

———. 2010. *Writing the Self: The Life and Philosophy of a Dissenting Guru.* New Delhi: Oxford University Press.

O'Shaughnessy, B. 1957. "The Location of Sound." *Mind* (n. s.) 66(264):471–90.

Packert, C. 2010. *The Art of Loving Krishna: Ornamentation and Devotion.* Bloomington: Indiana University Press.

Palmer, G. B., and W. R. Jankowiak. 1996. "Performance and Imagination: Toward an Anthropology of the Spectacular and the Mundane." *Cultural Anthropology* 11(2):225–58.

Palmer, G. B., and D. J. Occhi. 1999. "Introduction: Linguistic Anthropology and Emotional Experience." In *Languages of Sentiment: Cultural Constructions of Emotional Substrates*, edited by G. B. Palmer and D. J. Occhi (1–24). Amsterdam: John Benjamins.

Pandey, G. 1995. "The Appeal of Hindu History." In *Representing Hinduism: The Construction of Religious Traditions and National Identity*, edited by V. Dalmia and H. V. Steintencron (369–88). New Delhi: Sage.

Panopoulos, P. 2003. "Animal Bells as Symbols: Sound and Hearing in a Greek Island Village." *Journal of the Royal Anthropological Institute* (n. s.) 9:639–56.

Parry, J. 1985. "The Brahmanical Tradition and the Technology of the Intellect." In *Reason and Morality*, edited by J. Overing (200–25). London: Tavistock.

———. 1994. *Death in Banaras*. Cambridge: Cambridge University Press.

Pasnau, R. 1999. "What Is Sound?" *Philosophical Quarterly* 49(196):309–24.

Peabody, N. 1991. "In Whose Turban Does the Lord Reside? The Objectification of Charisma and the Fetishism of Objects in the Hindu Kingdom of Kota." *Comparative Studies in Society and History* 33(4):726–54.

Peraino, J. A. 2003. "Listening to the Sirens: Music as Queer Ethical Practice." *Journal of Lesbian and Gay Studies* 9(4):433–70.

Persson, A. 2007. "Intimate Immensity: Phenomenology of Place and Space in an Australian Yoga Community." *American Ethnologist* 34(1):44–56.

Pike, A. 1970. "A Phenomenological Analysis of Musical Experience and Other Related Essays." *Journal of Musical Theory* 14(2):237–46.

Pinch, V. 2003. "*Bhakti* and the British Empire." *Past and Present* 179:159–96.

Prabhupad, A. C. B. S. 1986. *Bhagavad-Gita As It Is*. Mumbai: Bhaktivedanta Book Trust.

———. 1987. *Chant and Be Happy*. Mumbai: Bhaktivedanta Book Trust.

Price, R. 1983. *First-Time: The Historical Vision of an Afro-American People*. Baltimore, MD: Johns Hopkins University Press.

Radi, K. 2004. *Nabadvip Mahima* [The Spiritual Significance of Navadvip]. Navadvip: Navadvip Purattatva Parishad.

Ratnagar, S. 2004. "Archaeology at the Heart of a Political Confrontation: The Case of Ayodhya." *Current Anthropology* 45(2):239–59.

Ray, S. C. 1915–1931. *Pada-Kalpataru* [Collection of Kirtan Padas]. Calcutta: Bangiya Sahitya Parishad.

Robbins, J. 2006. "Anthropology and Theology: An Awkward Relationship?" *Anthropological Quarterly* 79(2):285–94.

Rochford, E. B., Jr. 1982. "Recruitment Strategies, Ideology and Organisation in the Hare Krishna Movement." *Social Problems* 29(4):399–410.

———. 1995. "Family Structure, Commitment, and Involvement in the Hare Krishna Movement." *Sociology of Religion* 56(2):153–75.

———. 2007. *Hare Krishna Transformed*. New York: New York University Press.

Rodaway, P. 1994. *Sensuous Geographies: Body, Sense and Place*. London: Routledge.

Rodman, M. C. 2003. "Empowering Place: Multilocality and Multivocality." In *The Anthropology of Space and Place: Locating Culture*, edited by S. M. Low and D. Lawrence-Zuniga (204–23). Malden: Blackwell.

Rosaldo, M. Z. 1984. "Toward an Anthropology of Self and Feeling." In *Culture Theory: Essays on Mind, Self and Emotion*, edited by R. A. Shweder and R. A. LeVine (137–57). Cambridge: Cambridge University Press.

Rosen, S. 2008. *The Yoga of Kirtan: Conversations on the Sacred Art of Chanting*. Nyack, NY: Folk Books.

Rosen, S. J., ed. 1992. *Vaisnavism: Contemporary Scholars Discuss the Gaudiya Tradition*. New York: Folk Books.

Rosenstein, L. 1998. "The Radhavallabha and the Haridasi Sampradayas: A Comparison." *Journal of Vaisnava Studies* 7(1):5–18.

———. 2000. "Radha in the Haridasi Sampradaya." *Journal of Vaisnava Studies* 8(2):119–29.

Sadoski, M. 1992. "Imagination, Cognition, and Persona." *Rhetoric Review* 10(2):266–78.

Salomon, C. 1994. "The Cosmogonic Riddles of Lalan Fakir." In *Gender, Genre and Power in South Asian Expressive Traditions*, edited by A. Appadurai, F. J. Korom, and M. A. Willis (267–304). New Delhi: Motilal Banarssidas.

———. 1995. "*Baul* Songs." In *Religions of India in Practice*, edited by D. S. Lopez Jr. (187–208). Princeton, NJ: Princeton University Press.

Sanderson, A. 1985. "Purity and power among the Brahmans of Kashmir." In *The Category of the Person: Anthropology, Philosophy, History*, edited by M. Carrithers, S. Lukes, and S. Collins (190–216). Cambridge: Cambridge University Press.

Sanyal, H. R. 1989. *Bangla Kirtaner Itihash* [The History of Bengali Kirtan]. Kolkata: KP Bagchi.

Sarbadhikary, S. 2013. "Discovering *Gupta*-Vrindavan: Finding Selves and Places in the Storied Landscape." *Contributions to Indian Sociology* 47(1):113–40.

———. 2015. "Hearing the Transcendental Place: Sound, Spirituality and Sensuality in the Musical Practices of an Indian Devotional Order." In *Music and Transcendence*, edited by F. Stone-Davis. Ashgate.

Sarkar, S. 1989. "The Kalki-Avatar of Bikrampur: A Village Scandal in Early Twentieth Century Bengal." In *Subaltern Studies VI*, edited by R. Guha (1–53). Delhi: Oxford University Press.

———. 1992. "'Kaliyuga', 'Chakri' and 'Bhakti': Ramakrishna and his Times." *Economic and Political Weekly* 27(29):1543–59, 1561–66.

Sarkar, T. 2011. "Holy Infancy: Love and Power in a 'Low Caste' Sect in Bengal." *South Asian History and Culture* 2(3):337–51.

Sarukkai, S. 2002. "Inside/Outside: Merleau-Ponty/Yoga." *Philosophy East and West* 52(4):459–78.

Saso, M. 1997. "The Taoist Body and Cosmic Prayer." In *Religion and the Body*, edited by S. Coakley (231–47). Cambridge: Cambridge University Press.

Sax, W. S. 1990. "The Ramnagar Ramlila: Text, Performance, Pilgrimage." *History of Religions* 30(2):129–53.

Scarry, E. 1987. *The Body in Pain: The Making and Unmaking of the World*. New York: Oxford University Press.

Scheper-Hughes, N., and M. M. Lock. 1987. "The Mindful Body: A Prolegomenon to Future Work in Medical Anthropology." *Medical Anthropology Quarterly* 1(1):6–41.

Schimmel, A. 1997. "'I Take Off the Dress of the Body': Eros in Sufi Literature and Life." In *Religion and the Body*, edited by S. Coakley (262–88). Cambridge: Cambridge University Press.

Schomer, K., and W. H. McLeod. 1987. *The Sants: Studies in a Devotional Tradition of India*. Delhi: Motilal Banarssidas.

Schryer, C. 1992. "Sound Ecology." *Leonardo* 25(2):219–20.

Schultz, A. 2002. "Hindu Nationalism, Music and Embodiment in Marathi Rashtriya Kirtan." *Ethnomusicology* 46(2):307–22.

Schweig, G. M. 2002. "Humility and Passion: A Caitanyite Vaishnava Ethics of Devotion." *Journal of Religious Ethics* 30(3):421–44.

———. 2005. *Dance of Divine Love: India's Classic Sacred Love Story: The Rasa Lila of Krishna*. Princeton, NJ: Princeton University Press.

Sen, S. 1935. *History of Brajabuli Literature*. Calcutta: Calcutta University Press.

Shannon, J. H. 2004. "The Aesthetics of Spiritual Practice and the Creation of Moral and Musical Subjectivities in Aleppo, Syria." *Ethnology* 43(4):381–91.

Shaw, M. 1994. *Passionate Enlightenment: Women in Tantric Buddhism*. Princeton, NJ: Princeton University Press.

Shiraishi, F. 1999. "Calvin Brainerd Cady: Thought and Feeling in the Study of Music." *Journal of Research in Musical Education* 47(2):150–62.

Siegel, L. 1983. *Fires of Love, Waters of Peace: Passion and Renunciation in Indian Culture*. Honolulu: University of Hawaii Press.

Sil, N. P. 2009. "Hites Ranjan Sanyal's History of Bangla Kirtan." *Journal of Vaisnava Studies* 17(2):73–93.

Simmer-Brown, J. 2001. *Dakini's Warm Breath: The Feminine Principle in Tibetan Buddhism*. Boston: Shambhala.

Slawek, S. M. 1988. "Popular Kirtan in Benaras: Some 'Great' Aspects of a Little Tradition." *Ethnomusicology* 32(2):77–92.

Smith, M., J. Davidson, L. Cameron, and L. Bondi, eds. 2009. *Emotion, Place and Culture*. Farnham: Ashgate.

Sneath, D., M. Holbraad, and M. A. Pederson. 2009. "Technologies of the Imagination: An Introduction." *Ethnos* 74(1):5–30.

Sontheimer, G. D. 1991. "Bhakti in the Khandoba Cult." In *Devotion Divine: Bhakti Traditions from the Regions of India, Studies in Honour of Charlotte Vaudeville*, edited by D. L. Eck and F. Mallison (389–400). Paris: Groningen/ Egbert Forsten, Ecole Francaise Extreme-Orient.

Srinivas, S. 2008. *In the Presence of Sai Baba: Body, City, and Memory in a Global Religious Movement*. Leiden: Brill.

Srinivas, T. 2010. *Winged Faith: Rethinking Globalization and Religious Pluralism through the Sathya Sai Movement*. New York: Columbia University Press.

Stephen, M. 1995. *A'aisa's Gifts: A Study of Magic and the Self*. Berkeley: University of California Press.

Stewart, T. K. 1995. "The Exemplary Devotion of the 'Servant of Hari'." In *Religions of India in Practice*, edited by D. S. Lopez Jr. (564–77). Princeton, NJ: Princeton University Press.

————, ed. 1999. *Caitanya Caritamrta of Krsnadasa Kaviraja: A Translation and Commentary*. Cambridge, MA: Harvard University Press.

————. 2005. "Reading for Krishna's Pleasure: Gaudiya Vaisnava Meditation, Literary Interiority, and the Phenomenology of Repetition." *Journal of Vaisnava Studies* 14(1):243–80.

————. 2010. *The Final Word: The Caitanya Caritamrta and the Grammar of Religious Tradition*. New York: Oxford University Press.

————. 2011. "Replicating Vaisnava Worlds: Organising Devotional Space through the Architectonics of the Mandala." *South Asian History and Culture* 2(2):300–36.

Stoller, P. 1989. *The Taste of Ethnographic Things: The Senses in Anthropology*. Philadelphia: University of Pennsylvania Press.

Svami, H. H. B. 2004. *The Advent of Panca-Tattva*. Mayapur: ISKCON.

Svasek, M. 2005. "Introduction: Emotions in Anthropology." In *Mixed Emotions: Anthropological Studies of Feeling*, edited by K. Milton and M. Svasek (1–24). New York: Berg.

Swami, B. 2006. *Bhaktigiti Sanchayan* [Compilation of Devotional Songs]. Mayapur: Bhaktivedanta Book Trust.

Swami, G. P. 2009. *Namhatta Parichay* [Introduction to the Namhatta Program]. Mayapur: ISKCON, Sri Gourchandra Das Brahmachari.

Swami, M. 2002. *The Art of Chanting Hare Krishna: Japa Meditation Techniques*. New Delhi: Gokul Offset.

Swami, S. 1998. *The Apasampradayas*. Mayapur: Bhaktivedanta Academy.

Taussig, M. 1998. "Transgression." In *Critical Terms for Religious Studies*, edited by M. C. Taylor (348–64). Chicago, IL: University of Chicago Press.

Tedlock, D. 2002. "The Poetics of Time in Mayan Divination." In *A Reader in the Anthropology of Religion*, edited by M. Lambek (419–30). Oxford: Blackwell.

Thielemann, S. 1998. *Rasalila (A Musical Study of Religious Drama in Vraja)*. New Delhi: APH.

————. 2000. *Singing the Praises Divine: Music in the Hindu Tradition*. New Delhi: A.P.H.

Thrift, N. J. 2008. *Non-representational Theory: Space, Politics, Affect*. London: Routledge.

Tilley, C. 1994. *A Phenomenology of Landscape: Places, Paths and Monuments*. Oxford, USA: Berg.

————. 2008. *Body and Image: Explorations in Landscape Phenomenology 2*. Walnut Creek, CA: Left Coast Press.

Trawick, M. 1994. "Wandering Lost: A Landless Labourer's Sense of Place and Self." In *Gender, Genre and Power in South Asian Expressive Traditions*, edited by A. Appadurai, F. J. Korom, and M. A. Willis (224–66). New Delhi: Motilal Banarssidas.

Tuan, Y. 1974. *Topophilia: A Study of Environmental Perception, Attitudes, and Values*. New York: Columbia University Press.

Urban, H. B. 1998. "The Torment of Secrecy: Ethical and Epistemological Problems in the Study of Esoteric Traditions." *History of Religions* 37(3):209–48.

———. 2001. "The Marketplace and the Temple: Economic Metaphors and Religious Meanings in the Folk Songs of Colonial Bengal." *Journal of Asian Studies* 60(4):1085–1114.

———. 2003. "The Power of Impure: Transgression, Violence and Secrecy in Bengal Sakta Tantra and Modern Western Magic." *Numen* 50(3): 269–308.

———. 2010. *The Power of Tantra: Religion, Sexuality and Politics of South Asian Studies*. London: I. B. Tauris.

Valpey, K. R. 2006. *Attending Krsna's Image: Caitanya Vaisnava Murti-seva as Devotional Truth*. London: Routledge.

van der Veer, P. 1987. "Taming the Ascetic: Devotionalism in a Hindu Monastic Order." *Man* (n. s.) 22(4):680–95.

———. 1988. *Gods on Earth: The Management of Religious Experience and Identity in a North Indian Pilgrimage Centre*. London: Athlone Press.

———. 1989. "The Power of Detachment: Disciplines of Body and Mind in the Ramanandi Order." *American Ethnologist* 16(3):458–70.

Warrier, M. 2003. "The *Seva* Ethic and the Spirit of Institution Building in the Mata Amritanandamayi Mission." In *Hinduism in Public and Private: Reform, Hindutva, Gender and Sampraday*, edited by A. Copley (254–89). New Delhi: Oxford University Press.

———. 2005. *Hindu Selves in the Modern World: Guru Faith in the Mata Amritanandamayi Mission*. London: Routledge-Curzon.

Watt, C. A. 2005. *Serving the Nation: Cultures of Service, Association, and Citizenship in Colonial India*. New Delhi: Oxford University Press.

Wedlock, T. 2008. "The Dilemmas of Walking: A Comparative View." In *Ways of Walking: Ethnography and Practice on Foot*, edited by T. Ingold and L. Vergunst (51–66). Hampshire: Ashgate.

Weiss, A. S., and R. H. Mendoza. 1990. "Effects of Acculturation into the Hare Krishna Movement on Mental Health and Personality." *Journal for the Scientific Study of Religion* 29(2):173–84.

White, D. G. 1996. *The Alchemical Body: Siddha Traditions in Medieval India*. London: University of Chicago Press.

———, ed. 2000. *Tantra in Practice*. Princeton, NJ: Princeton University Press.

———. 2009. *Sinister Yogis*. Chicago, IL: University of Chicago Press.

Whitehouse, H., and J. Laidlaw, eds. 2004. *Ritual and Memory: Toward a Comparative Anthropology of Religion*. Oxford: Altamira Press.

Whitridge, P. 2004. "Landscapes, Houses, Bodies, Things: 'Place' and the Archaeology of Inuit Imaginaries." *Journal of Archaeological Method and Theory* 11(2):213–50.

Williams, P. 1997. "Some Mahayana Buddhist Perspectives on the Body." In *Religion and the Body*, edited by S. Coakley (205–30). Cambridge: Cambridge University Press.

Williams, R. B. 2001. *An Introduction to Swaminarayan Hinduism*. Cambridge: Cambridge University Press.

Willis, R. J. 1979. "Meditation to Fit the Person: Psychology and the Meditative Way." *Journal of Religion and Health* 18(2):93–119.

Winer, M. 2001. "Landscapes, Fear and Land Loss on the 19th Century South African Colonial Frontier." In *Contested Landscapes: Movement, Exile and Place*, edited by B. Bender and M. Winer (257–72). Oxford: Berg.

Wolf, R. K. 2006. "The Poetics of 'Sufi' Practice: Drumming, Dancing and Complex Agency at Mado Lal Husain and Beyond." *American Ethnologist* 33(2):246–68.

Wolfson, E. R. 2004. "Weeping, Death and Spiritual Ascent in Sixteenth-Century Jewish Mysticism." In *Religion and Emotion: Approaches and Interpretations*, edited by J. Corrigan (271–304). New York: Oxford University Press.

Wulff, D. M. 1982. "Prolegomenon to a Psychology of the Goddess." In *The Divine Consort: Radha and the Goddesses of India*, edited by J. S. Hawley and D. M. Wulff (283–97). Berkeley, CA: Graduate Theological Union.

———. 1984. *Drama as a Mode of Religious Realization: The Vidagdhamadhava of Rupa Gosvami*. Chicago, IL: Scholars Press.

———. 2009. "The Debate over Improvisation's Legitimacy in Bengali Devotional Performance." *Journal of Vaisnava Studies* 17(2):95–101.

Wulff, H. 2007. "The Cultural Study of Mood and Meaning." In *The Emotions: A Cultural Reader*, edited by H. Wulff (1–16). Oxford: Berg.

Zaidman-Dvir, N., and S. Sharot. 1992. "The Response of Israeli Society to New Religious Movements: ISKCON and Teshuvah." *Journal for the Scientific Study of Religion* 31(3):279–95.

Index

CPSIA information can be obtained at www.ICGtesting.com
Printed in the USA
LVOW01s1613120815

449843LV00008B/42/P